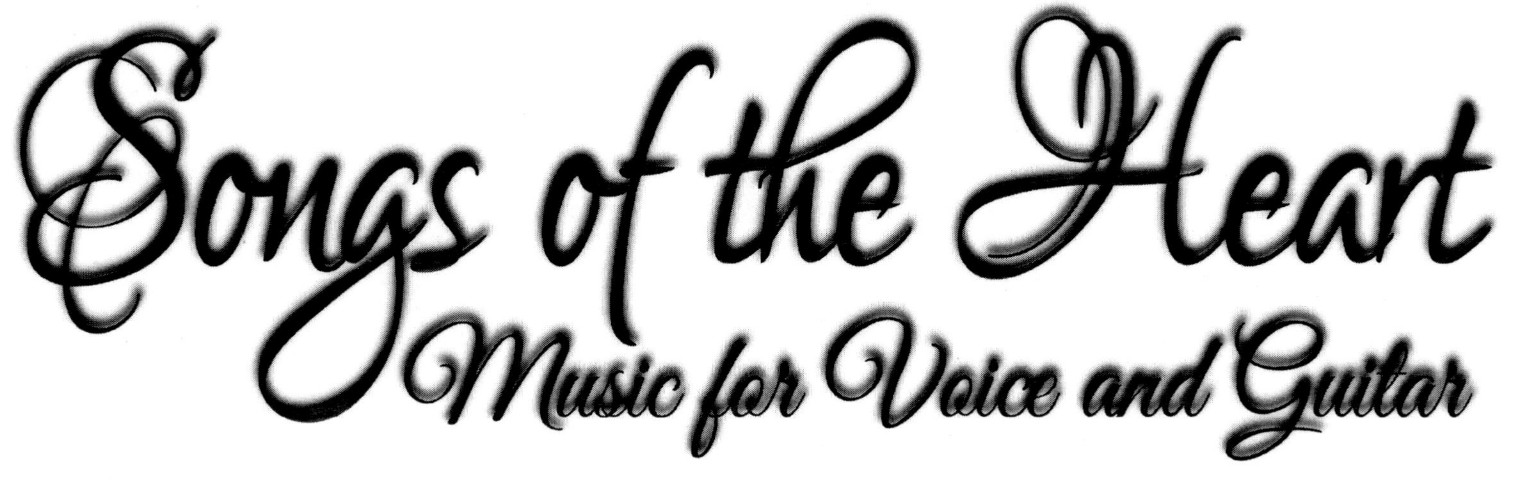

Giovanni De Chiaro

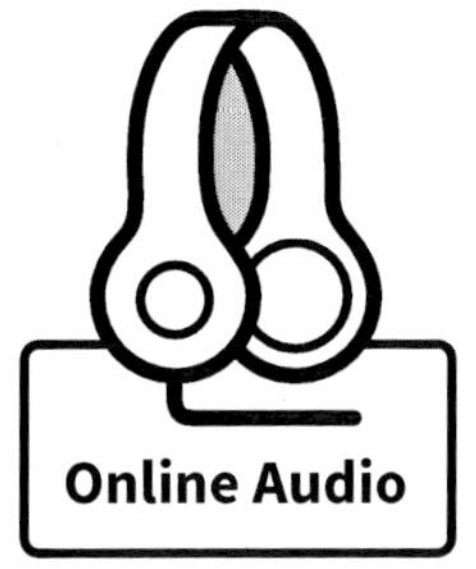

To access the online audio go to:
WWW.MELBAY.COM/30897MEB

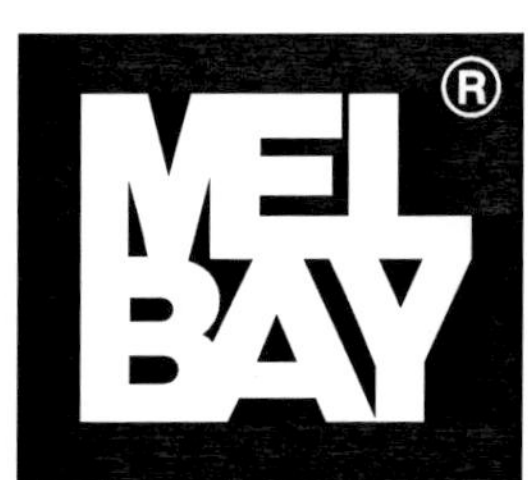

WWW.MELBAY.COM

Preface

In the classical guitar repertoire, there is a need for voice and guitar music by master composers. This anthology addresses this deficiency by providing vocal masterpieces by Schubert, Mozart, and Giuliani as well as music by important but lesser-known mid-nineteenth-century English composers.

Many of the selections included in this varied collection consist of my transcriptions, orchestral reductions, and arrangements. Seven of the nine Schubert selections were transcribed from the keyboard settings to the guitar; the remaining two pieces feature guitar parts originally composed by Schubert himself, as he was known to play the guitar. It is fascinating to see and experience his abilities as a guitarist.

The three compositions by Mozart were taken from his opera, *Don Giovanni.* To closely approximate Mozart's original intention, the transcriptions were created by first making a reduction of the complete orchestral score, including the string and wind parts, while still making the end result accessible to the guitar. As was the case in these orchestrations, many of the wind parts simply doubled the strings, creating the characteristic sound and color associated with Mozart's symphonic works.

Mauro Giuliani is best known for his concert pieces, etudes, and exercises for solo guitar. The selections included in this anthology— *Sei Ariette* (Six Short Arias)—are among his best and most important contributions to the vocal/ guitar repertoire.

The "Four English Songs" in this anthology were composed by noteworthy composers of this same genre and period. While the composer's names are not familiar to modern audiences, perhaps their inclusion here will give them the exposure they justly deserve, and at least make them available for singers and guitarists wishing to perform these short, beautiful works. To facilitate technical and rhythmic clarity, guitar accompaniment parts were revised for these songs in a manner more familiar to modern guitarists.

Throughout this collection, I deliberately avoided making fingering suggestions; I have discovered over the years that digitation is a very personal matter for which every guitarist has their own individual and unique approach.

Giovanni De Chiaro

Acknowledgements

I am deeply grateful to soprano, Kate Rawls for lending her exquisite vocal skills to the companion recording for this project and for her expertise in proofing and editing the vocal parts of all selections.

Special thanks to Kermit Poling for his work as recording engineer, editor, and producer of the accompanying recording.

Mr. De Chiaro performs on a guitar built by retired steelworker and luthier Joe Benevides.

Contents

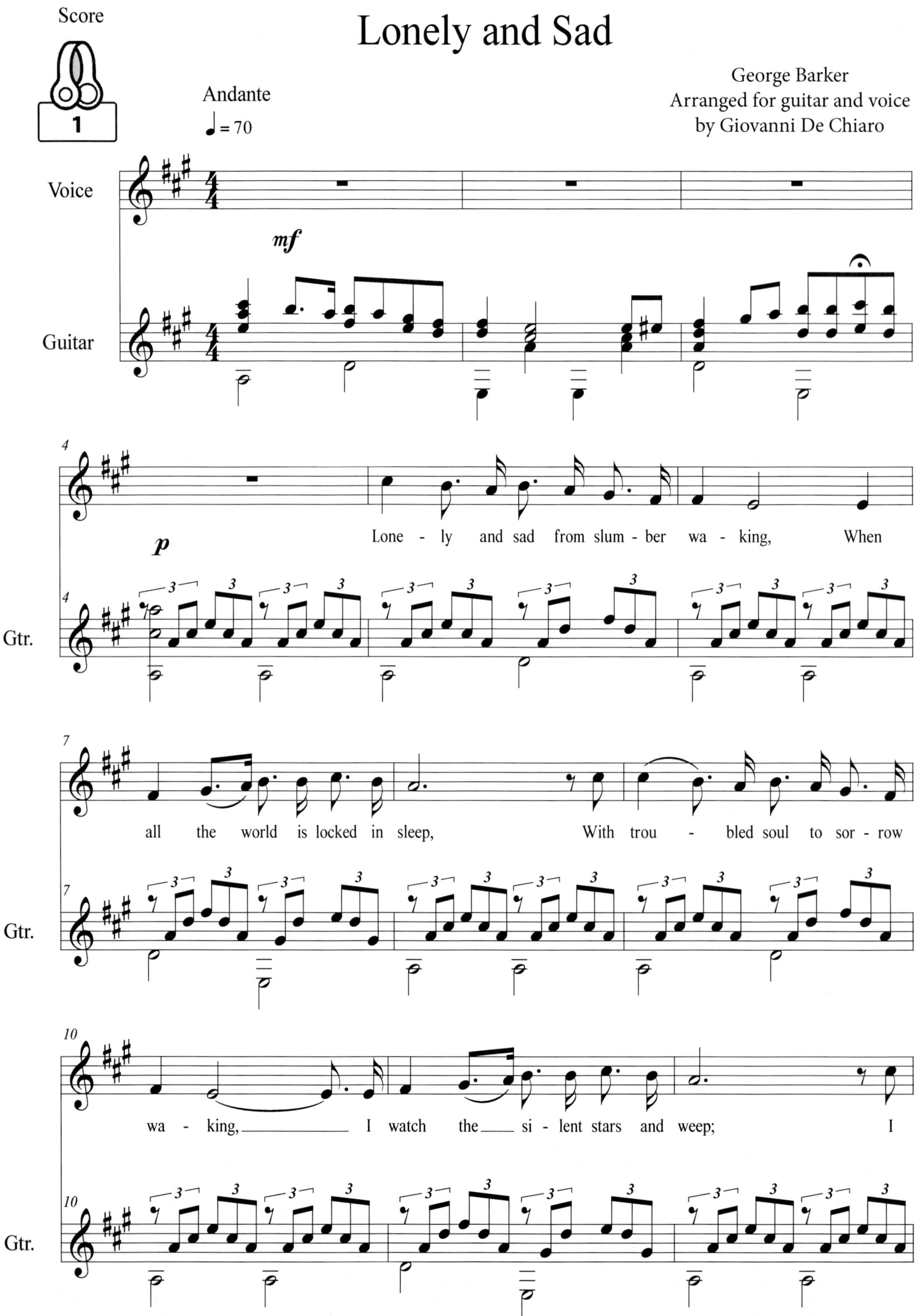
Score
1
Lonely and Sad
George Barker
Arranged for guitar and voice
by Giovanni De Chiaro
Andante
♩ = 70
Voice
Guitar
mf
p
Gtr.
Lone - ly and sad from slum - ber wa - king, When
all the world is locked in sleep, With trou - bled soul to sor - row
wa - king, I watch the si - lent stars and weep; I

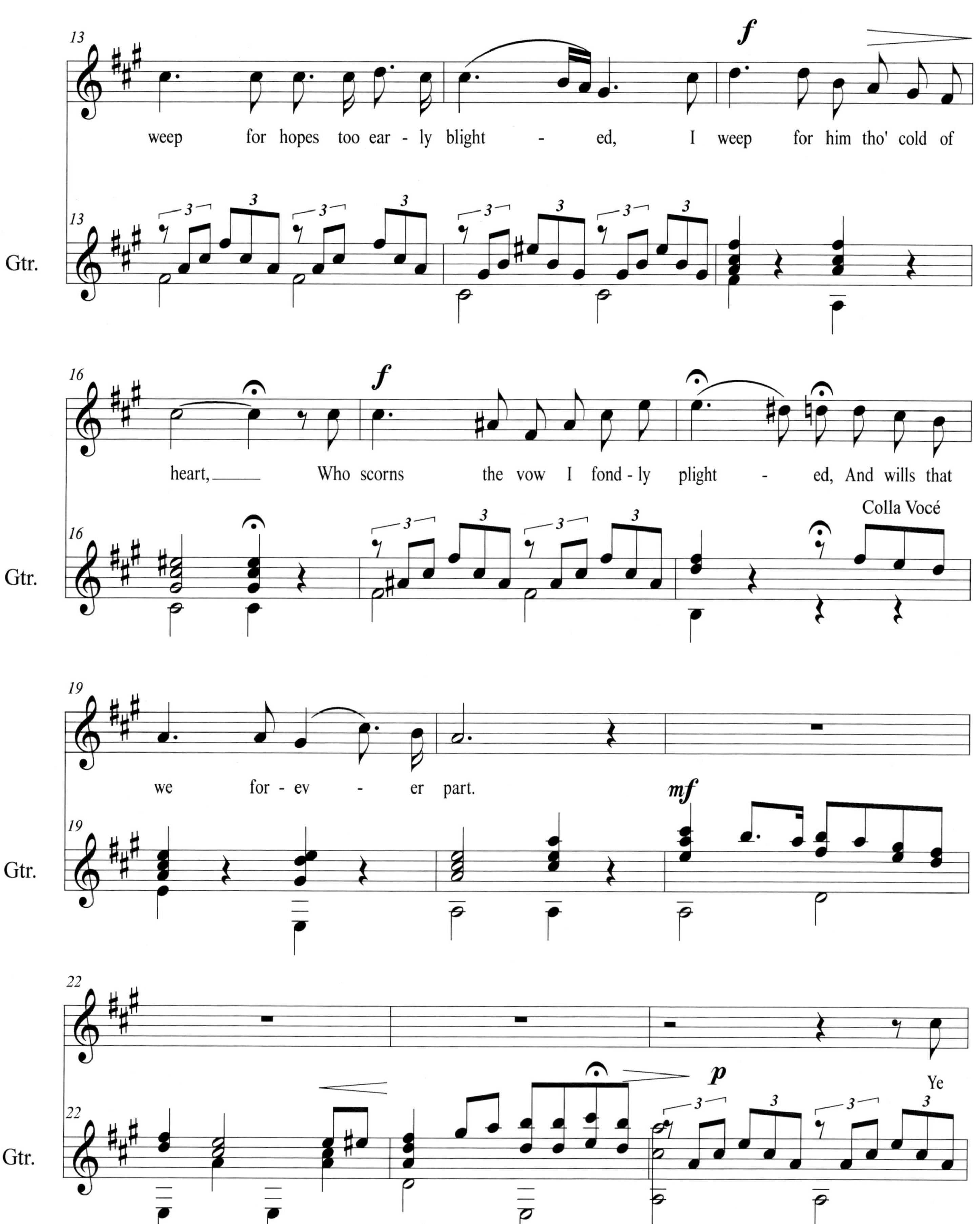
13
weep for hopes too ear - ly blight - ed, I weep for him tho' cold of
Gtr.
16
heart, Who scorns the vow I fond - ly plight - ed, And wills that
Colla Vocé
19
we for - ev - er part.
22
Ye

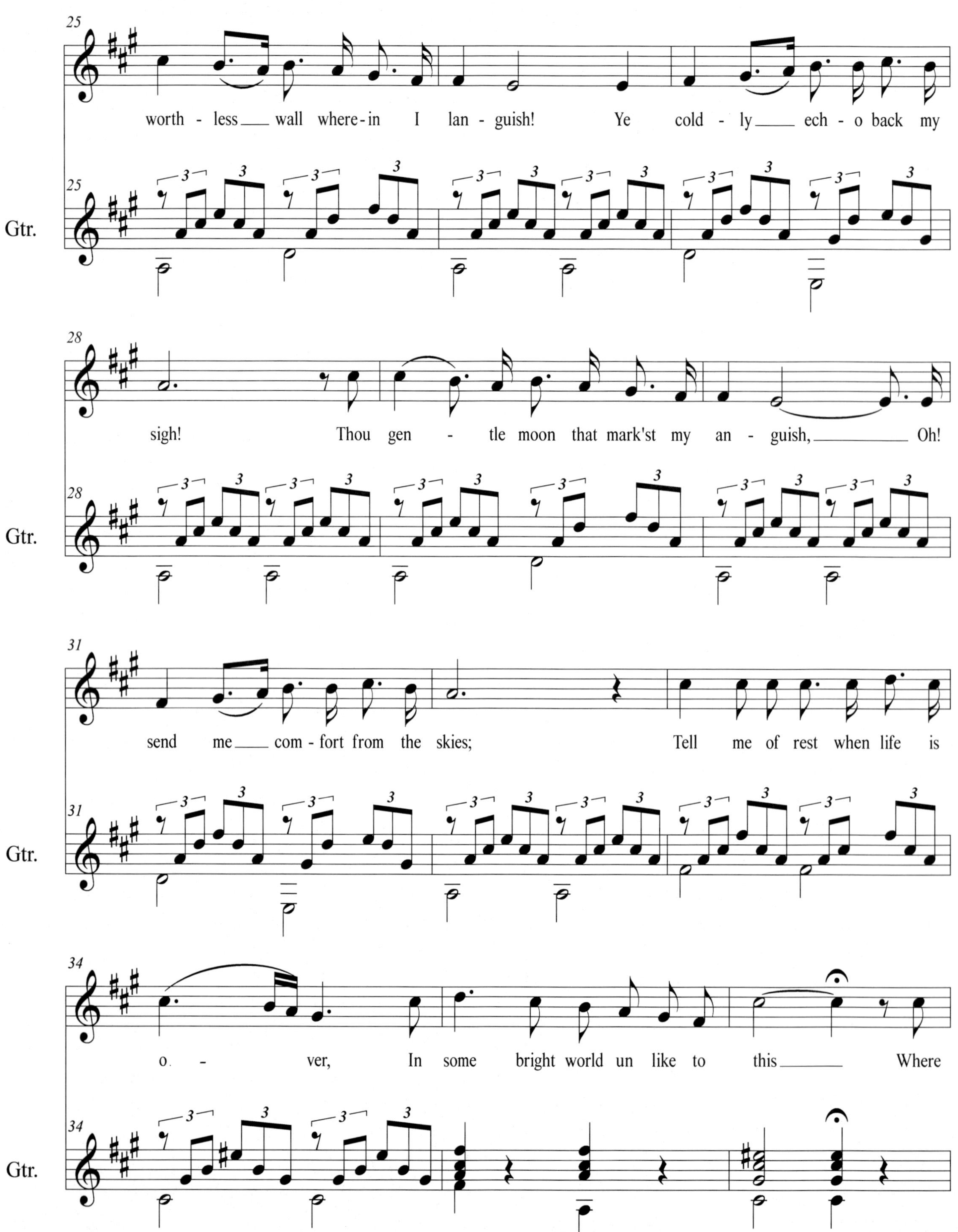
25
worth - less wall where-in I lan - guish! Ye cold - ly ech - o back my
Gtr.
28
sigh! Thou gen - tle moon that mark'st my an - guish, Oh!
Gtr.
31
send me com - fort from the skies; Tell me of rest when life is
Gtr.
34
o - ver, In some bright world un like to this Where
Gtr.

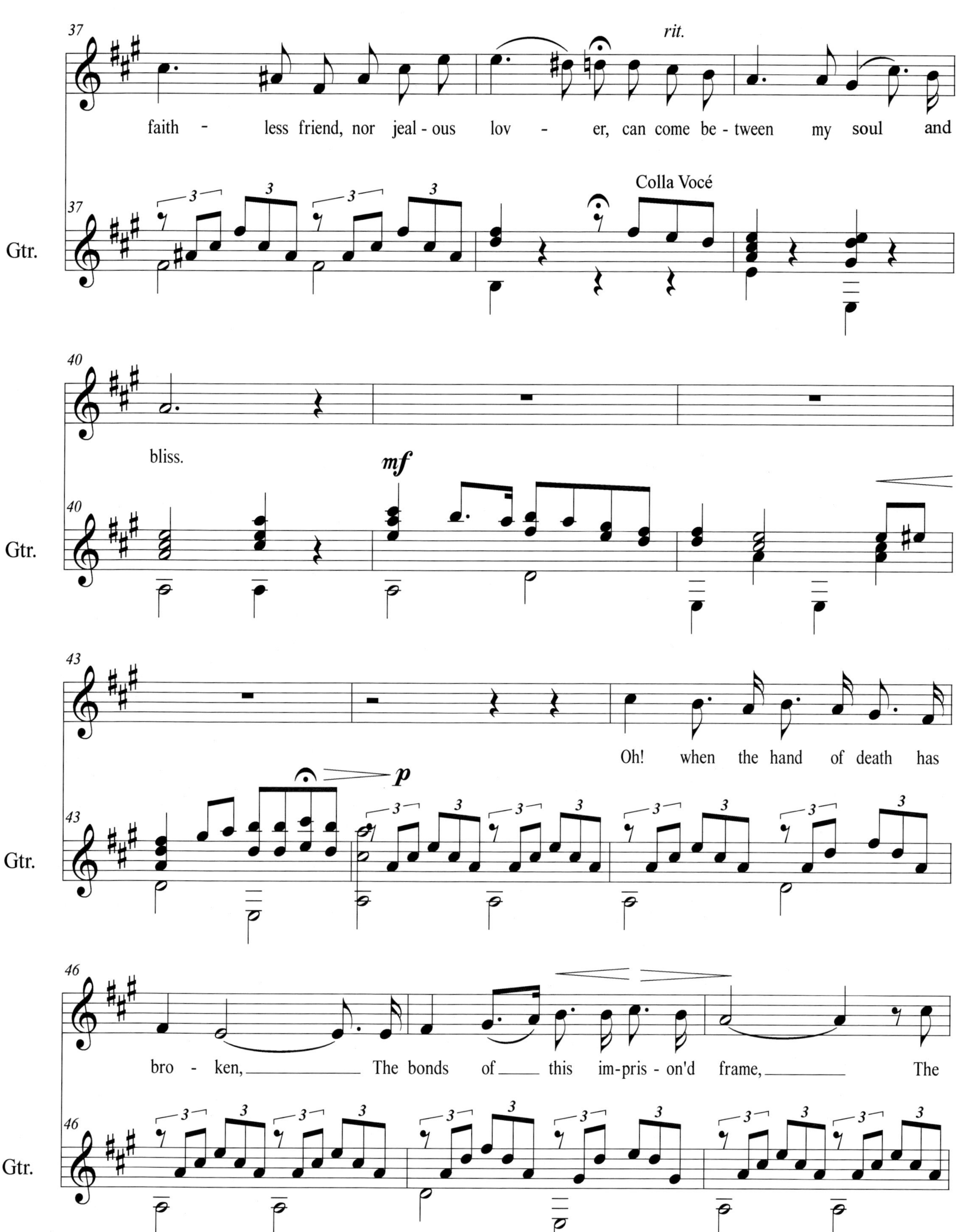
37
rit.
faith - less friend, nor jeal - ous lov - er, can come be - tween my soul and
Gtr.
Colla Vocé
40
bliss.
mf
43
Oh! when the hand of death has
p
46
bro - ken, The bonds of this im-pris - on'd frame, The

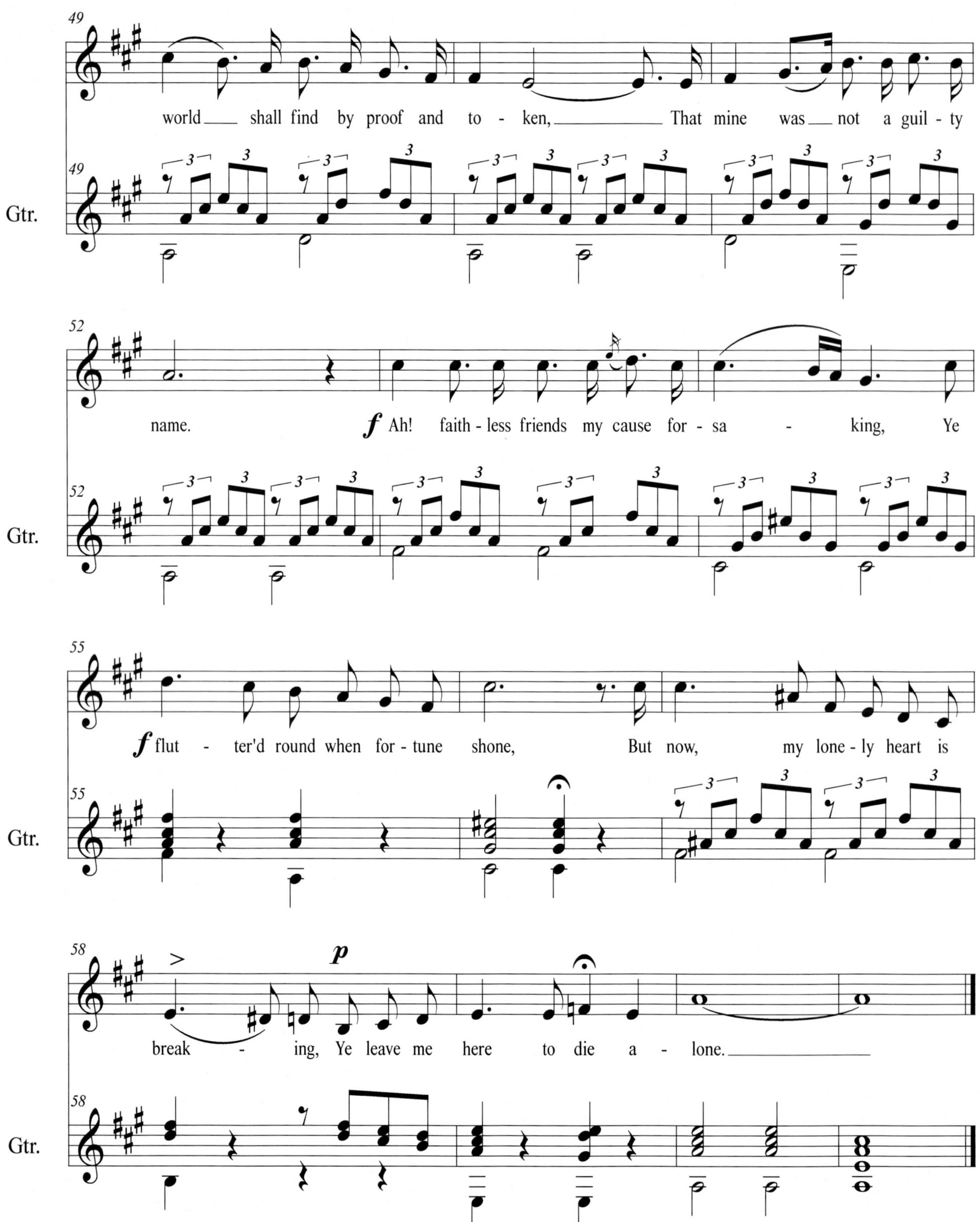
49
world shall find by proof and to - ken, That mine was not a guil - ty
Gtr.
52
name. f Ah! faith - less friends my cause for - sa - king, Ye
Gtr.
55
f flut - ter'd round when for - tune shone, But now, my lone - ly heart is
Gtr.
58
p
break - ing, Ye leave me here to die a - lone.
Gtr.

Come Away Love

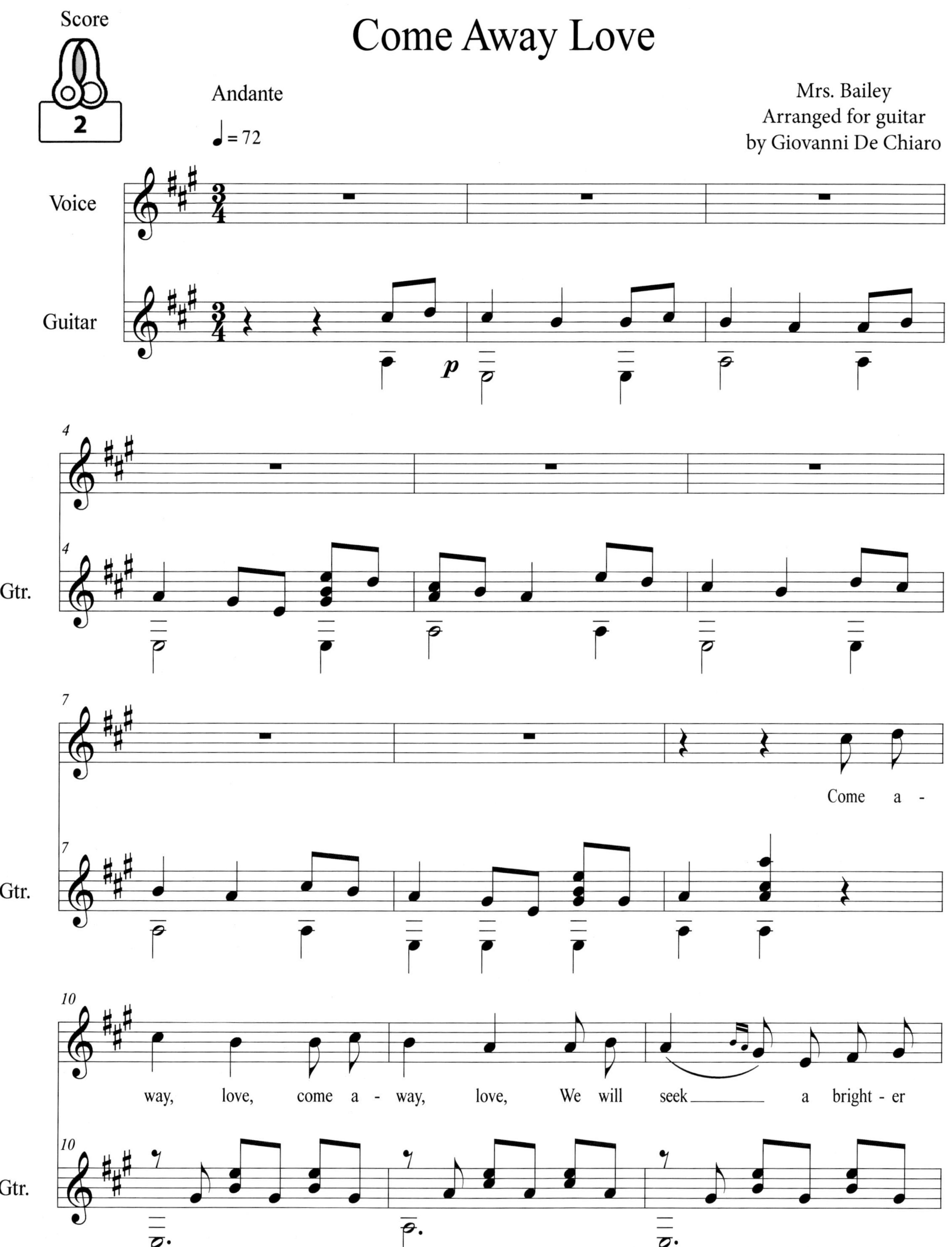

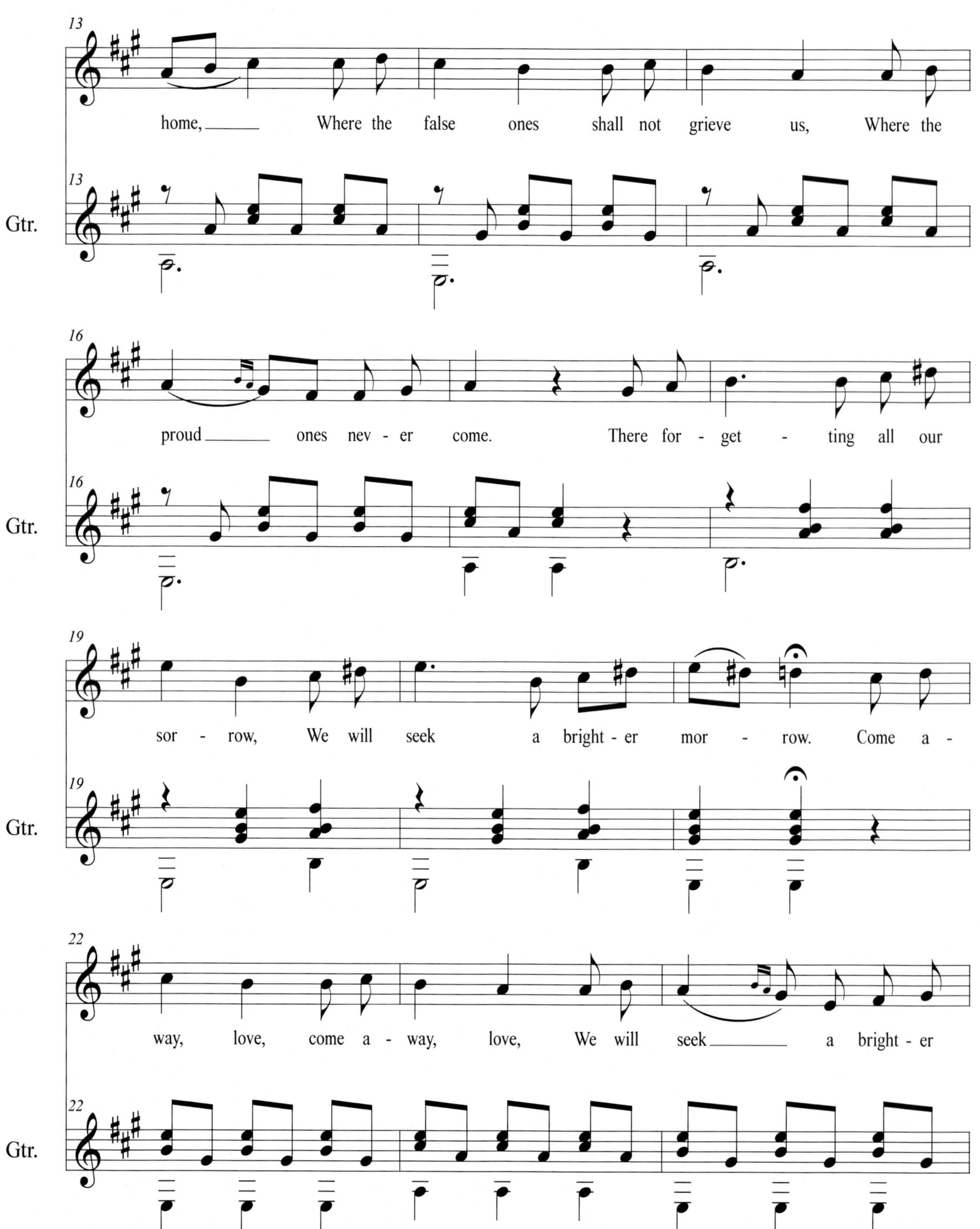
13
home, Where the false ones shall not grieve us, Where the
Gtr.
16
proud ones nev - er come. There for - get - ting all our
Gtr.
19
sor - row, We will seek a bright - er mor - row. Come a -
Gtr.
22
way, love, come a - way, love, We will seek a bright - er
Gtr.

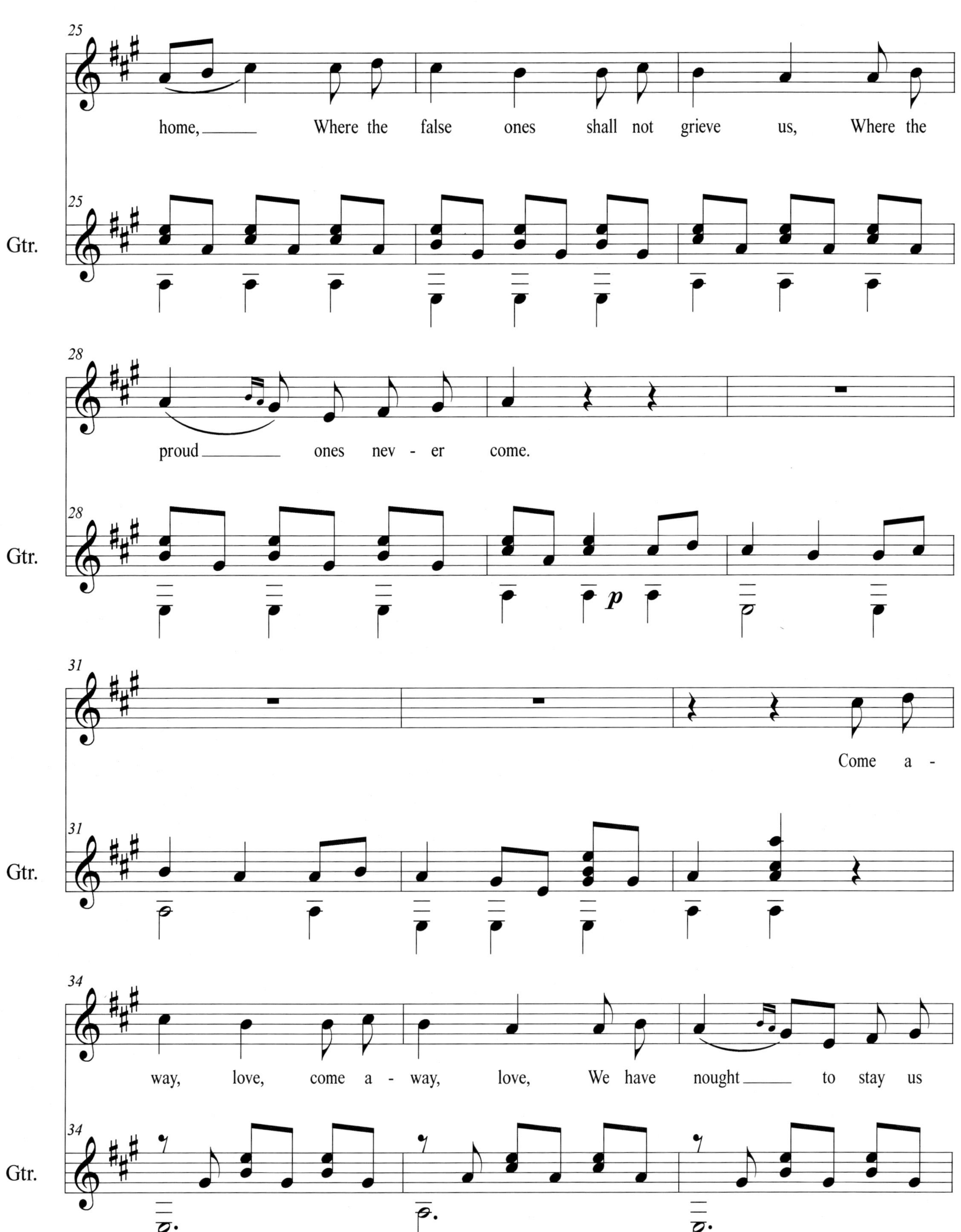

home, Where the false ones shall not grieve us, Where the
Gtr.
proud ones nev - er come.
Gtr.
p
Come a -
Gtr.
way, love, come a - way, love, We have nought to stay us
Gtr.

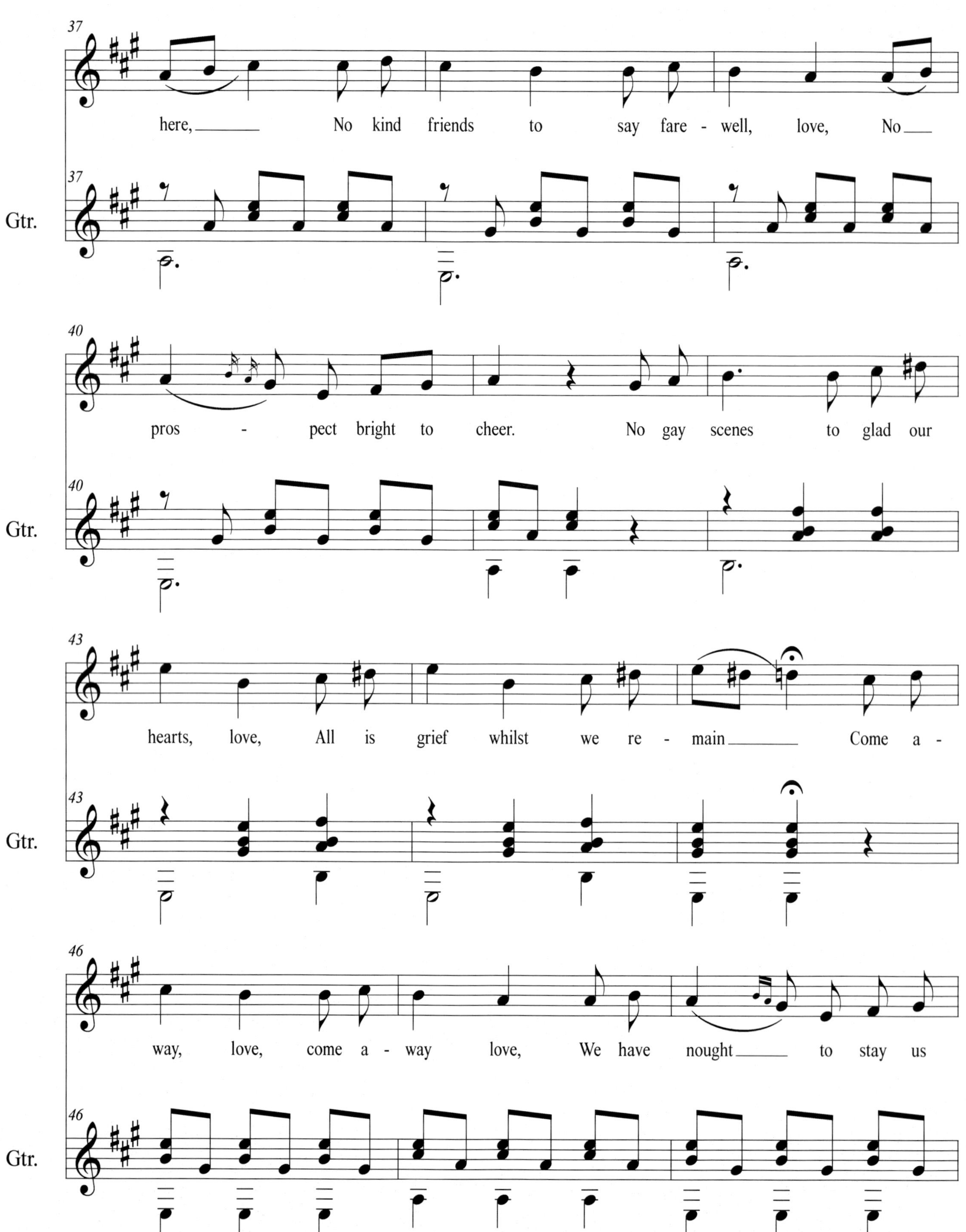
37
here, No kind friends to say fare - well, love, No
Gtr.
40
pros - pect bright to cheer. No gay scenes to glad our
Gtr.
43
hearts, love, All is grief whilst we re - main Come a -
Gtr.
46
way, love, come a - way love, We have nought to stay us
Gtr.

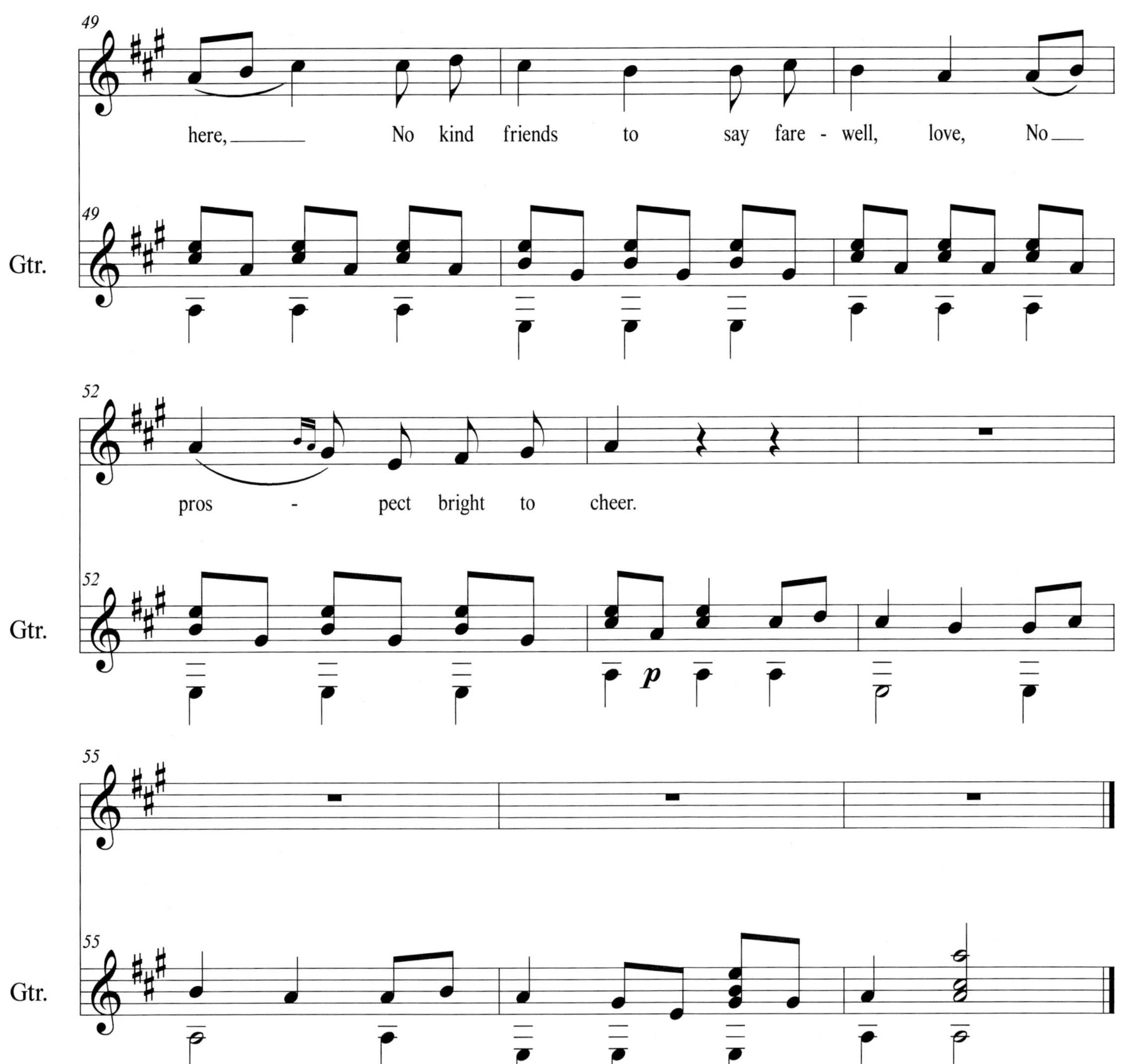
49
here, No kind friends to say fare - well, love, No
Gtr.
52
pros - pect bright to cheer.
p
55

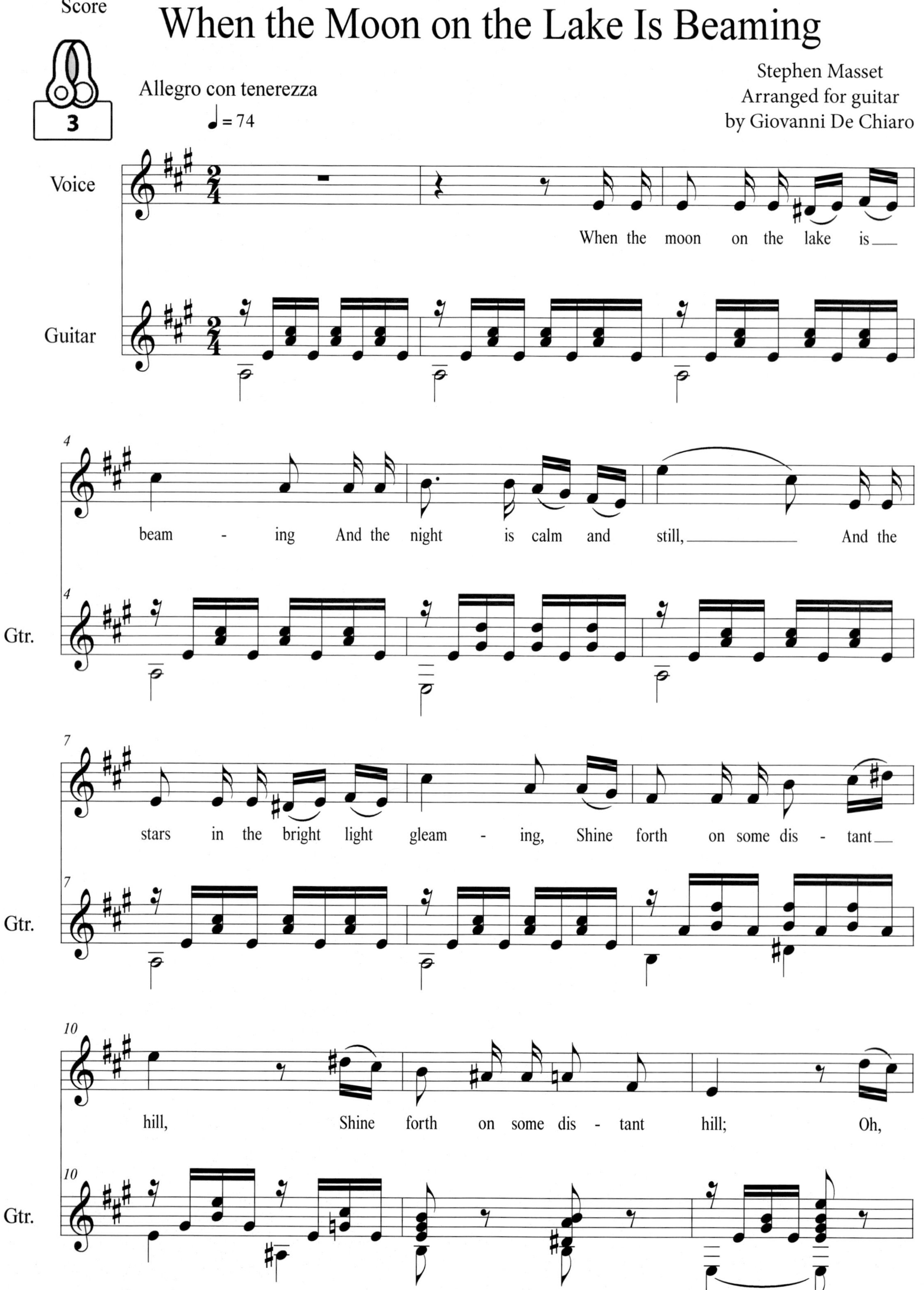
Score
3
When the Moon on the Lake Is Beaming
Allegro con tenerezza
♩ = 74
Stephen Masset
Arranged for guitar
by Giovanni De Chiaro
Voice
Guitar
When the moon on the lake is
beam - ing And the night is calm and still, And the
Gtr.
stars in the bright light gleam - ing, Shine forth on some dis - tant
hill, Shine forth on some dis - tant hill; Oh,

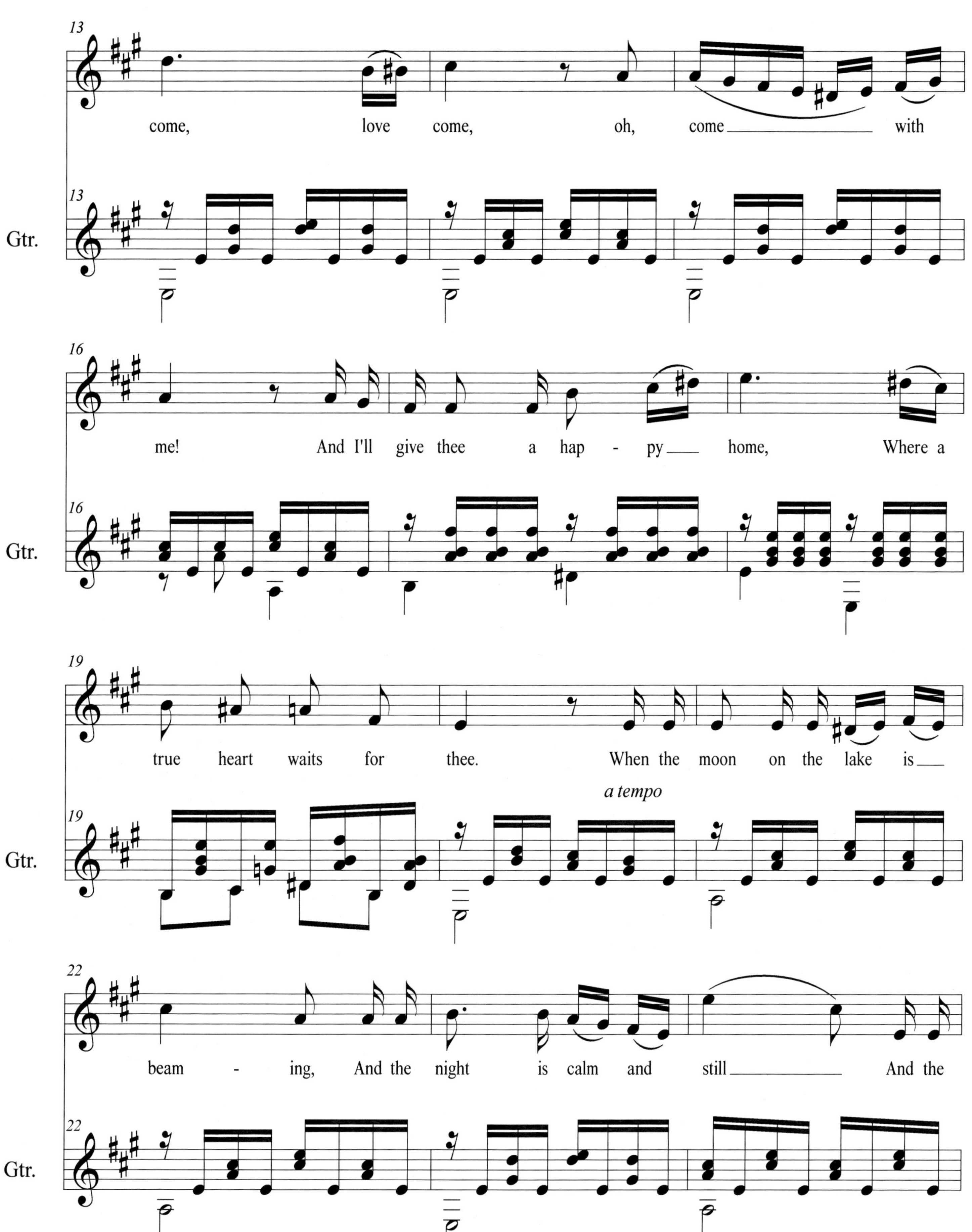
13
come, love come, oh, come with
Gtr.
16
me! And I'll give thee a hap - py home, Where a
19
true heart waits for thee. When the moon on the lake is
a tempo
22
beam - ing, And the night is calm and still And the

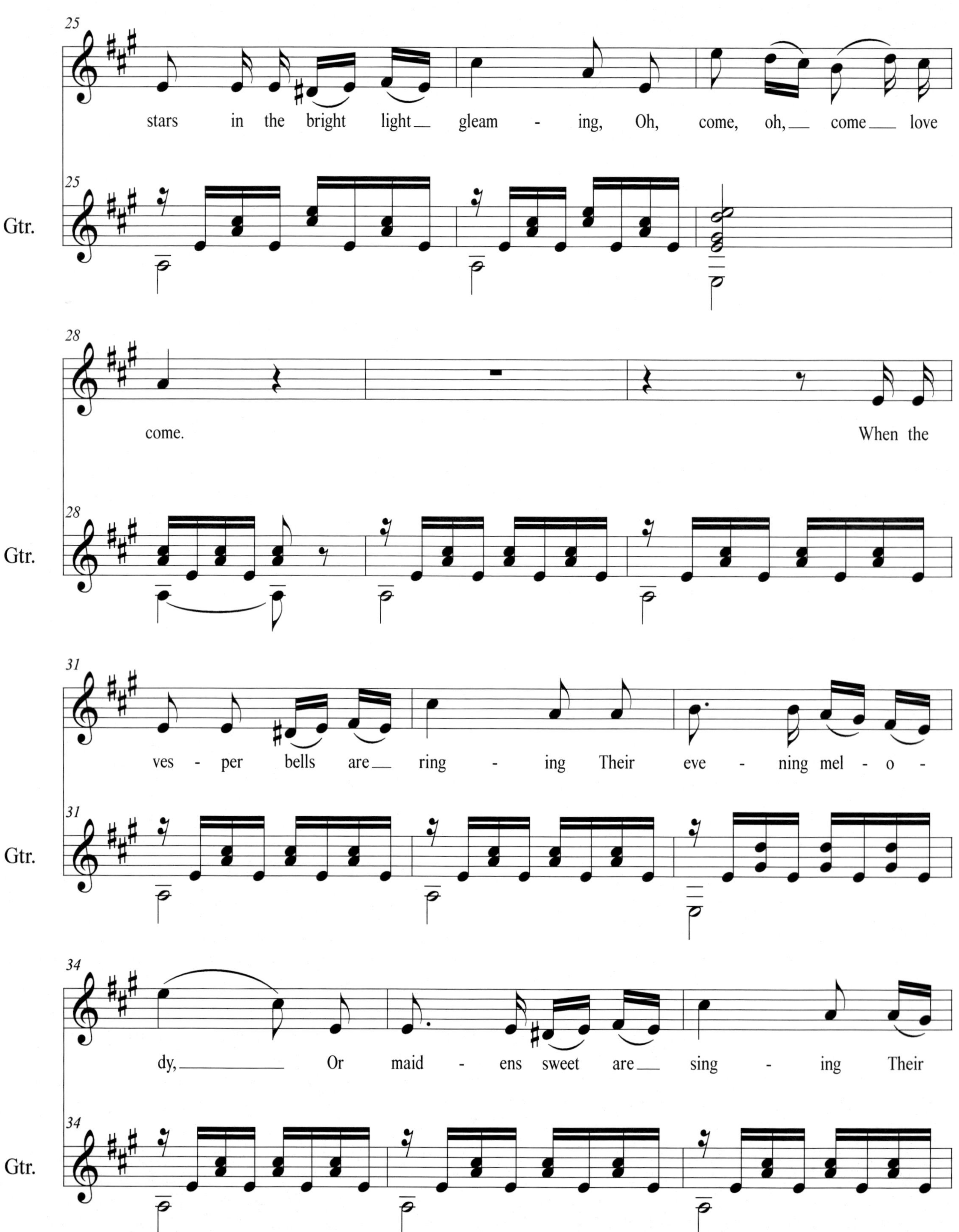
25
stars in the bright light gleam - ing, Oh, come, oh, come love
Gtr.
28
come.
When the
Gtr.
31
ves - per bells are ring - ing Their eve - ning mel - o -
Gtr.
34
dy, Or maid - ens sweet are sing - ing Their
Gtr.

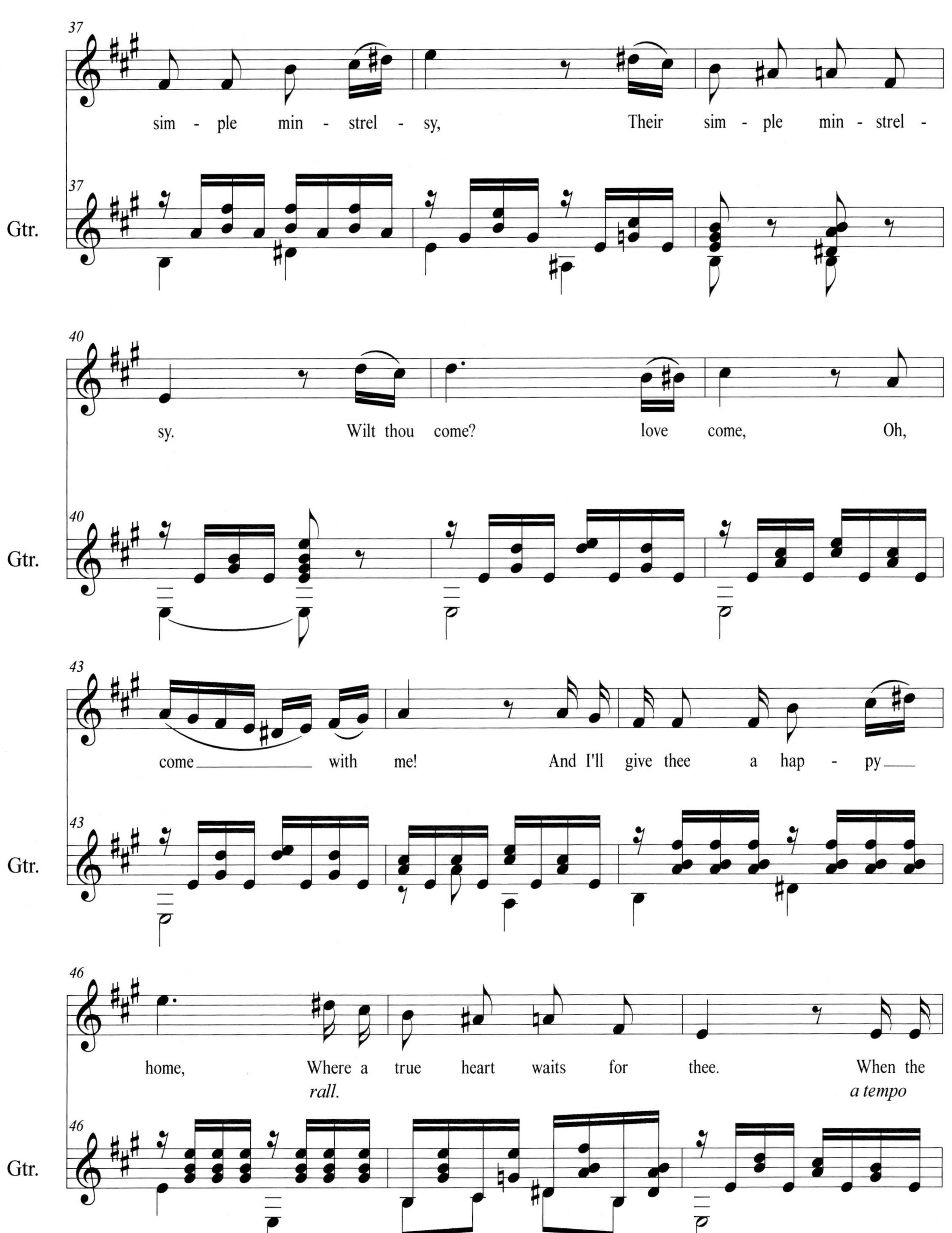
37
sim - ple min - strel - sy, Their sim - ple min - strel -
Gtr.
40
sy. Wilt thou come? love come, Oh,
Gtr.
43
come with me! And I'll give thee a hap - py
Gtr.
46
home, Where a true heart waits for thee. When the
rall.
a tempo
Gtr.

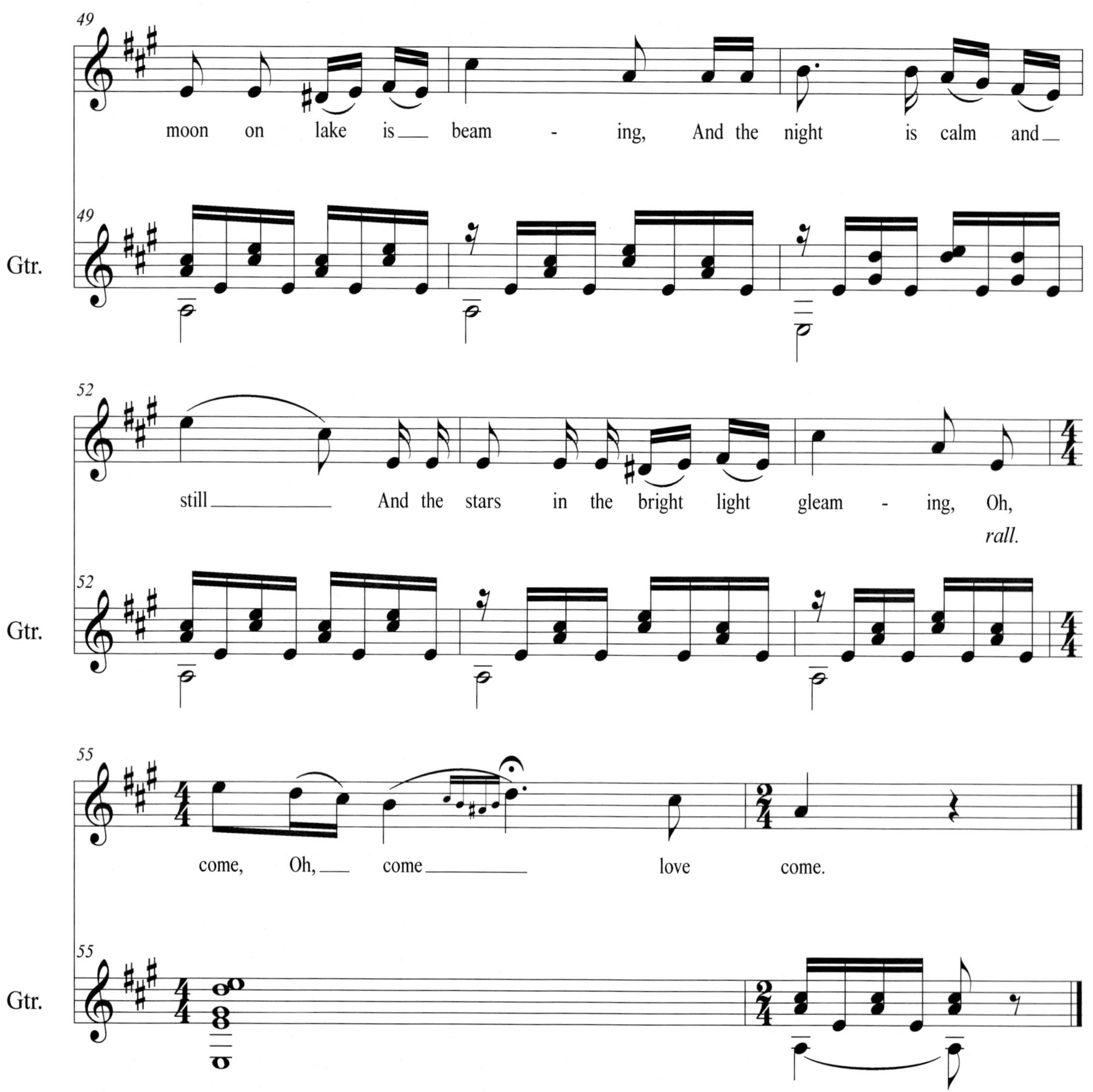
49
moon on lake is beam - ing, And the night is calm and
49
Gtr.
52
still And the stars in the bright light gleam - ing, Oh,
rall.
52
Gtr.
55
come, Oh, come love come.
55
Gtr.

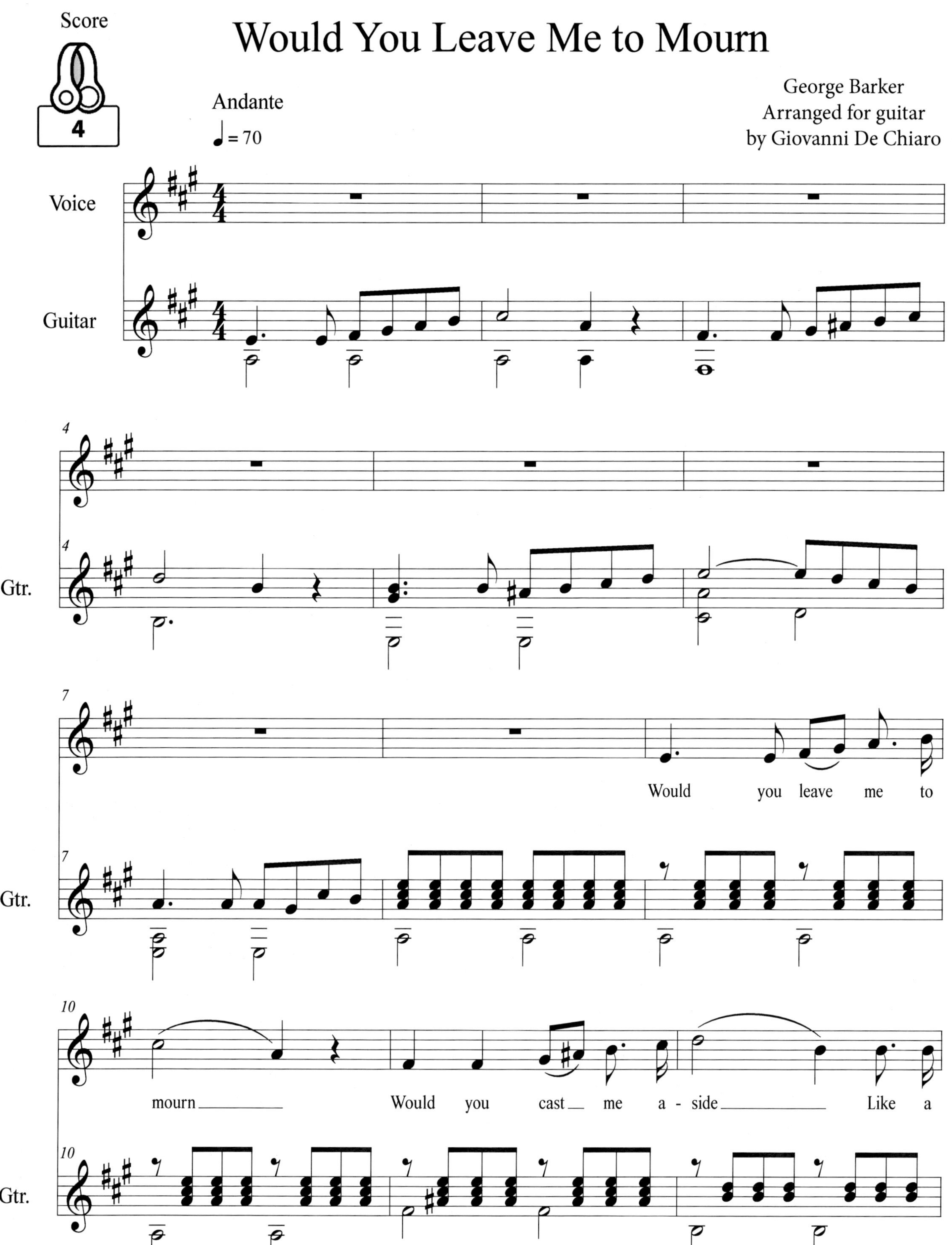
Score
4
Would You Leave Me to Mourn
Andante
♩ = 70
George Barker
Arranged for guitar
by Giovanni De Chiaro
Voice
Guitar
Gtr.
Would you leave me to
mourn
Would you cast me a - side
Like a

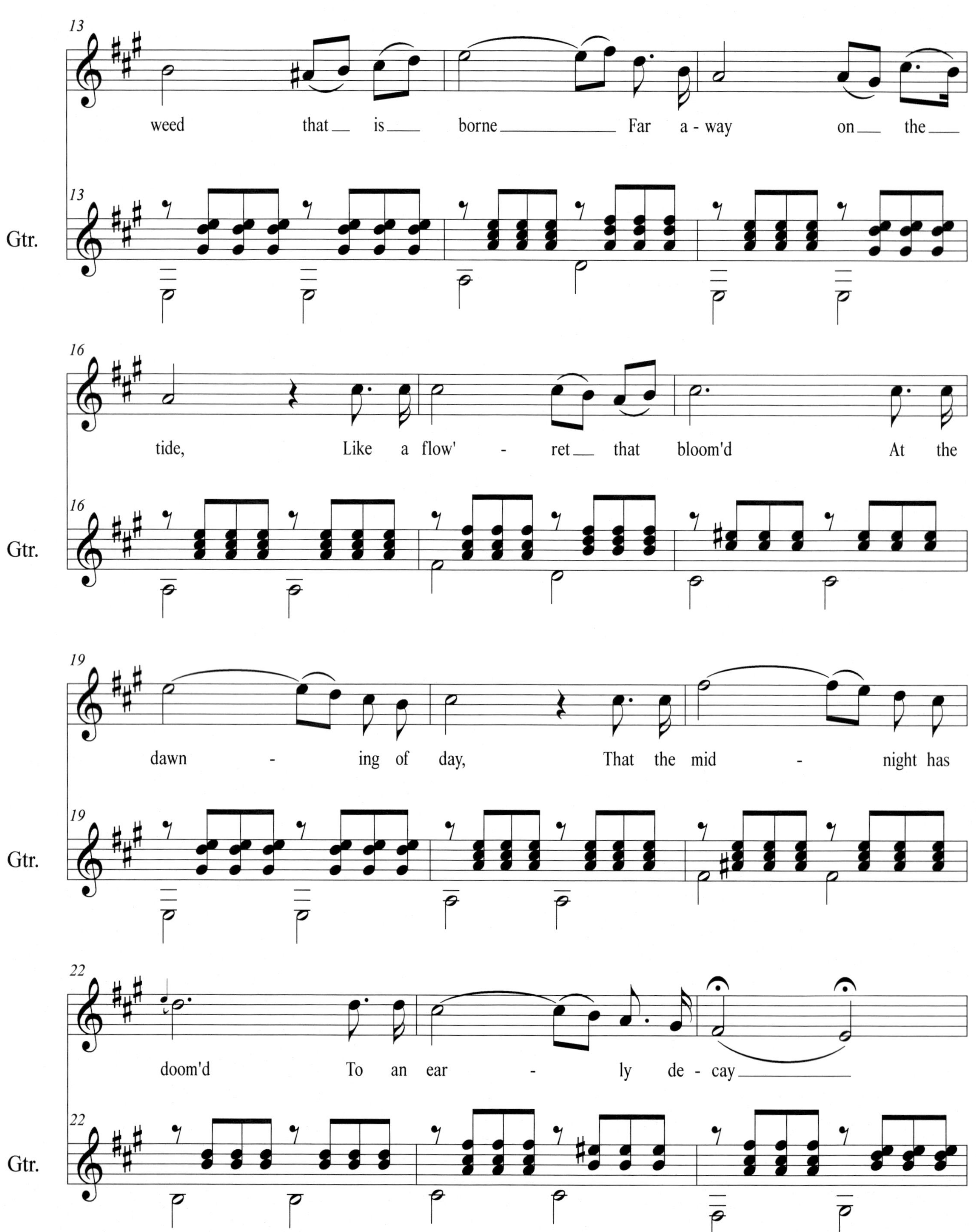
13
weed that is borne Far a - way on the
13
Gtr.
16
tide, Like a flow' - ret that bloom'd At the
16
Gtr.
19
dawn - ing of day, That the mid - night has
19
Gtr.
22
doom'd To an ear - ly de - cay
22
Gtr.

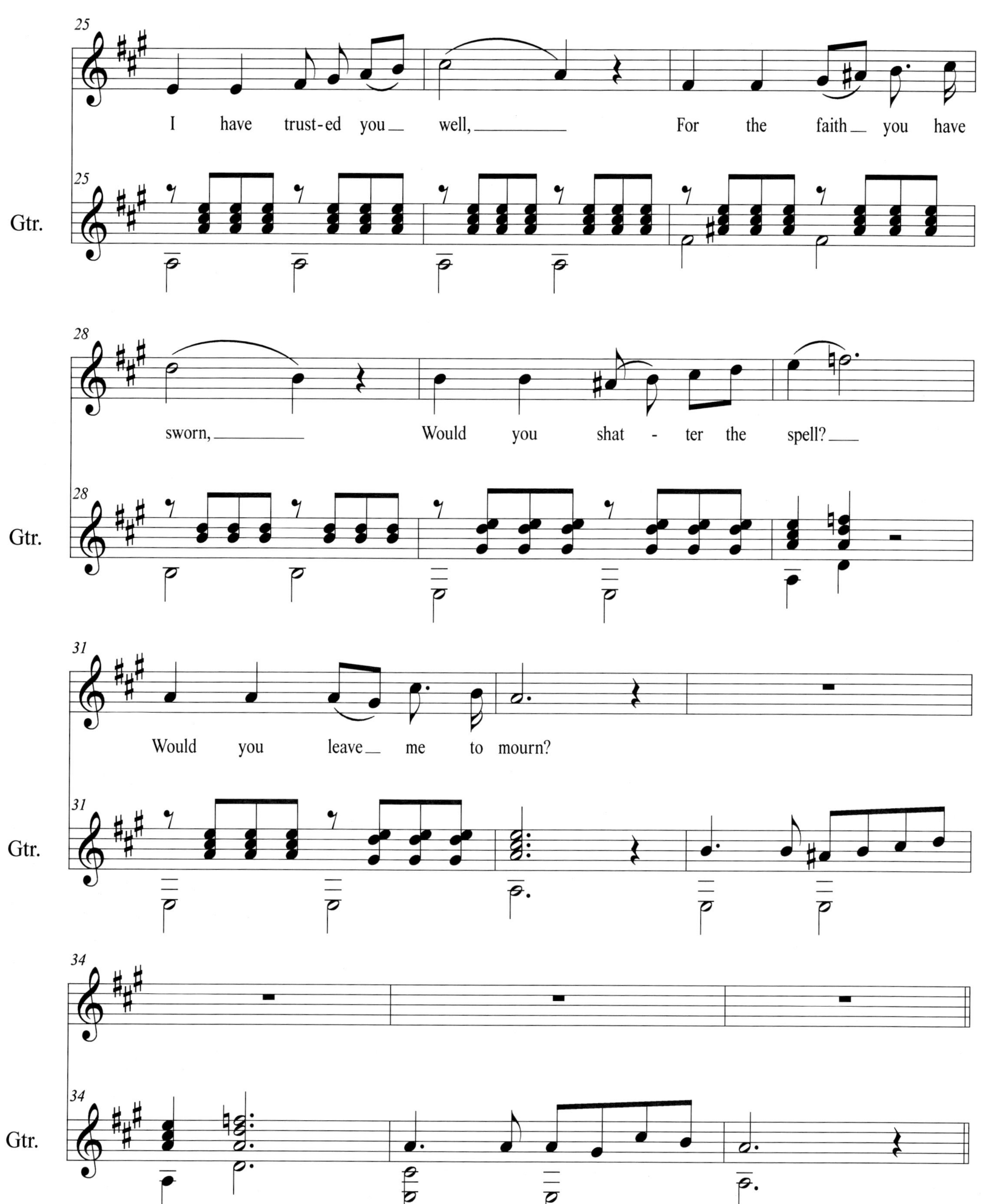
I have trust-ed you well,
For the faith you have
sworn,
Would you shat - ter the spell?
Would you leave me to mourn?
Gtr.
Gtr.
Gtr.
Gtr.

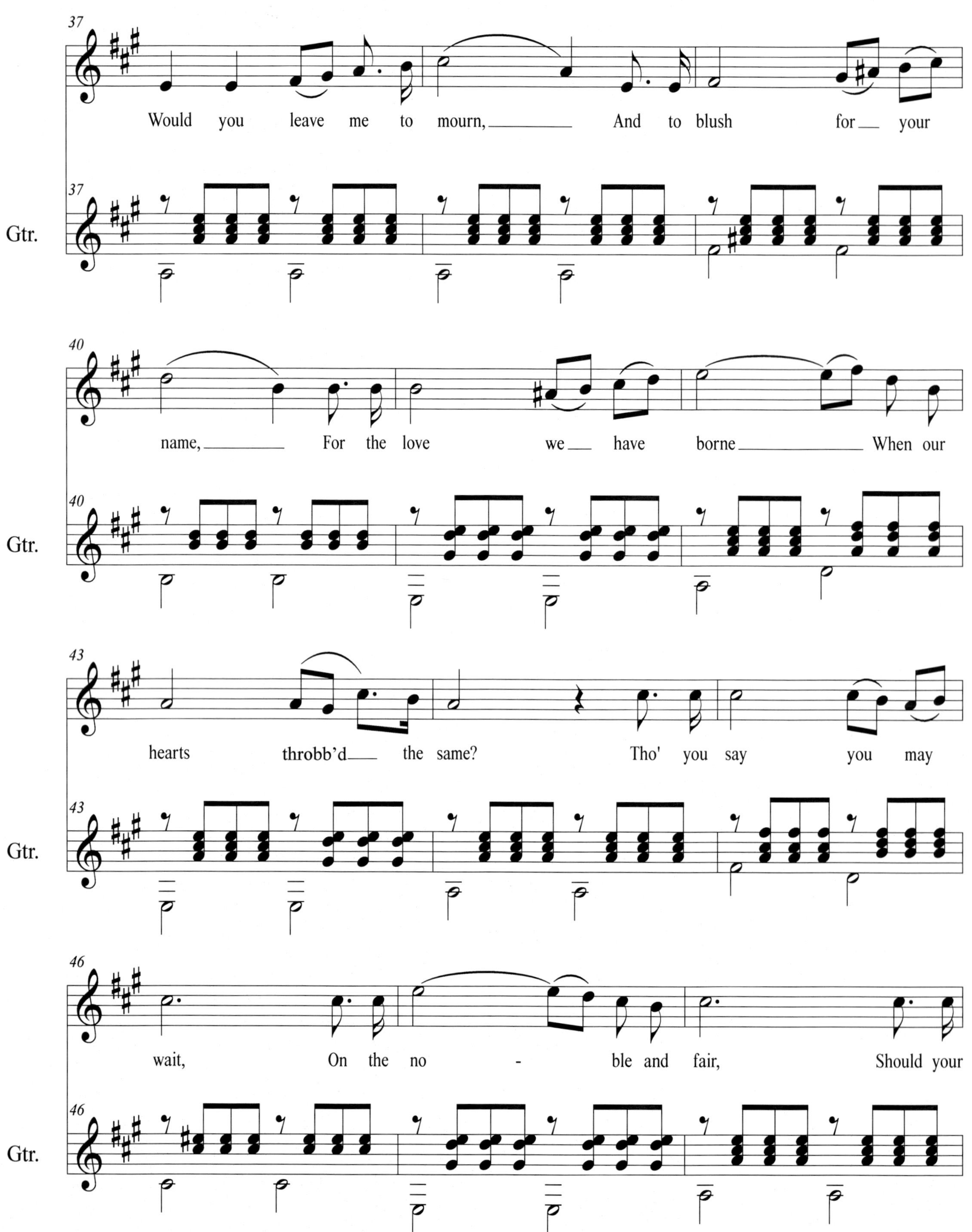
37
Would you leave me to mourn, And to blush for your
Gtr.
40
name, For the love we have borne When our
Gtr.
43
hearts throbb'd the same? Tho' you say you may
Gtr.
46
wait, On the no - ble and fair, Should your
Gtr.

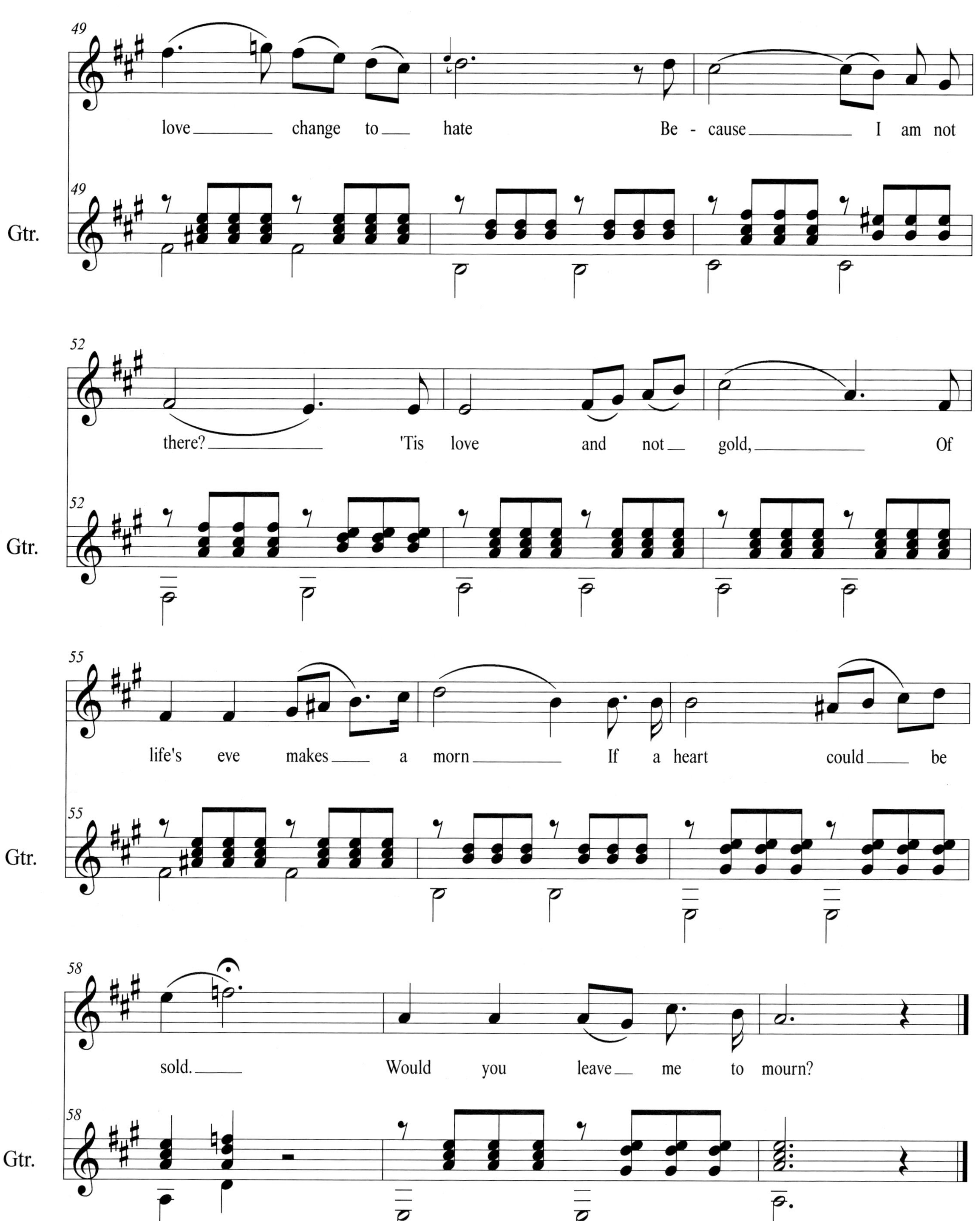
49
love change to hate Be - cause I am not
Gtr.
52
there? 'Tis love and not gold, Of
Gtr.
55
life's eve makes a morn If a heart could be
Gtr.
58
sold. Would you leave me to mourn?
Gtr.

Canzonetta

Wolfgang Amadeus Mozart
Transcribed for guitar
by Giovanni De Chiaro

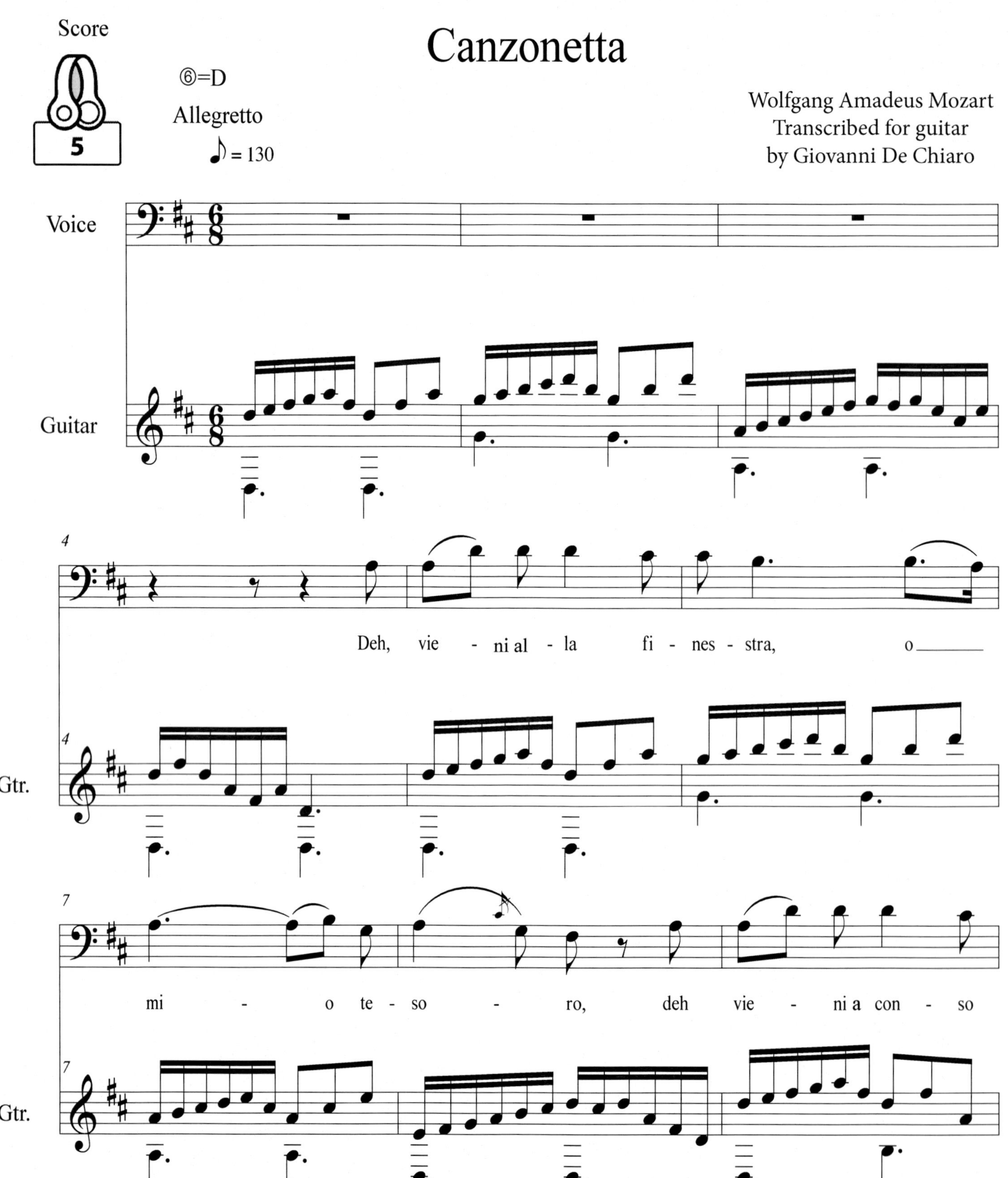

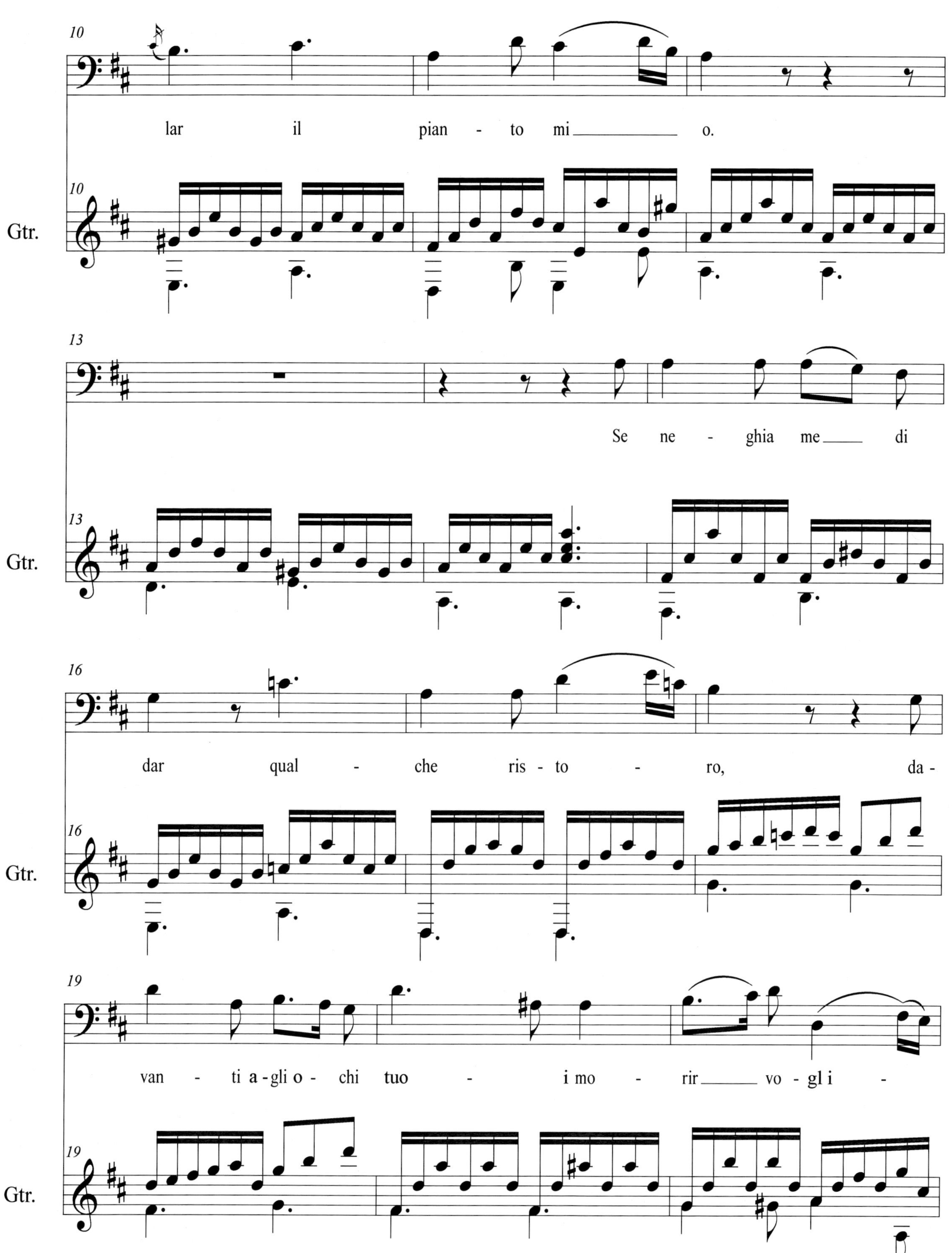
10
lar il pian - to mi o.
Gtr.
13
Se ne - ghia me di
16
dar qual - che ris - to - ro, da -
19
van - ti a - gli o - chi tuo - i mo - rir vo - gl i -

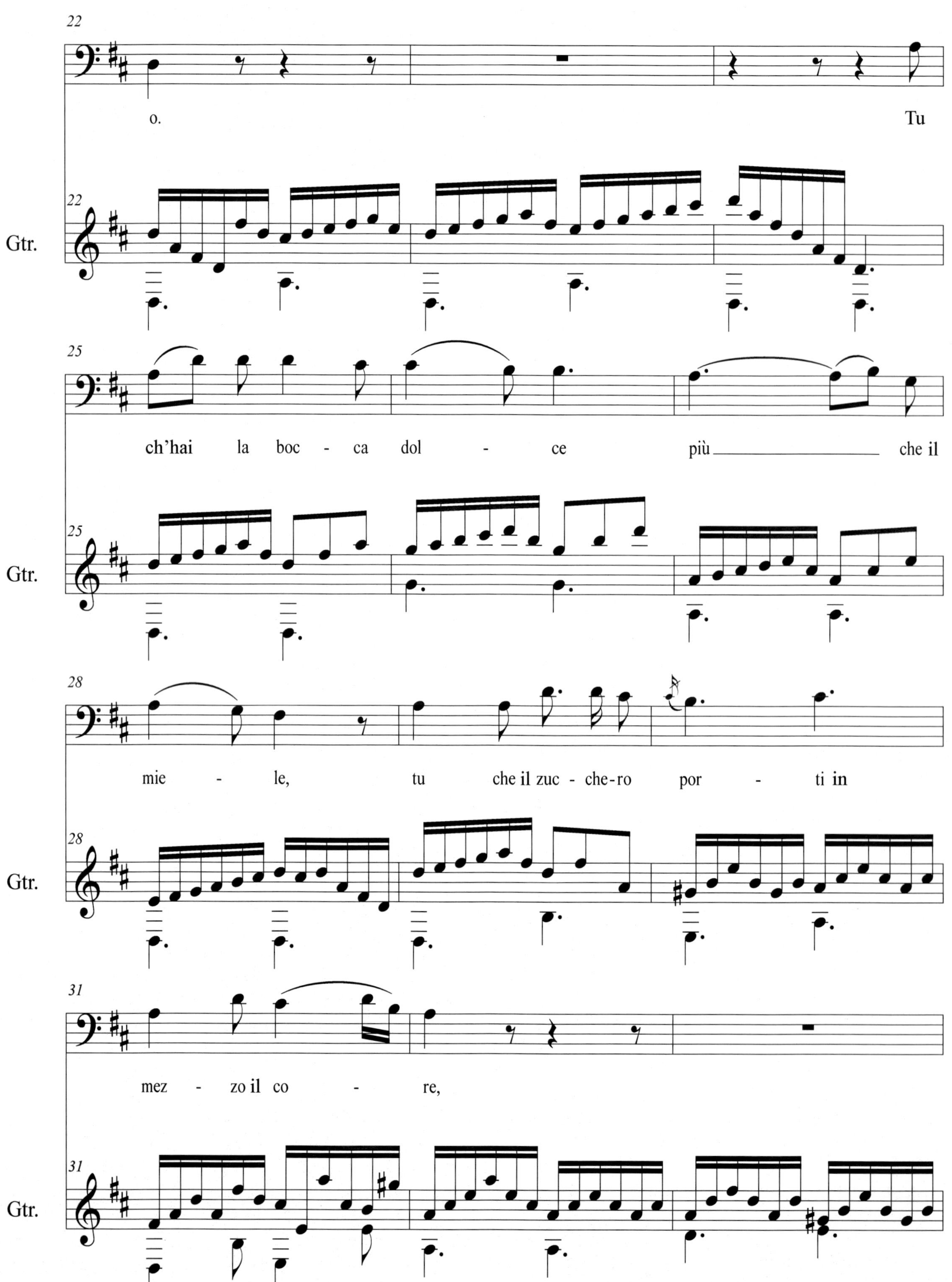
22
o.
Tu
Gtr.
25
ch'hai la boc - ca dol - ce più che il
28
mie - le, tu che il zuc - che-ro por - ti in
31
mez - zo il co - re,

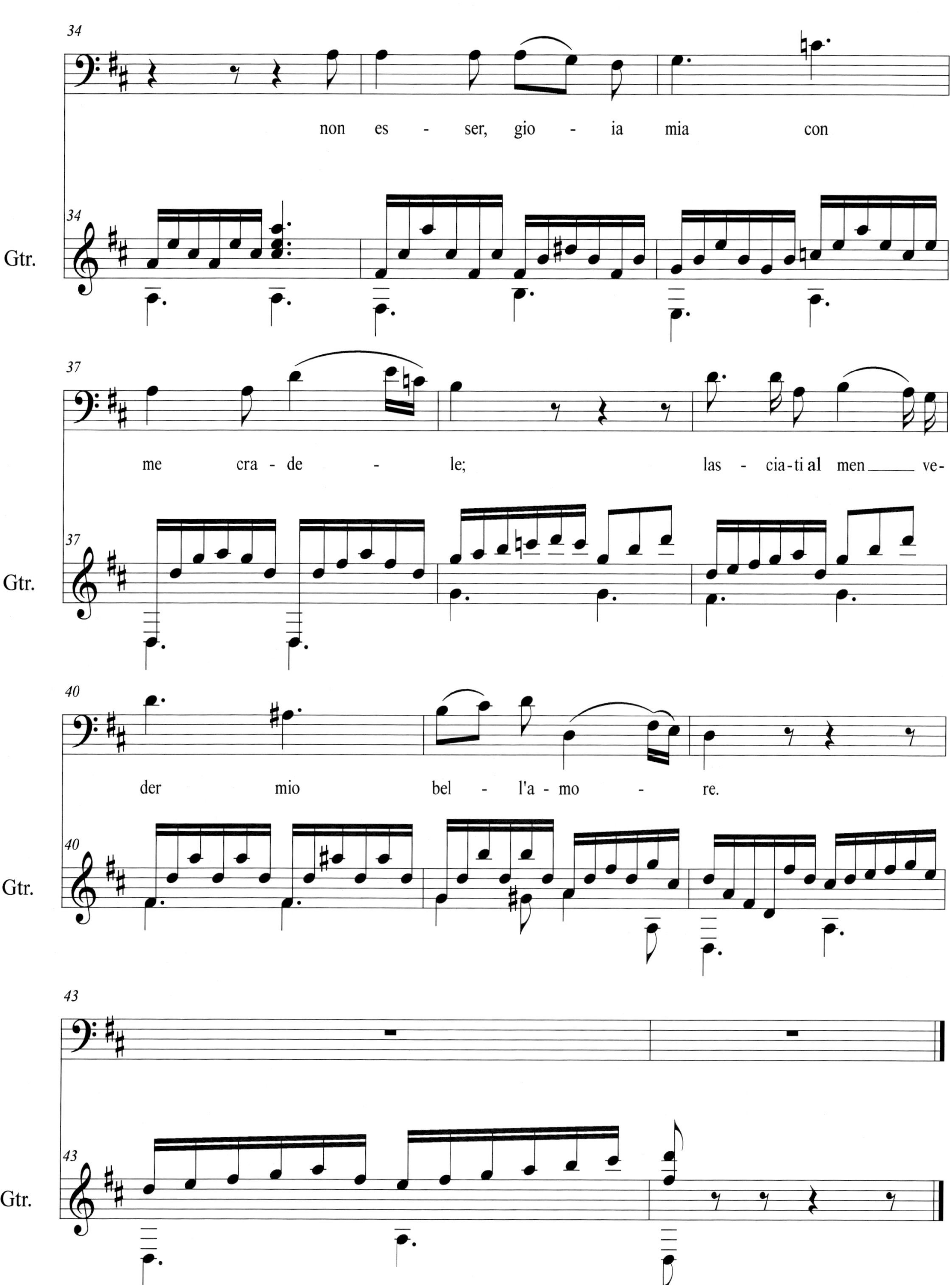
34
non es - ser, gio - ia mia con
Gtr.
37
me cra - de - le;
las - cia-ti al men ve-
40
der mio bel - l'a - mo - re.
43

Vedrai, Carino

Wolfgang Amadeus Mozart
Transcribed for guitar
by Giovanni De Chiaro

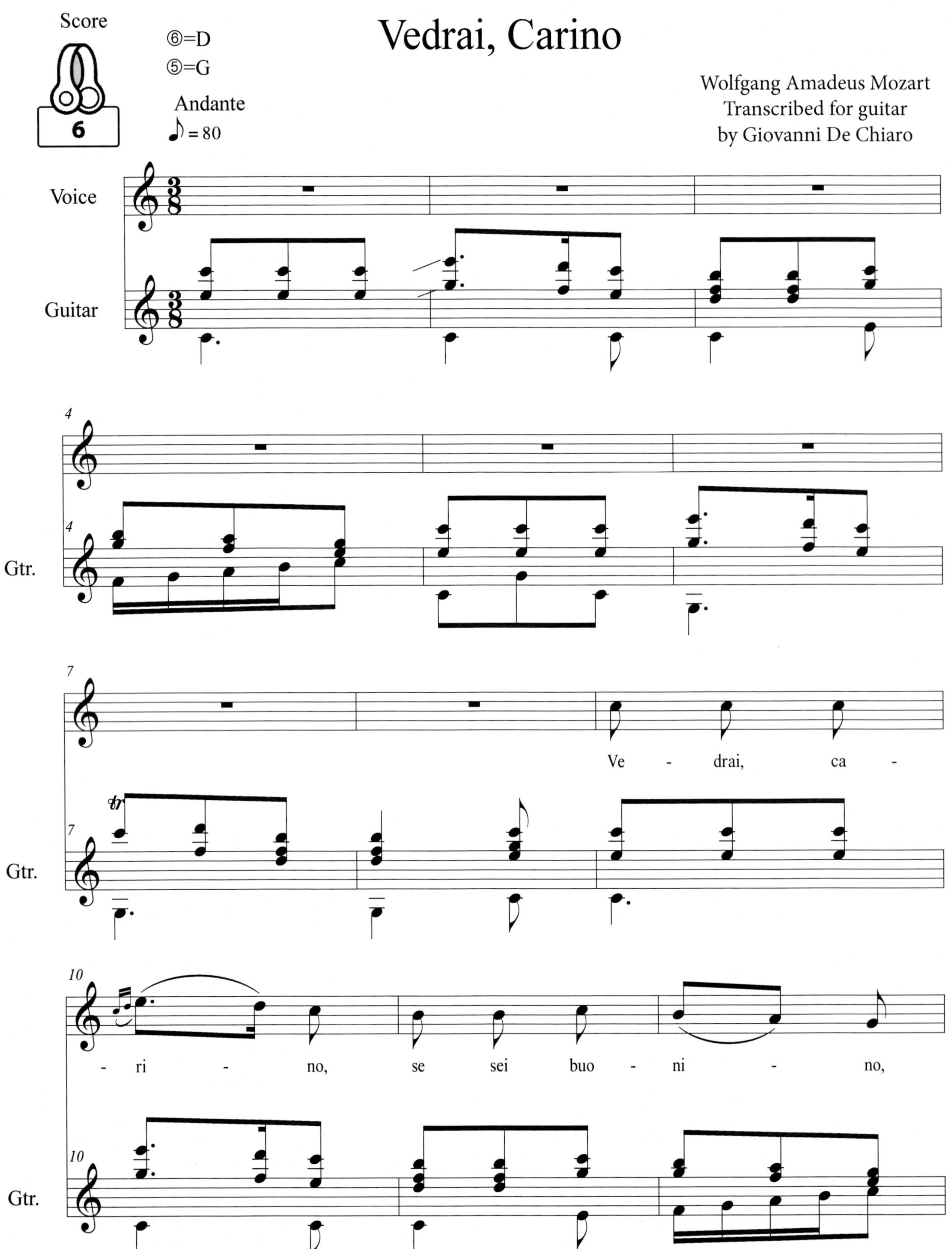

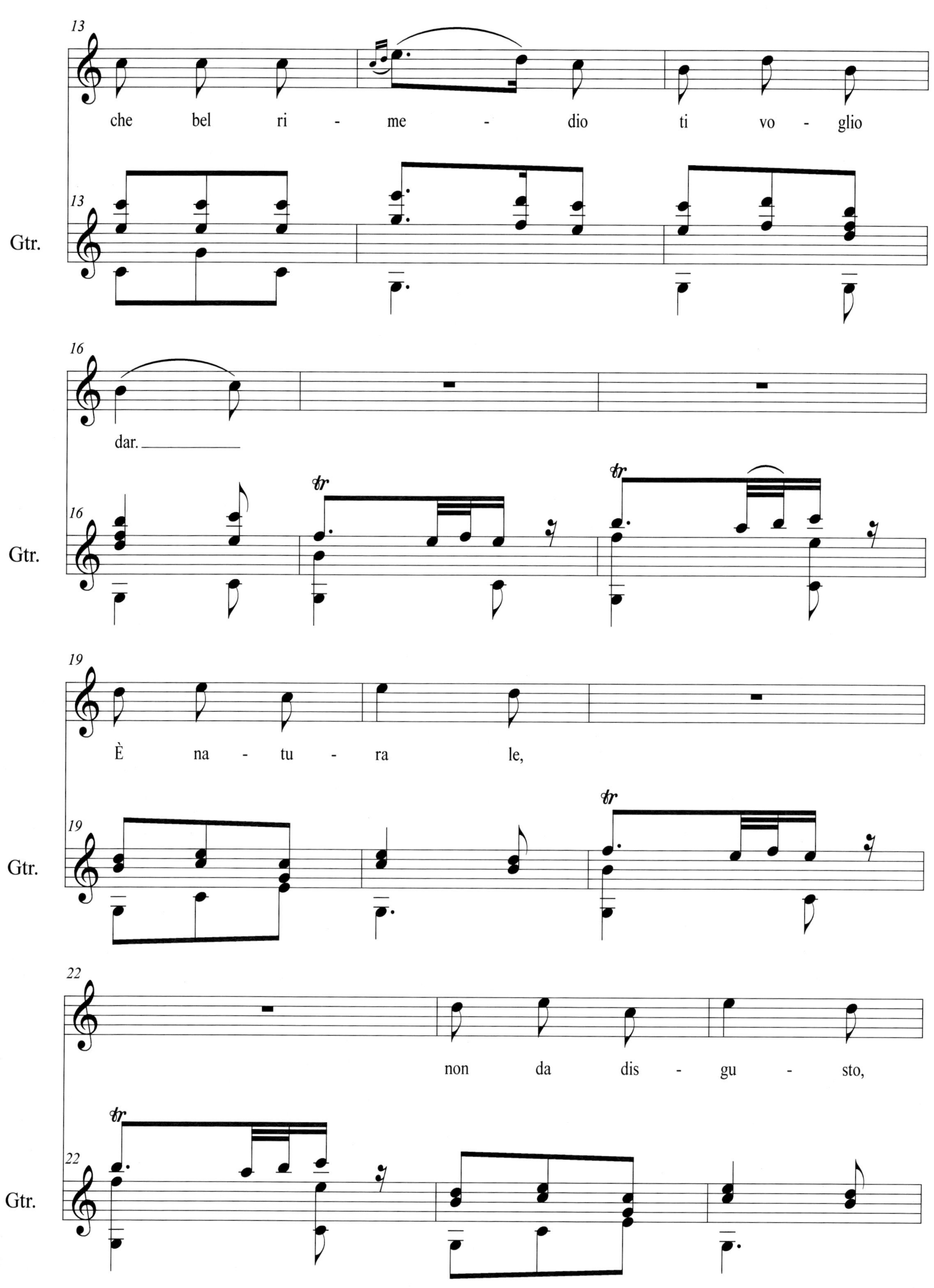
13
che bel ri - me - dio ti vo - glio
Gtr.
16
dar.
Gtr.
19
È na - tu - ra le,
Gtr.
22
non da dis - gu - sto,
Gtr.

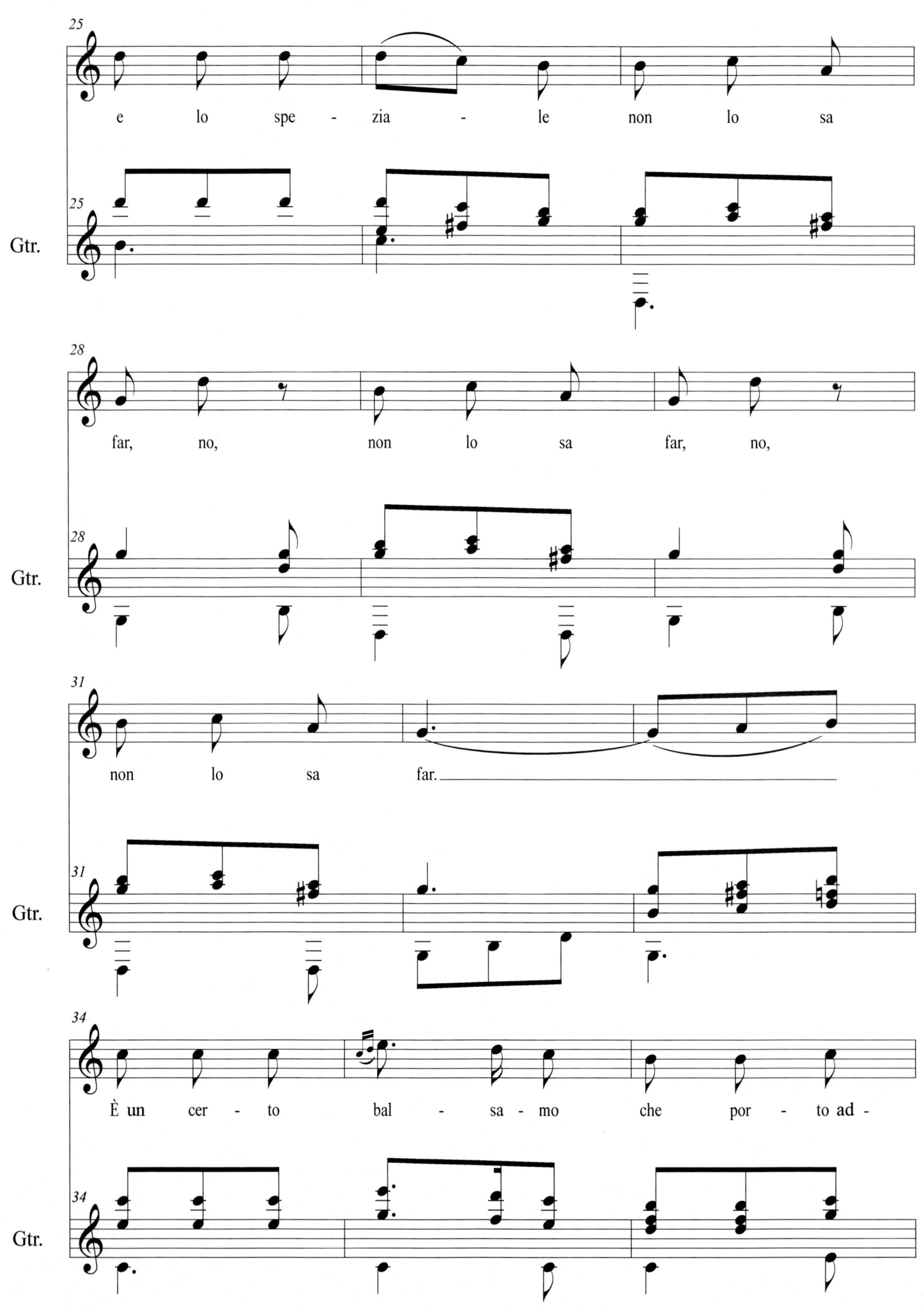
25
e lo spe - zia - le non lo sa
Gtr.
28
far, no, non lo sa far, no,
31
non lo sa far.
34
È un cer - to bal - sa - mo che por - to ad -

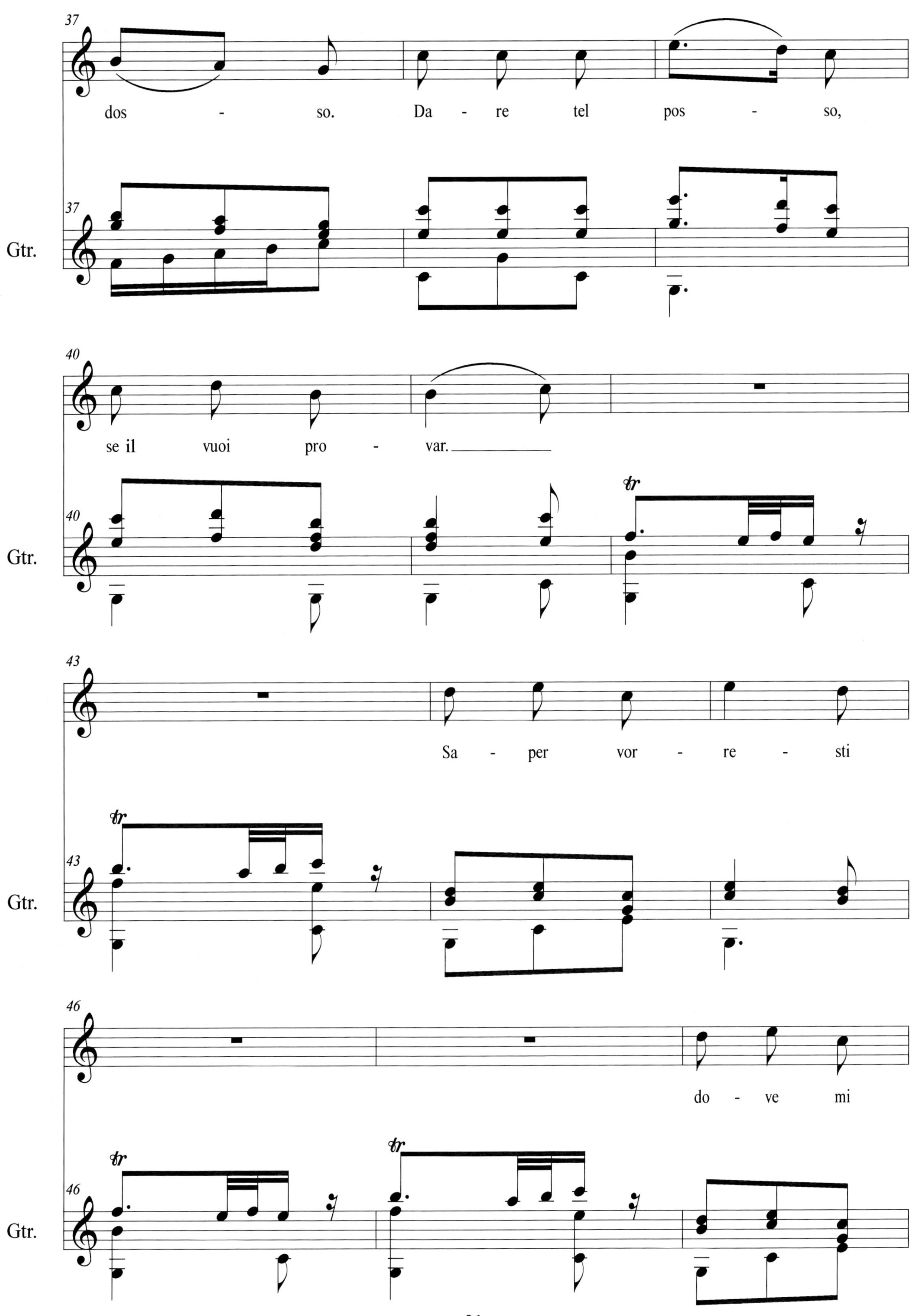
37
dos - so. Da - re tel pos - so,
37
Gtr.
40
se il vuoi pro - var.
40
Gtr.
tr
43
Sa - per vor - re - sti
tr
43
Gtr.
46
do - ve mi
tr
tr
46
Gtr.

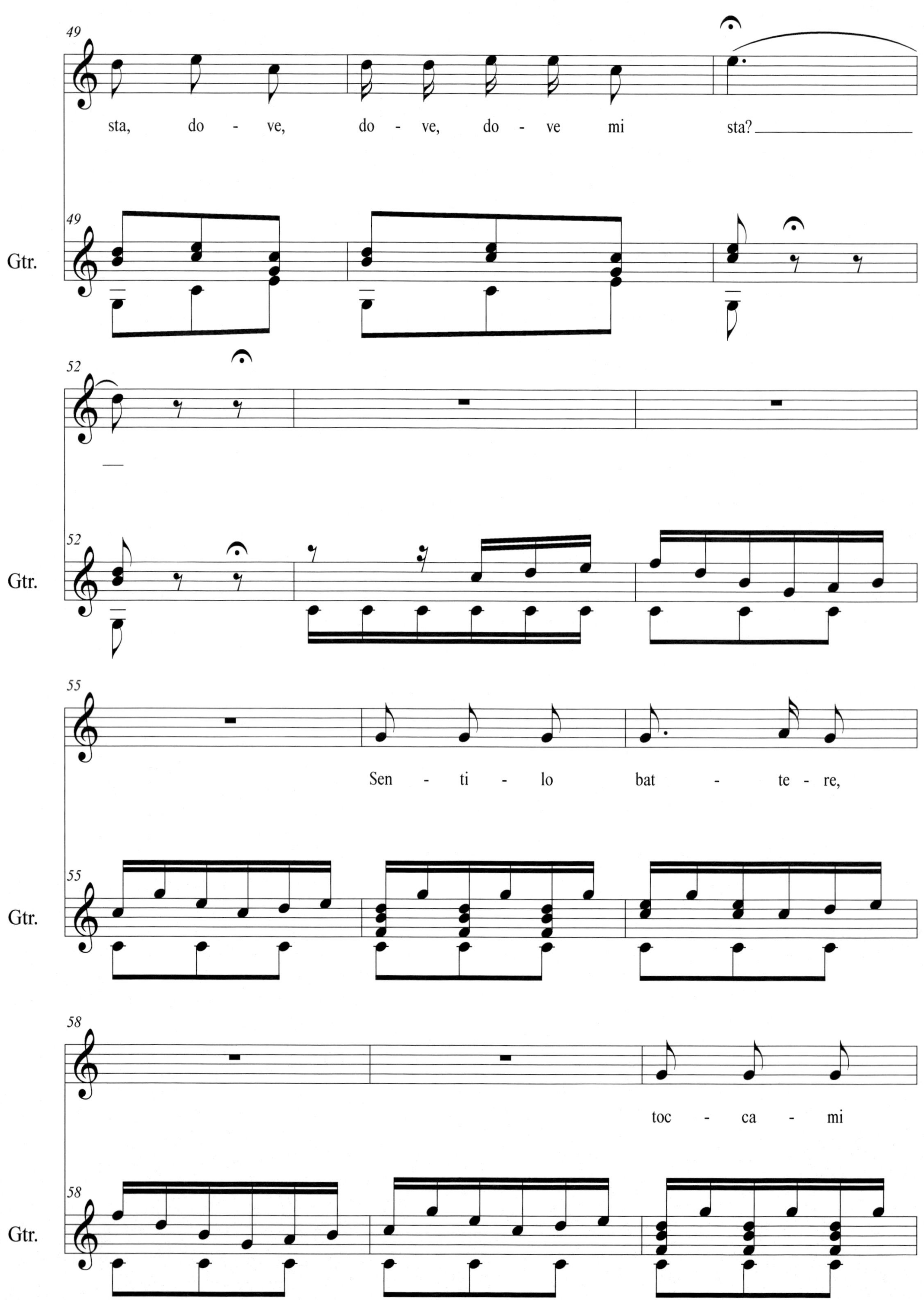
49
sta, do - ve, do - ve, do - ve mi sta?
Gtr.
52
55
Sen - ti - lo bat - te - re,
58
toc - ca - mi

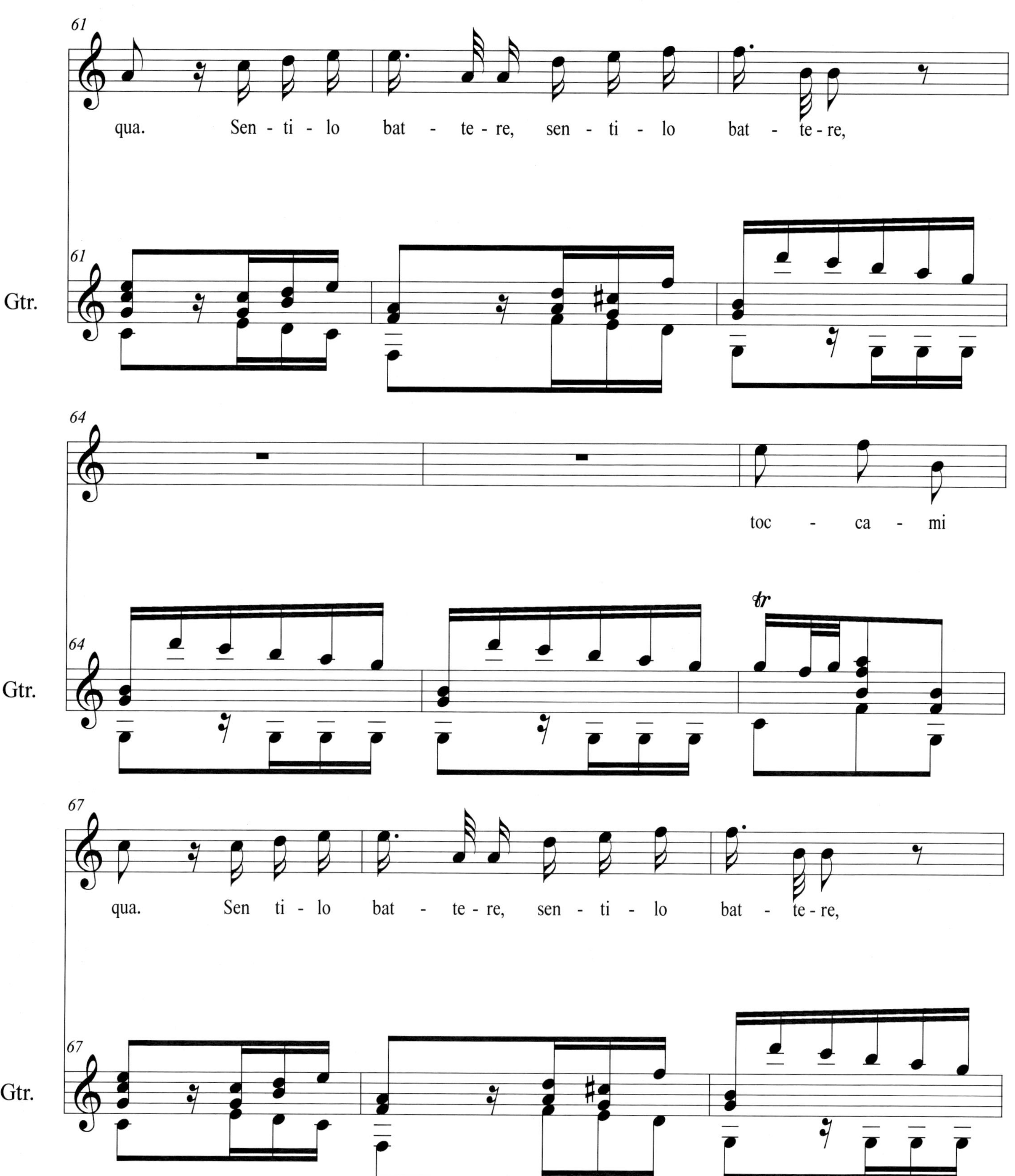
61
qua. Sen - ti - lo bat - te - re, sen - ti - lo bat - te - re,
61
Gtr.
64
toc - ca - mi
64
Gtr.
tr
67
qua. Sen ti - lo bat - te - re, sen - ti - lo bat - te - re,
67
Gtr.

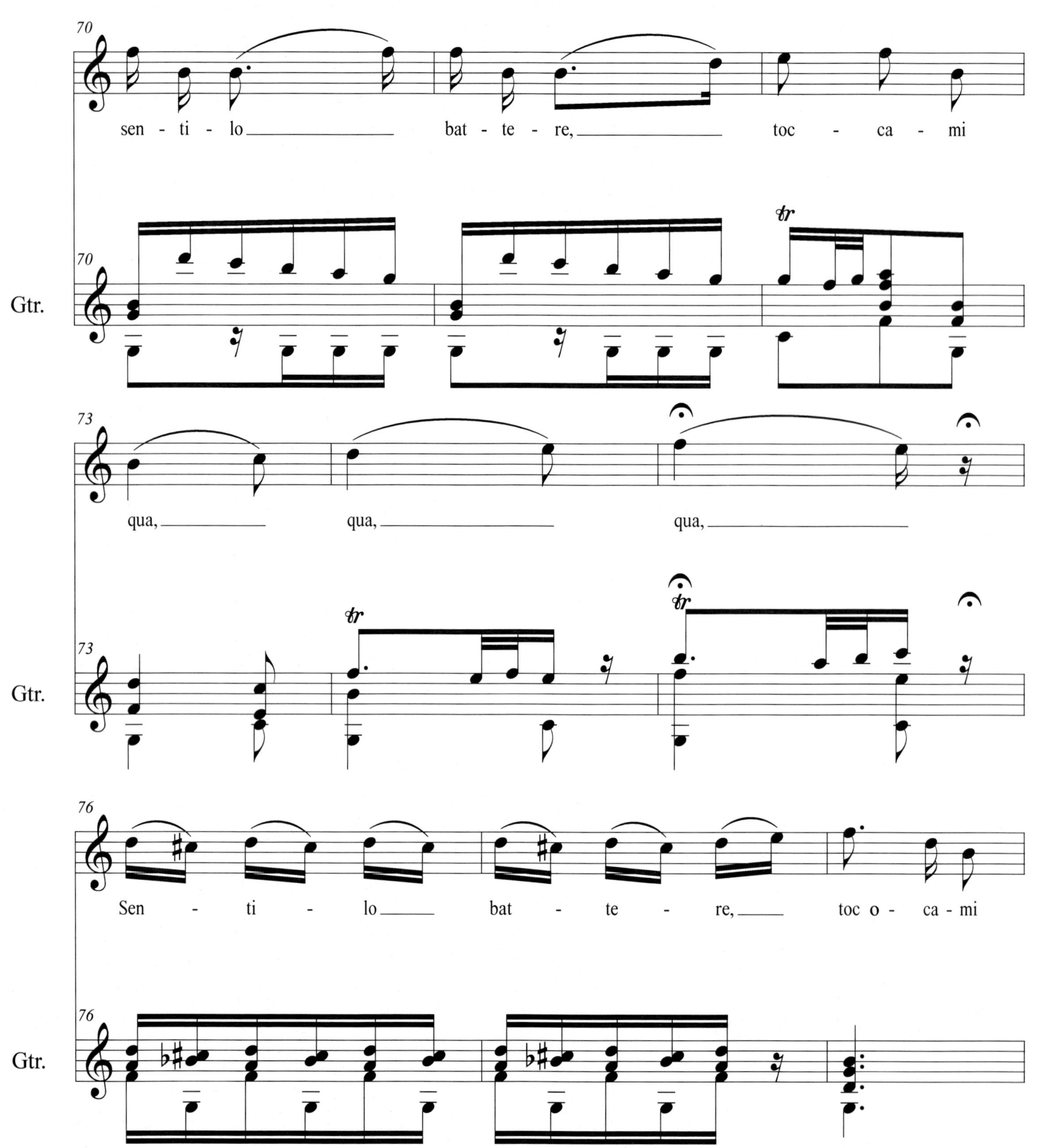
70
sen - ti - lo bat - te - re, toc - ca - mi
70
Gtr.
tr
73
qua, qua, qua,
73
Gtr.
tr
tr
76
Sen - ti - lo bat - te - re, toc o - ca - mi
76
Gtr.

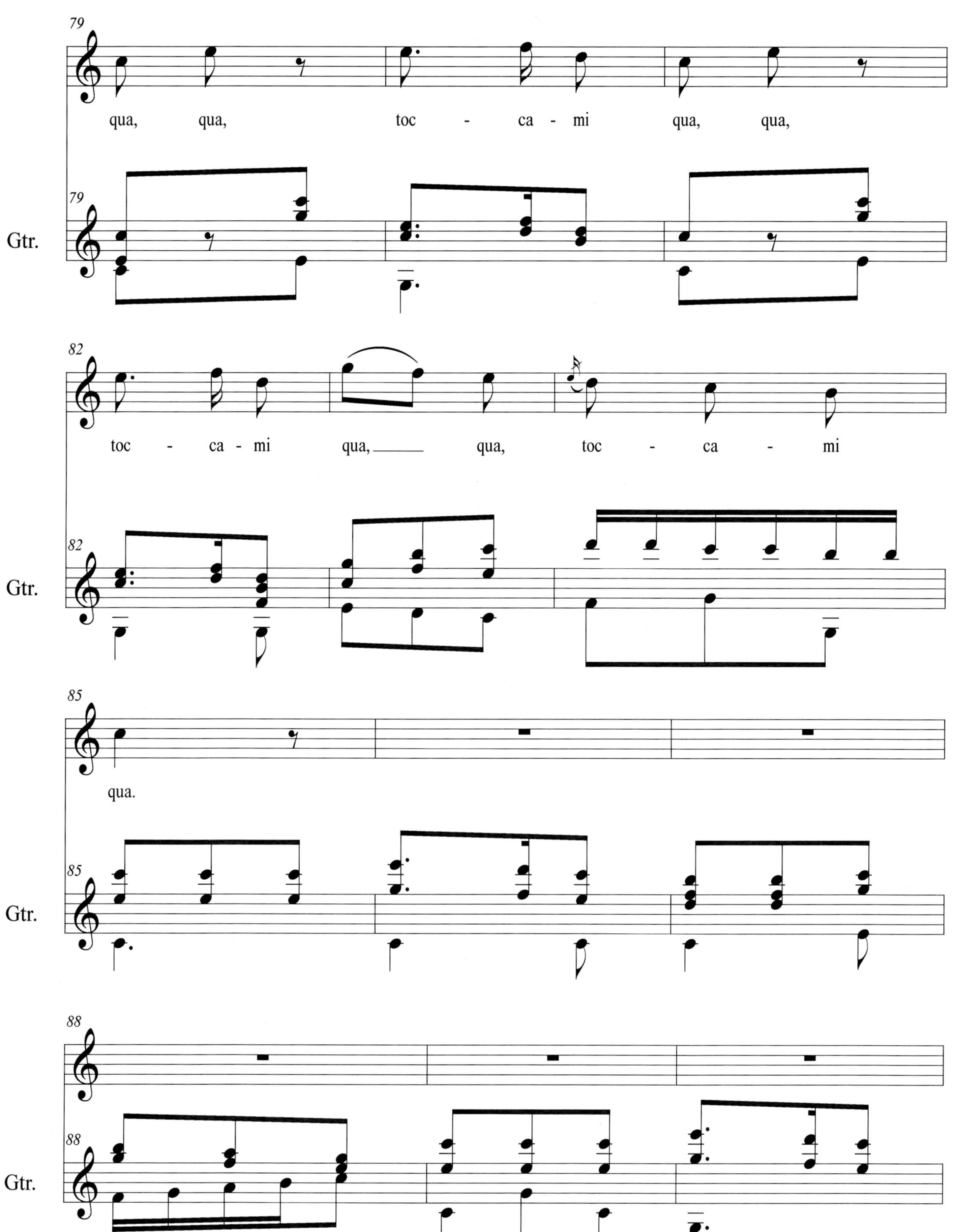
79
qua, qua, toc - ca - mi qua, qua,
79
Gtr.
82
toc - ca - mi qua, qua, toc - ca - mi
82
Gtr.
85
qua.
85
Gtr.
88
88
Gtr.

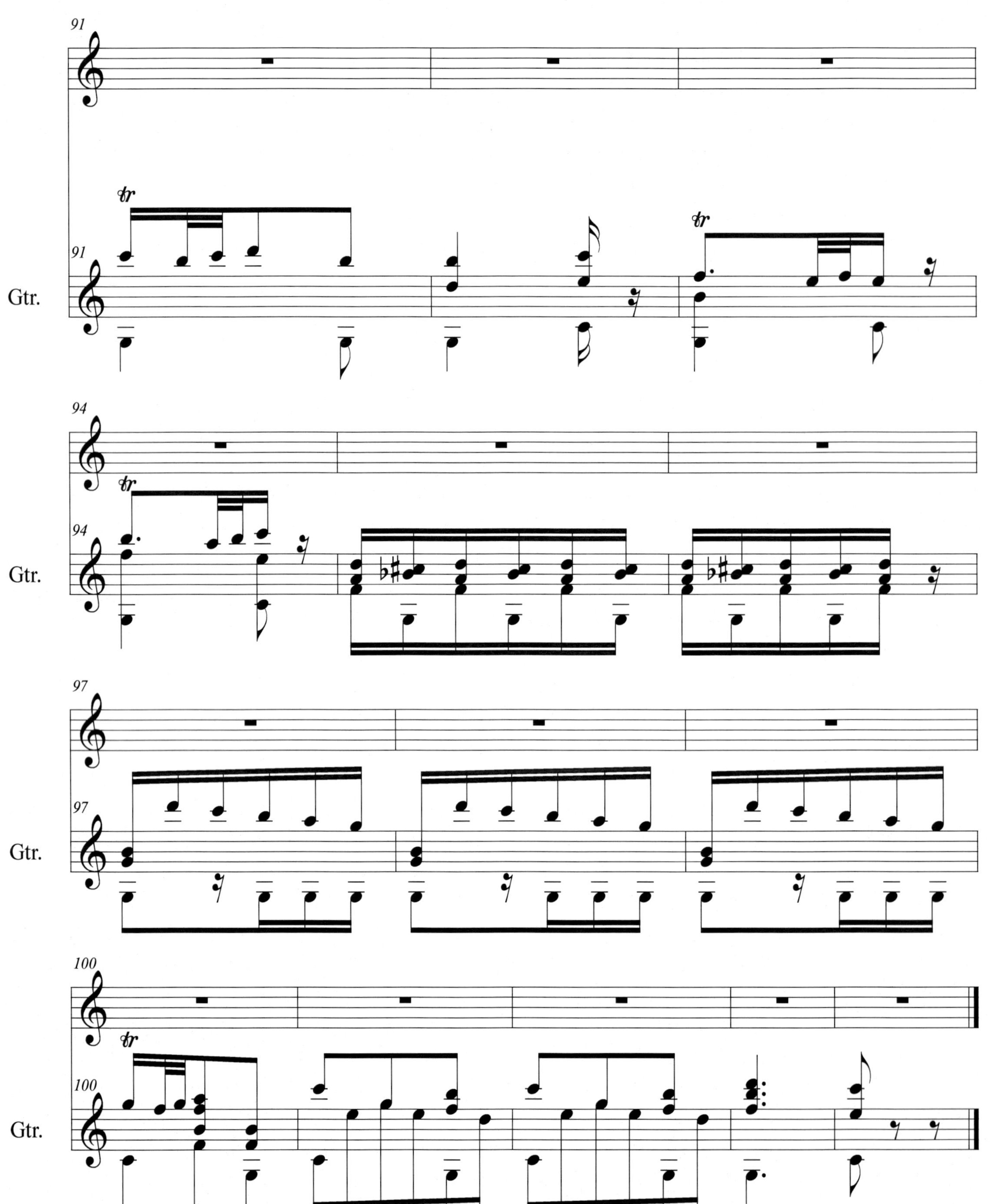
91
Gtr.
94
Gtr.
97
Gtr.
100
Gtr.

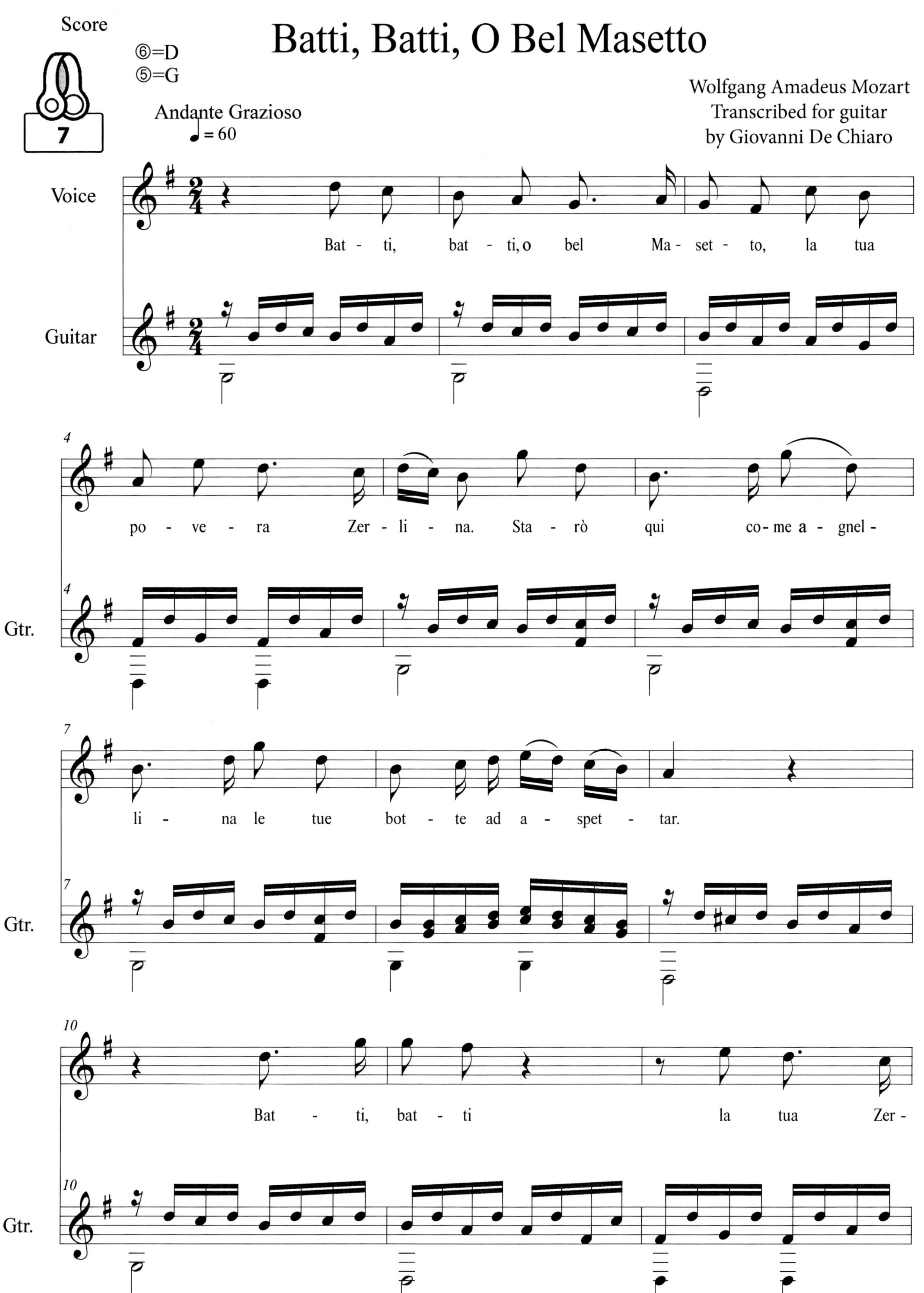
Score
7
Batti, Batti, O Bel Masetto
⑥=D
⑤=G
Wolfgang Amadeus Mozart
Transcribed for guitar
by Giovanni De Chiaro
Andante Grazioso
♩= 60
Voice
Guitar
Bat - ti, bat - ti, o bel Ma - set - to, la tua
po - ve - ra Zer - li - na. Sta - rò qui co - me a - gnel -
Gtr.
li - na le tue bot - te ad a - spet - tar.
Bat - ti, bat - ti la tua Zer -

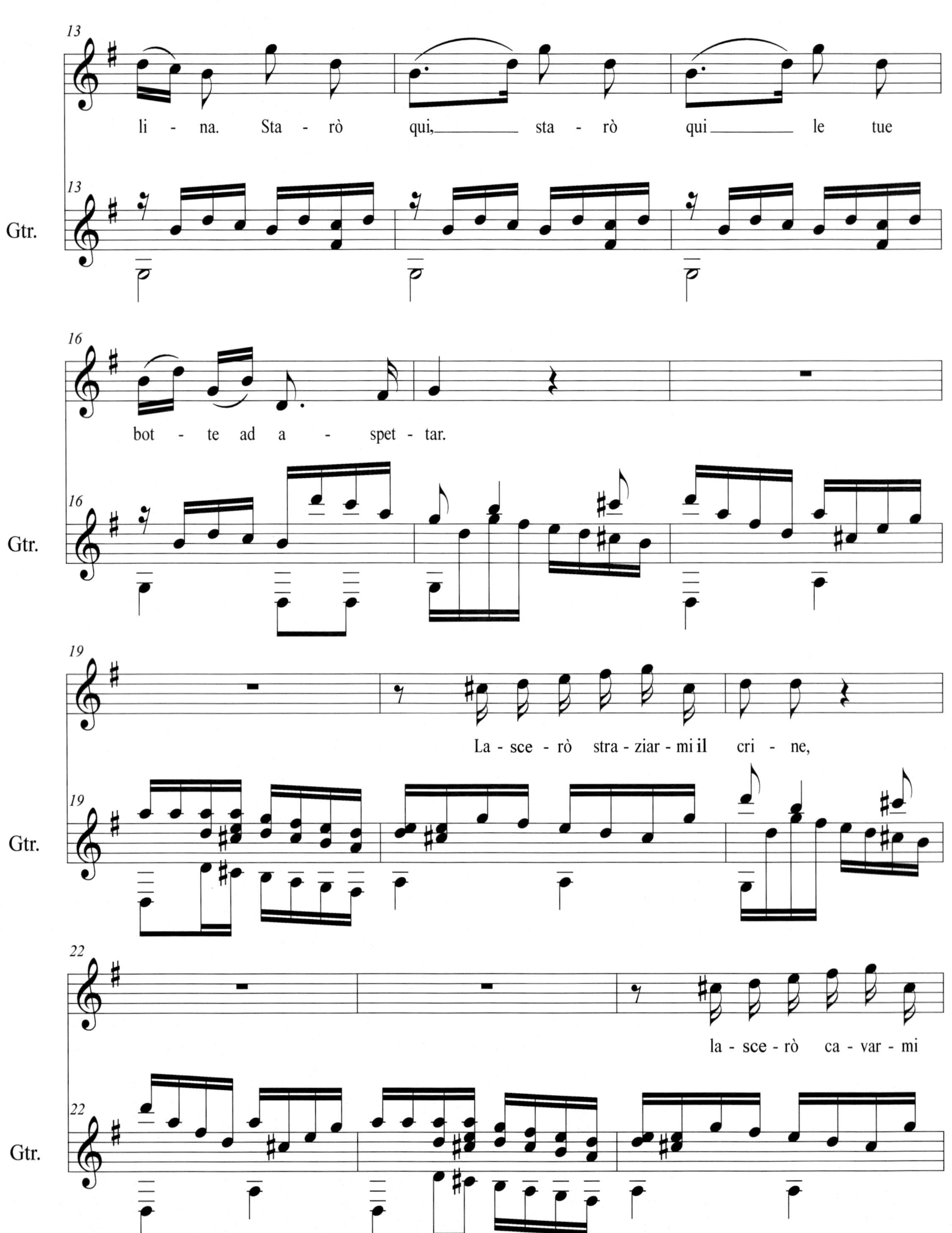
13
li - na. Sta - rò qui, sta - rò qui le tue
13
Gtr.
16
bot - te ad a - spet - tar.
16
Gtr.
19
La - sce - rò stra - ziar - mi il cri - ne,
19
Gtr.
22
la - sce - rò ca - var - mi
22
Gtr.

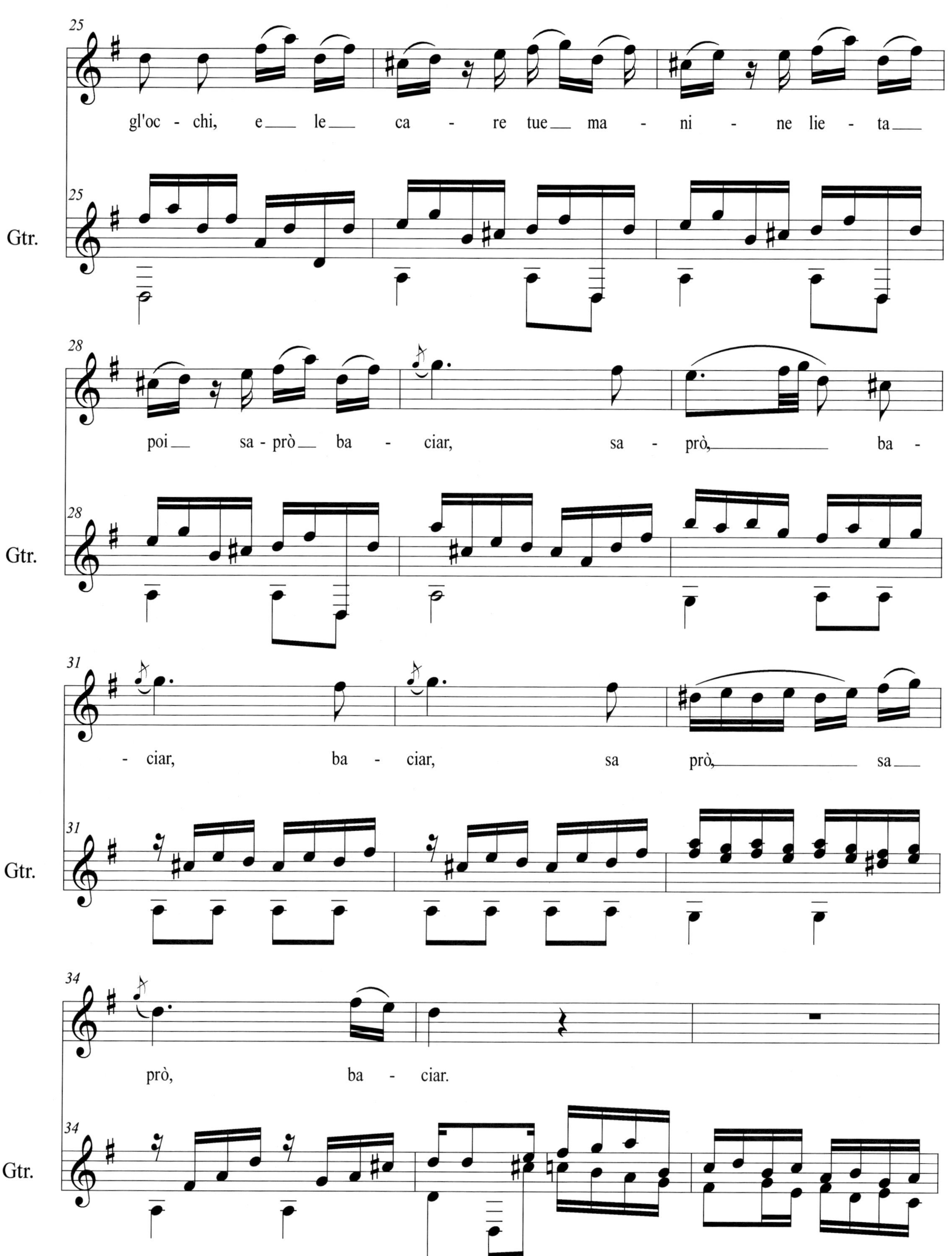
25
gl'oc - chi, e le ca - re tue ma - ni - ne lie - ta
25
Gtr.
28
poi sa - prò ba - ciar, sa - prò, ba -
28
Gtr.
31
- ciar, ba - ciar, sa prò, sa
31
Gtr.
34
prò, ba - ciar.
34
Gtr.

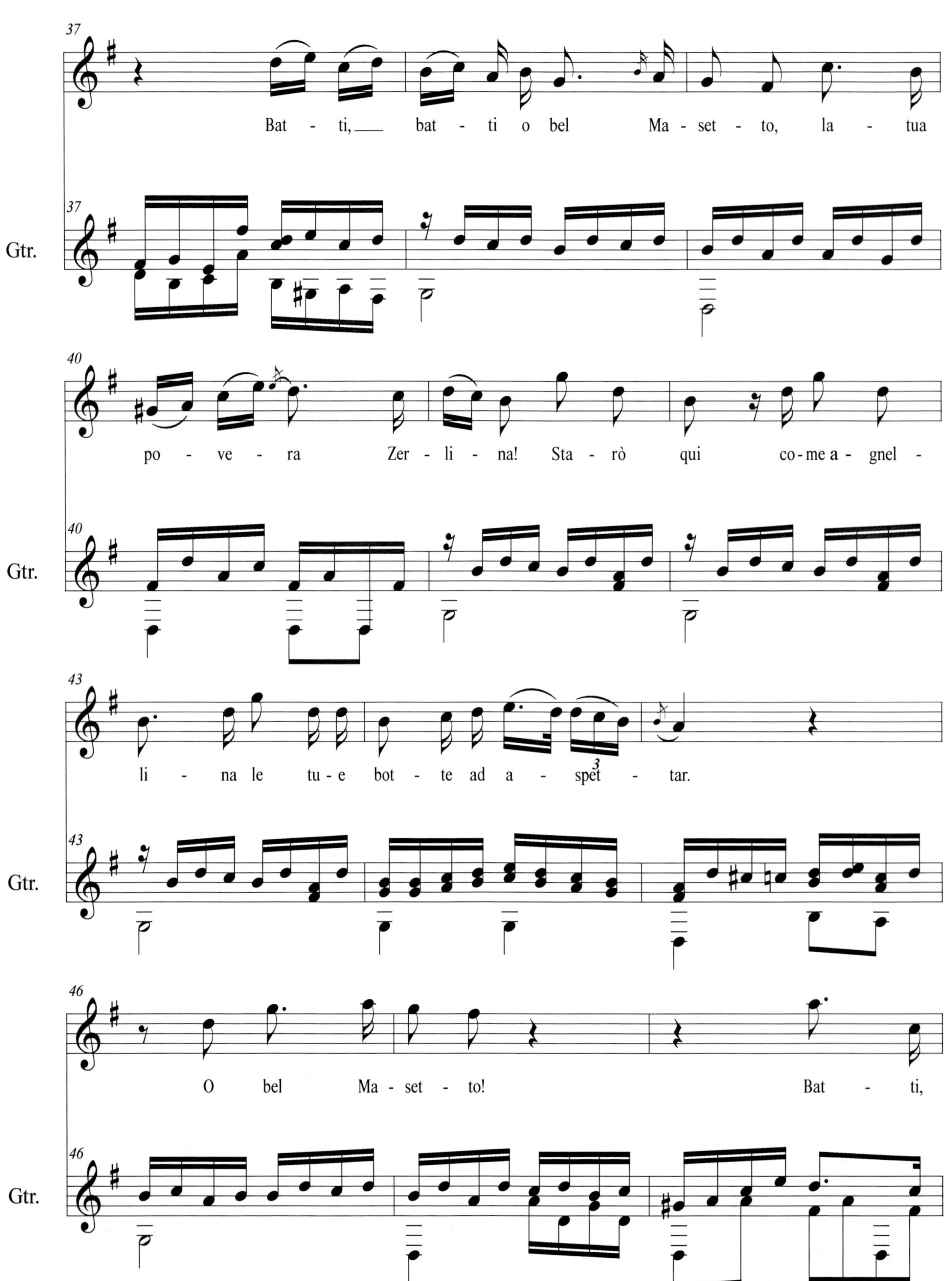
37
Bat - ti, bat - ti o bel Ma - set - to, la - tua
Gtr.
40
po - ve - ra Zer - li - na! Sta - rò qui co - me a - gnel -
Gtr.
43
li - na le tu - e bot - te ad a - spet - tar.
3
Gtr.
46
O bel Ma - set - to! Bat - ti,
Gtr.

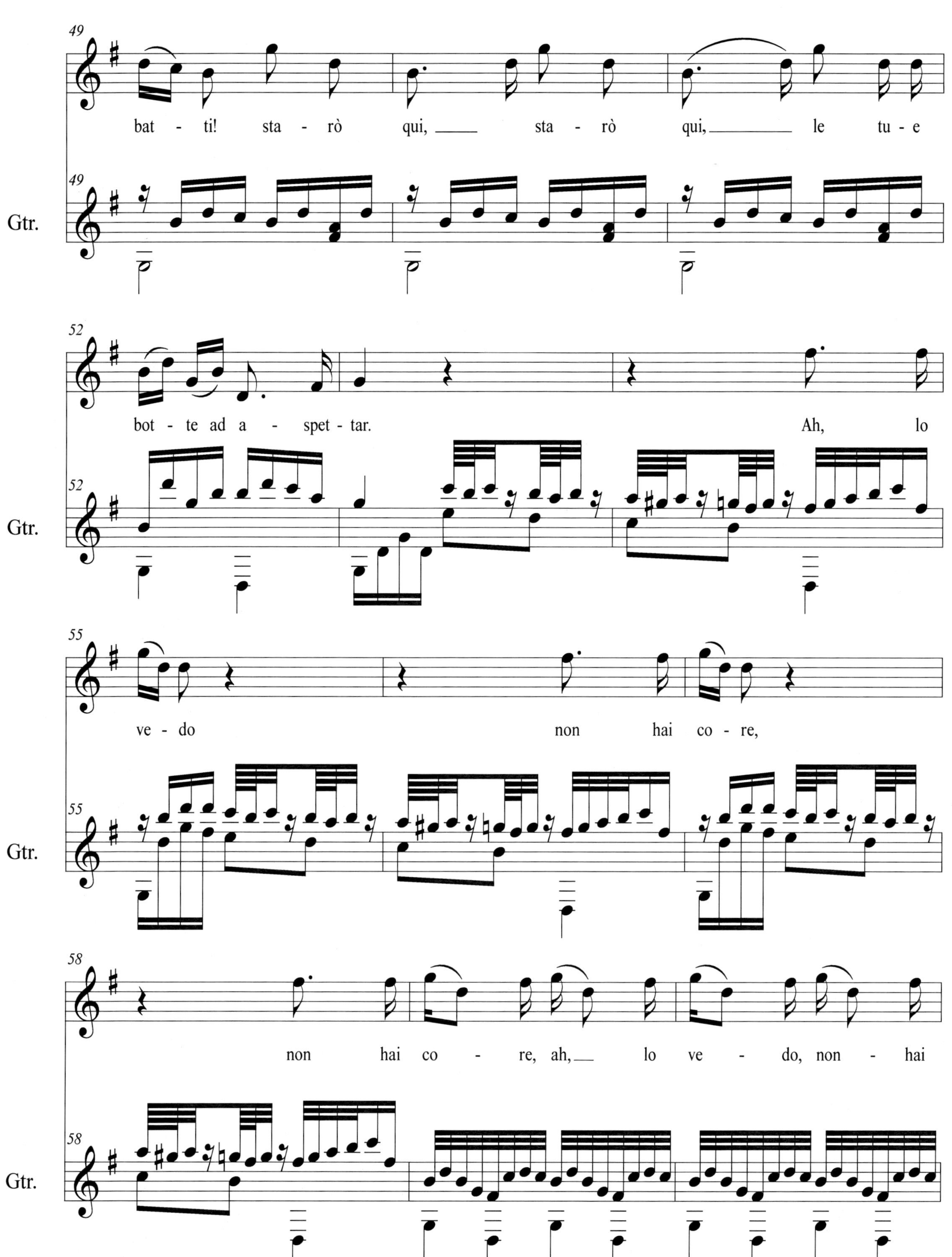
49
bat - ti! sta - rò qui, sta - rò qui, le tu - e
Gtr.
52
bot - te ad a - spet - tar. Ah, lo
Gtr.
55
ve - do non hai co - re,
Gtr.
58
non hai co - re, ah, lo ve - do, non - hai
Gtr.

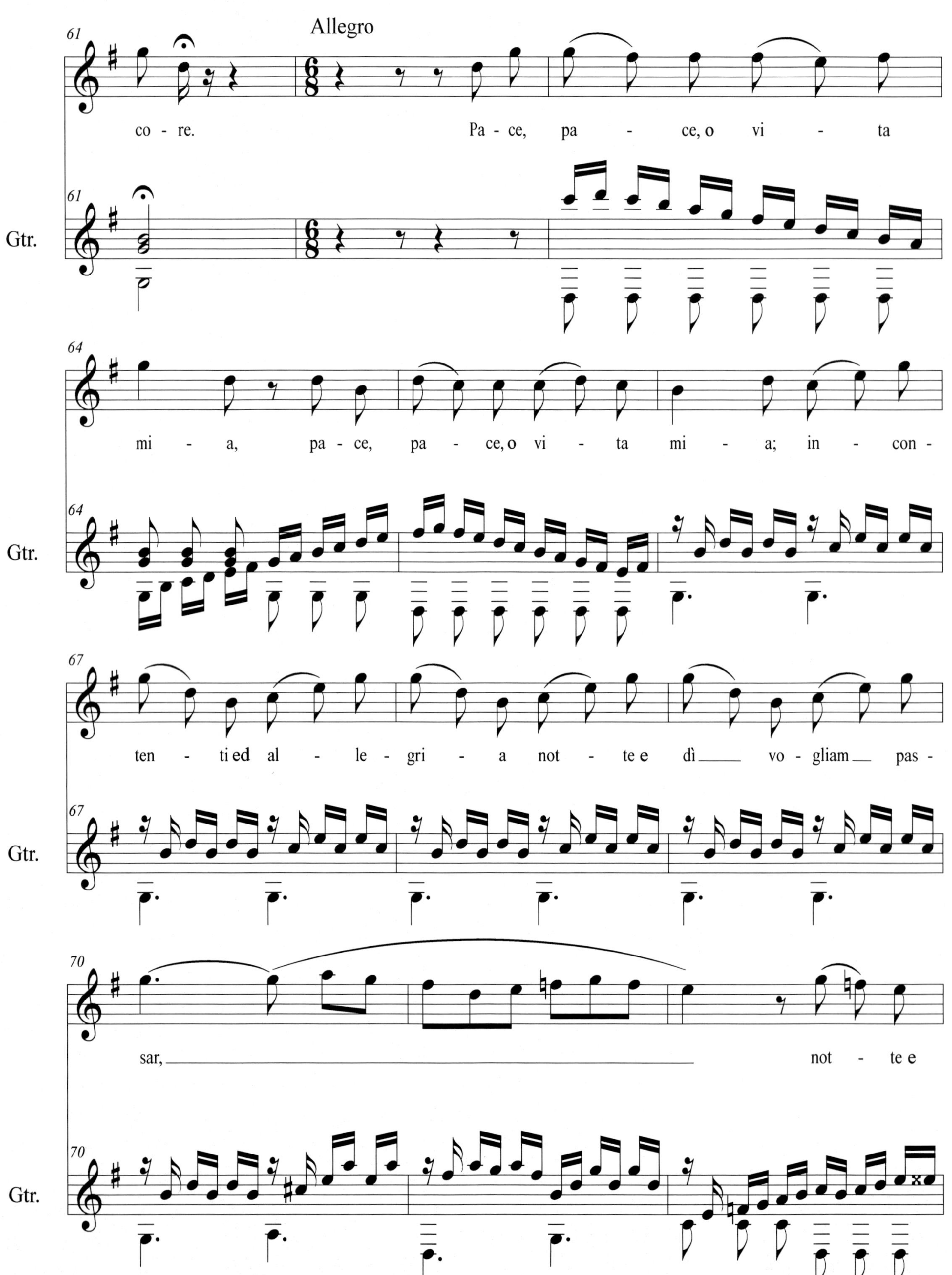
Allegro
co - re. Pa - ce, pa - ce, o vi - ta
Gtr.
mi - a, pa - ce, pa - ce, o vi - ta mi - a; in - con -
Gtr.
ten - ti ed al - le - gri - a not - te e dì vo - gliam pas -
Gtr.
sar, not - te e
Gtr.

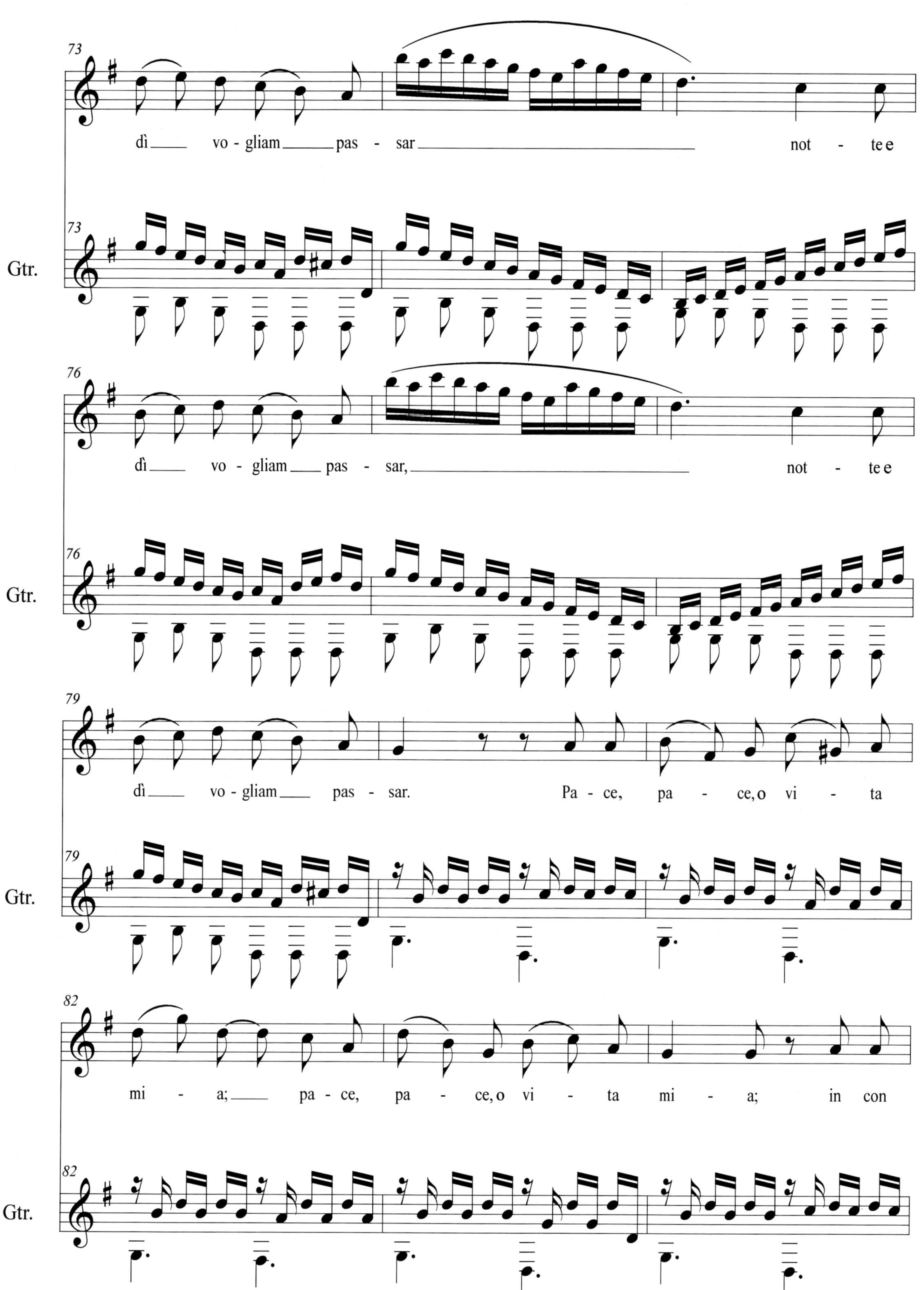
73
dì vo - gliam pas - sar not - te e
Gtr.
76
dì vo - gliam pas - sar, not - te e
Gtr.
79
dì vo - gliam pas - sar. Pa - ce, pa - ce, o vi - ta
Gtr.
82
mi - a; pa - ce, pa - ce, o vi - ta mi - a; in con
Gtr.

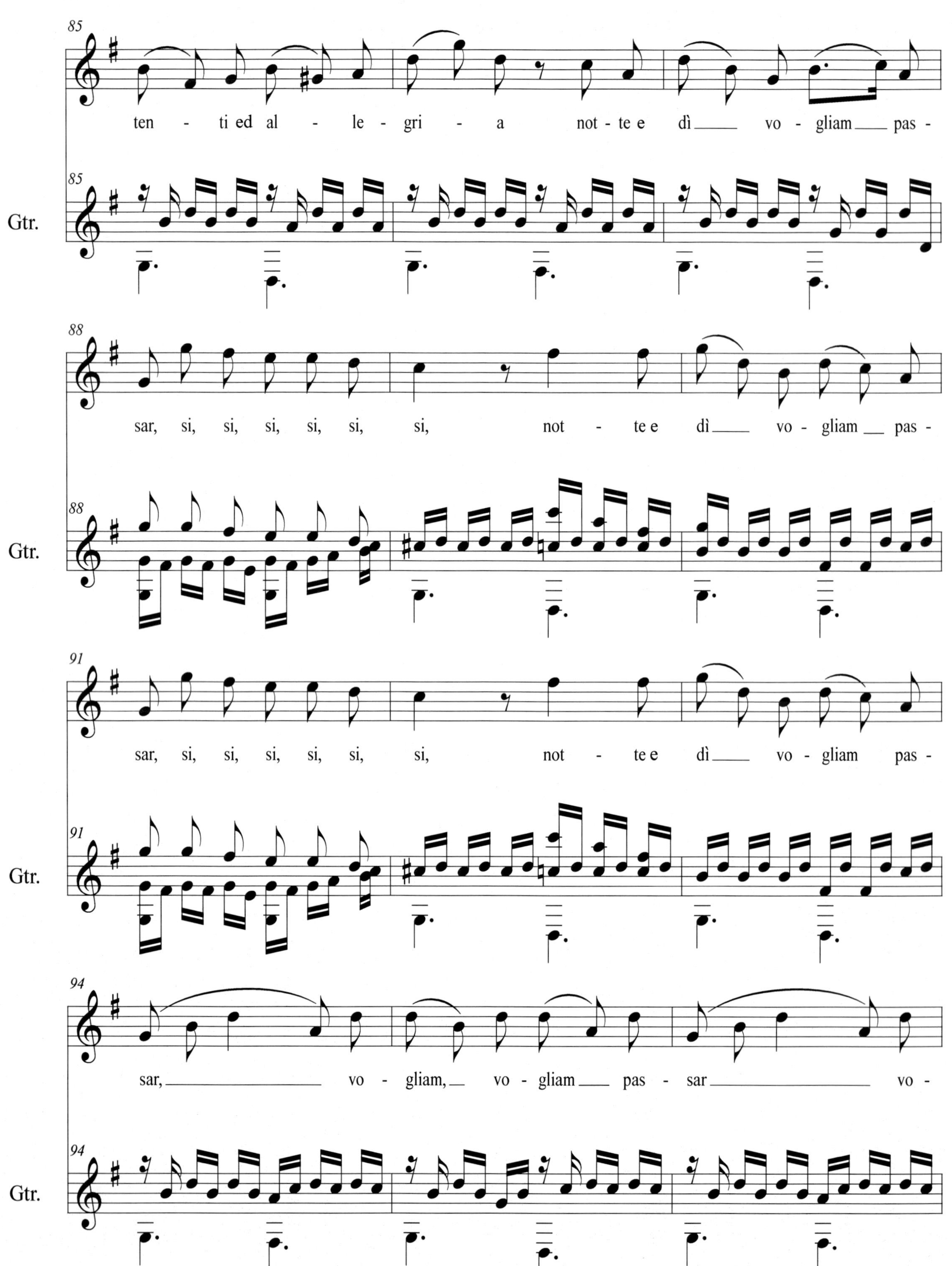
85
ten - ti ed al - le - gri - a not - te e dì vo - gliam pas -
85
Gtr.
88
sar, si, si, si, si, si, si, not - te e dì vo - gliam pas -
88
Gtr.
91
sar, si, si, si, si, si, si, not - te e dì vo - gliam pas -
91
Gtr.
94
sar, vo - gliam, vo - gliam pas - sar vo -
94
Gtr.

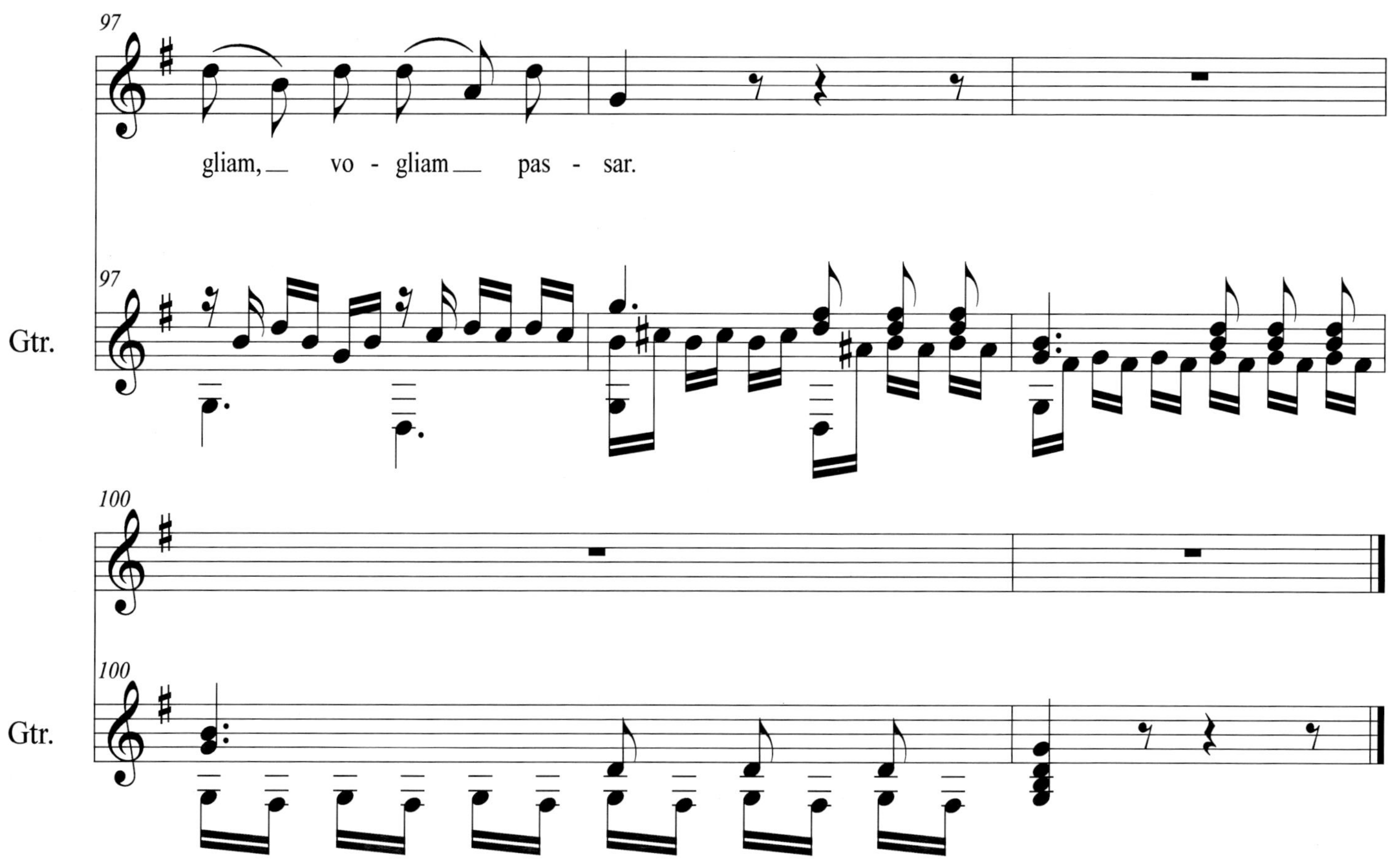
97
gliam, vo - gliam pas - sar.
97
Gtr.
100
100
Gtr.

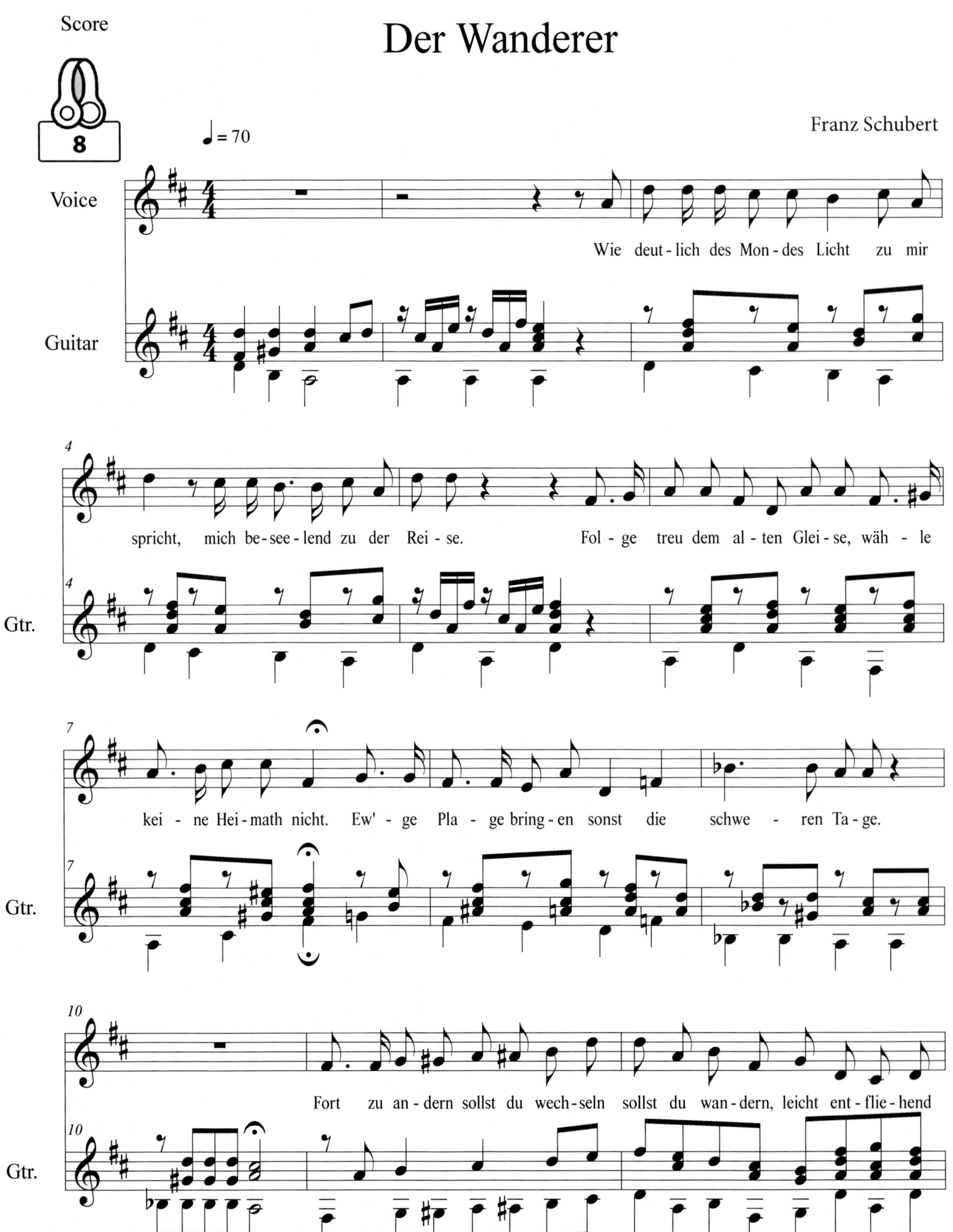
Score
Der Wanderer
8
Franz Schubert
♩ = 70
Voice
Guitar
Wie deut - lich des Mon - des Licht zu mir
Gtr.
spricht, mich be - see - lend zu der Rei - se. Fol - ge treu dem al - ten Glei - se, wäh - le
kei - ne Hei - math nicht. Ew' - ge Pla - ge bring - en sonst die schwe - ren Ta - ge.
Fort zu an - dern sollst du wech - seln sollst du wan - dern, leicht ent - flie - hend

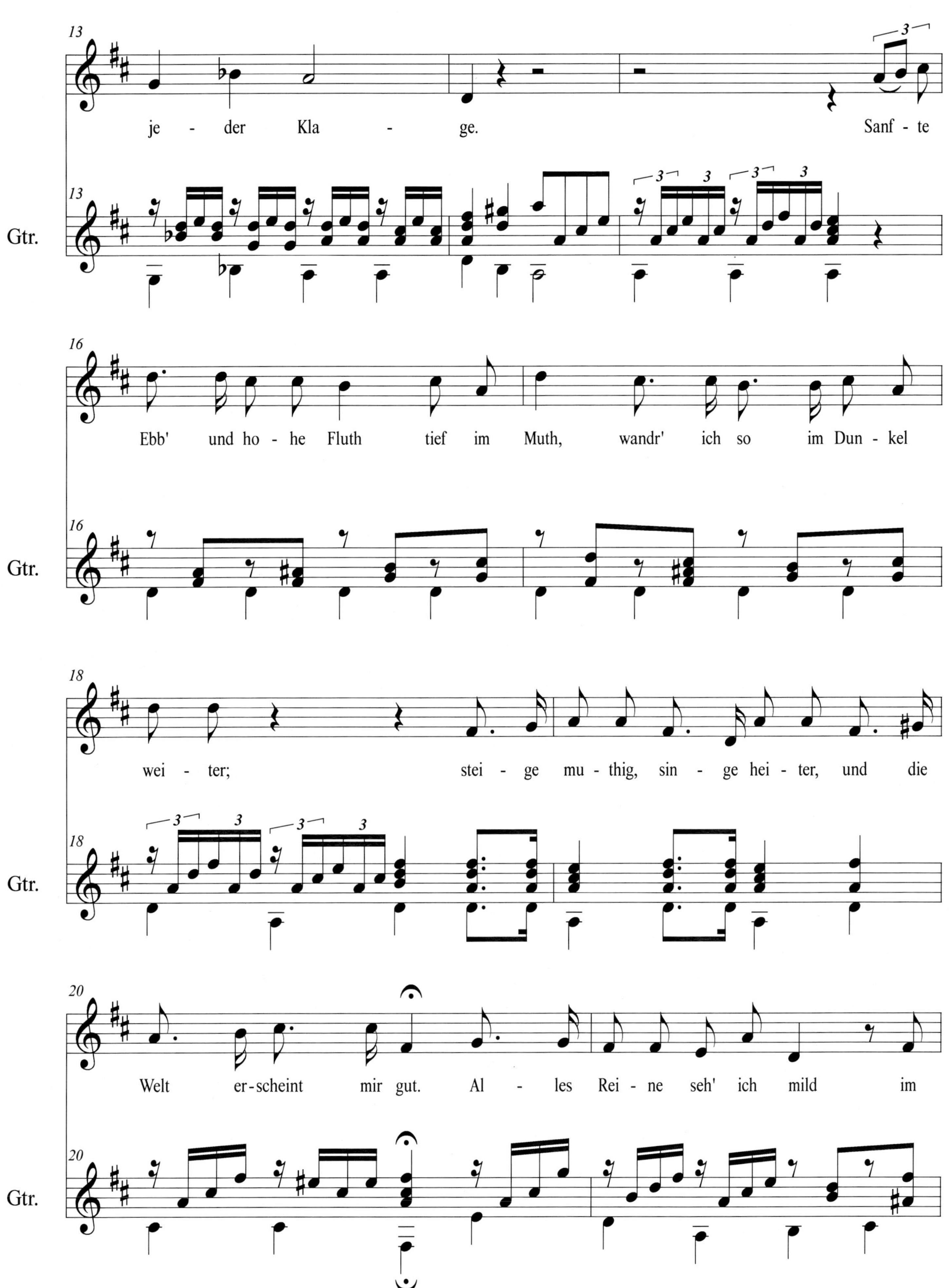
13
je - der Kla - ge. Sanf - te
Gtr.
16
Ebb' und ho - he Fluth tief im Muth, wandr' ich so im Dun - kel
Gtr.
18
wei - ter; stei - ge mu - thig, sin - ge hei - ter, und die
Gtr.
20
Welt er - scheint mir gut. Al - les Rei - ne seh' ich mild im
Gtr.

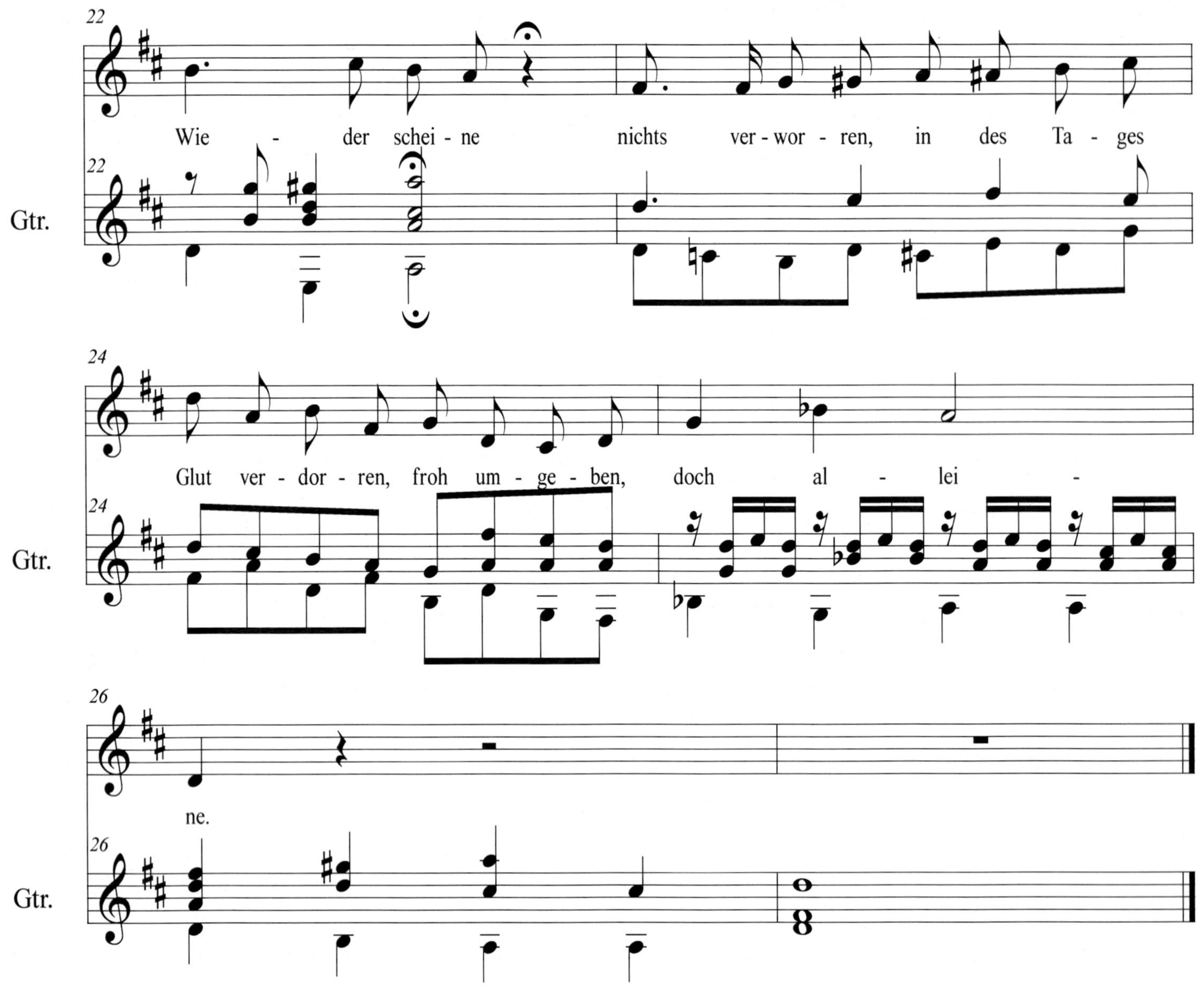
22
Wie - der schei - ne nichts ver - wor - ren, in des Ta - ges
Gtr.
24
Glut ver - dor - ren, froh um - ge - ben, doch al - lei -
Gtr.
26
ne.
Gtr.

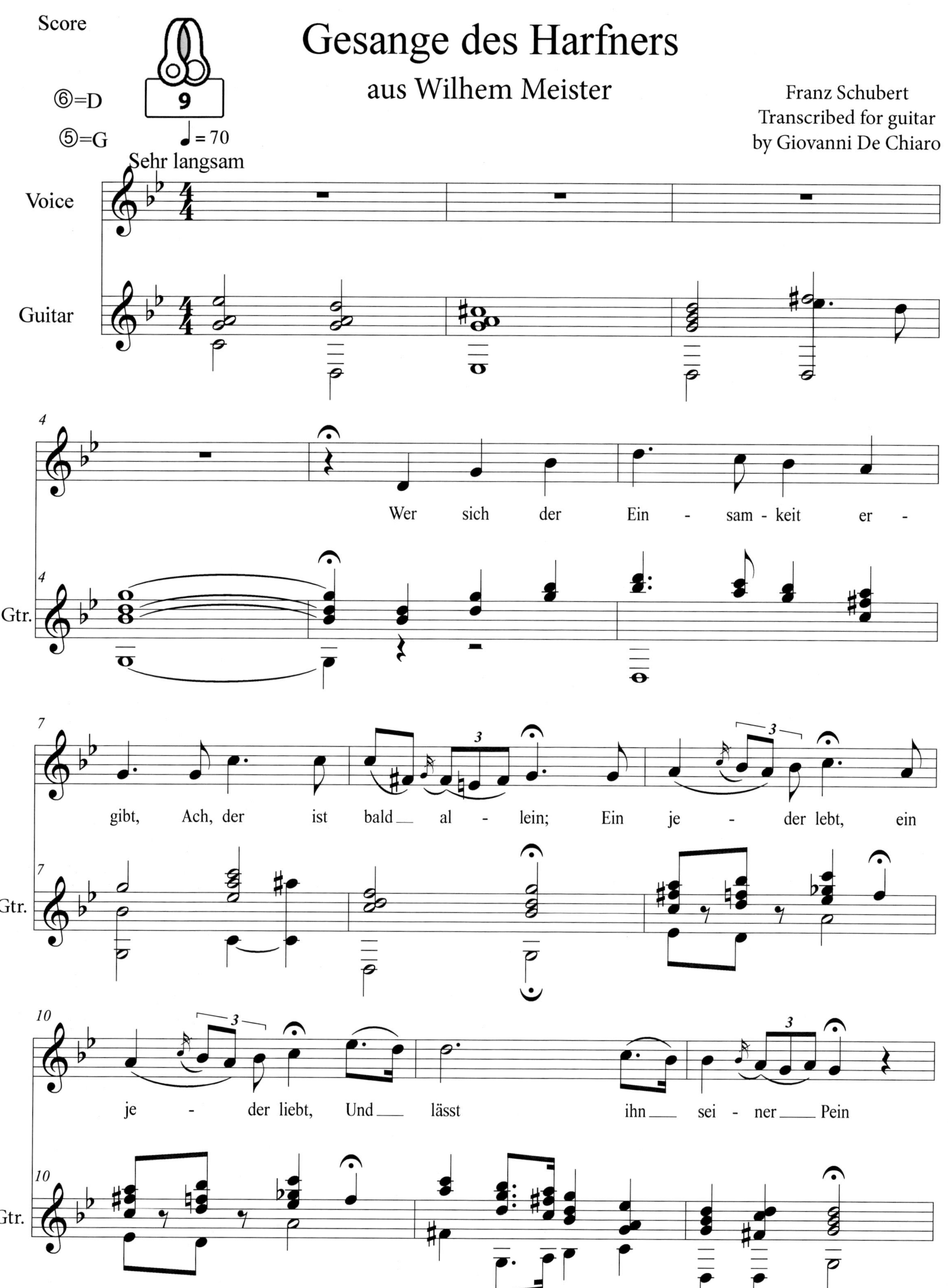
Score
⑥=D
⑤=G
9
♩= 70
Gesange des Harfners
aus Wilhem Meister
Franz Schubert
Transcribed for guitar
by Giovanni De Chiaro
Sehr langsam
Voice
Guitar
Gtr.
Wer sich der Ein - sam - keit er -
gibt, Ach, der ist bald al - lein; Ein je - der lebt, ein
je - der liebt, Und lässt ihn sei - ner Pein

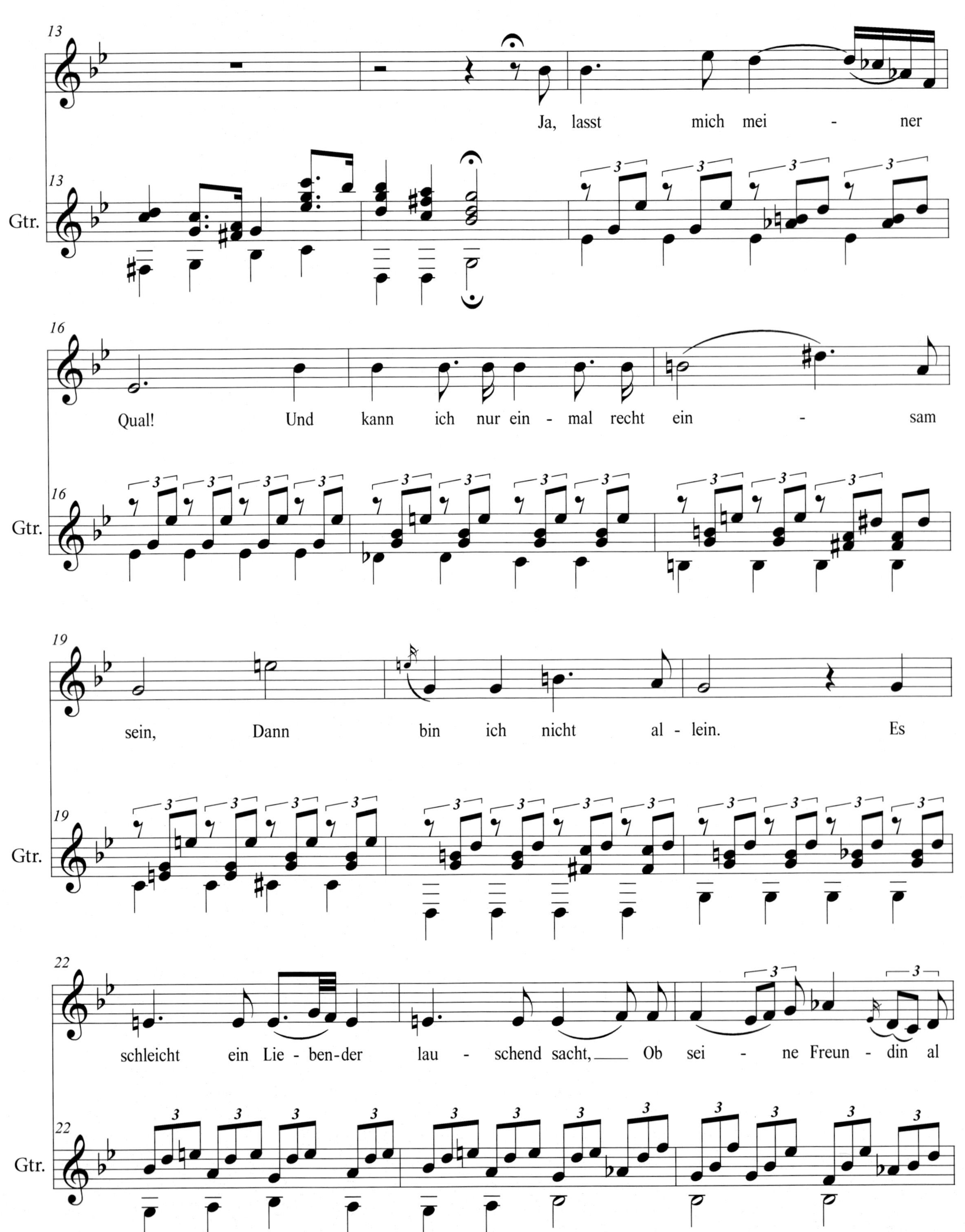
13
Ja, lasst mich mei - ner
13
Gtr.
16
Qual! Und kann ich nur ein - mal recht ein - sam
16
Gtr.
19
sein, Dann bin ich nicht al - lein. Es
19
Gtr.
22
schleicht ein Lie - ben-der lau - schend sacht, Ob sei - ne Freun - din al
22
Gtr.

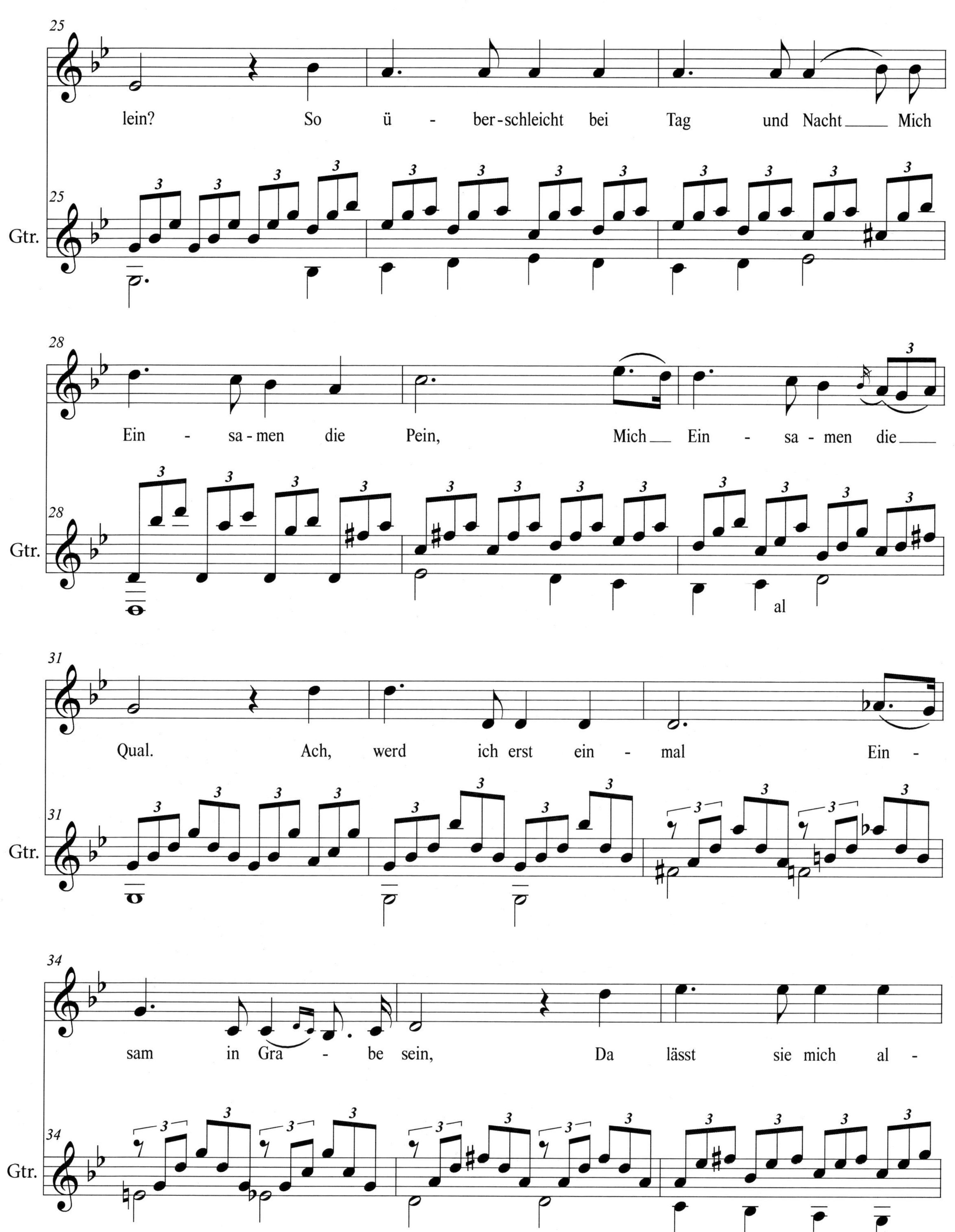
25
lein? So ü - ber-schleicht bei Tag und Nacht Mich
Gtr.
28
Ein - sa-men die Pein, Mich Ein - sa-men die
Gtr.
al
31
Qual. Ach, werd ich erst ein - mal Ein -
Gtr.
34
sam in Gra - be sein, Da lässt sie mich al -
Gtr.

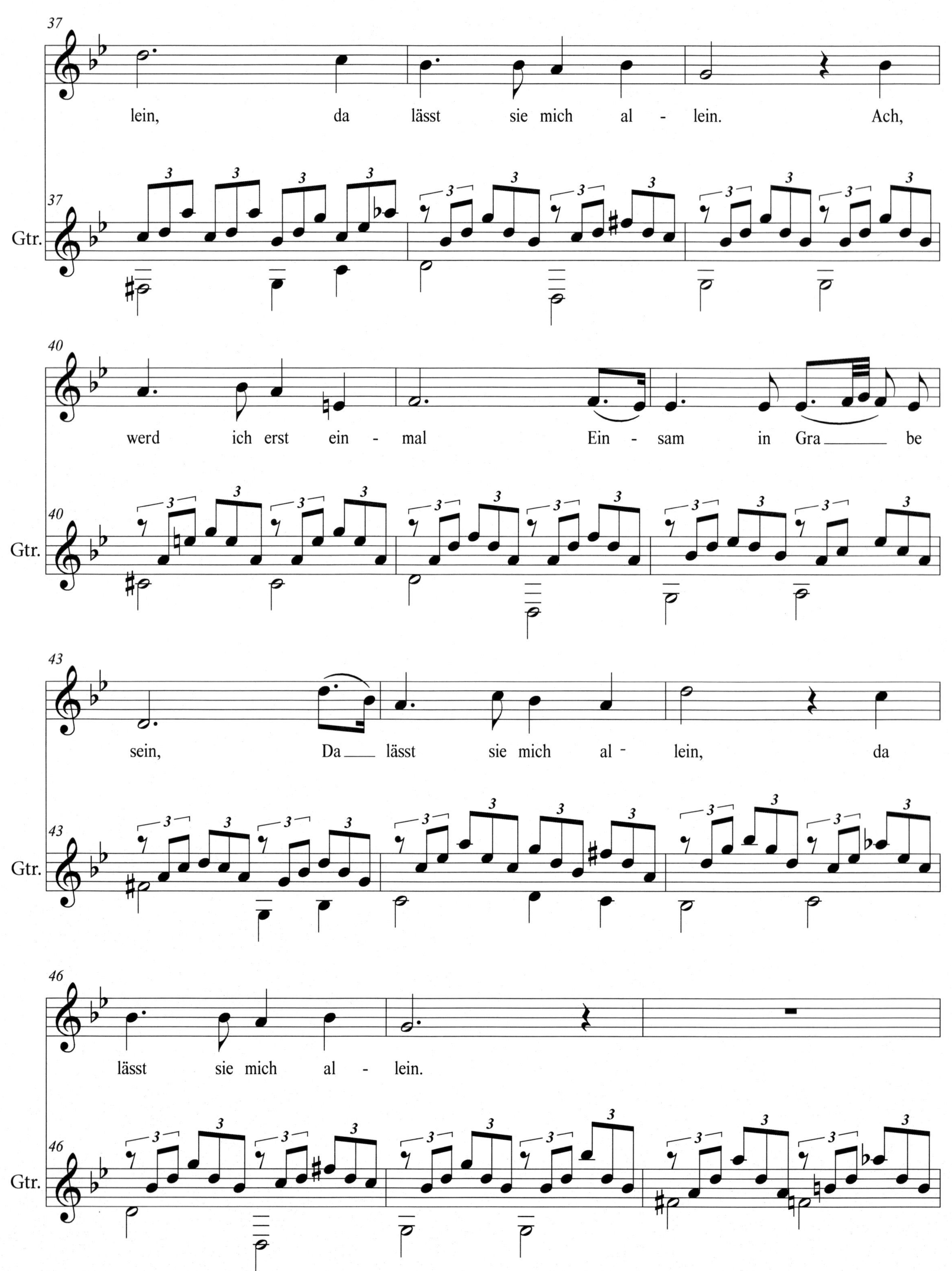
37
lein, da lässt sie mich al - lein. Ach,
Gtr.
40
werd ich erst ein - mal Ein - sam in Gra_ be
Gtr.
43
sein, Da_ lässt sie mich al - lein, da
Gtr.
46
lässt sie mich al - lein.
Gtr.

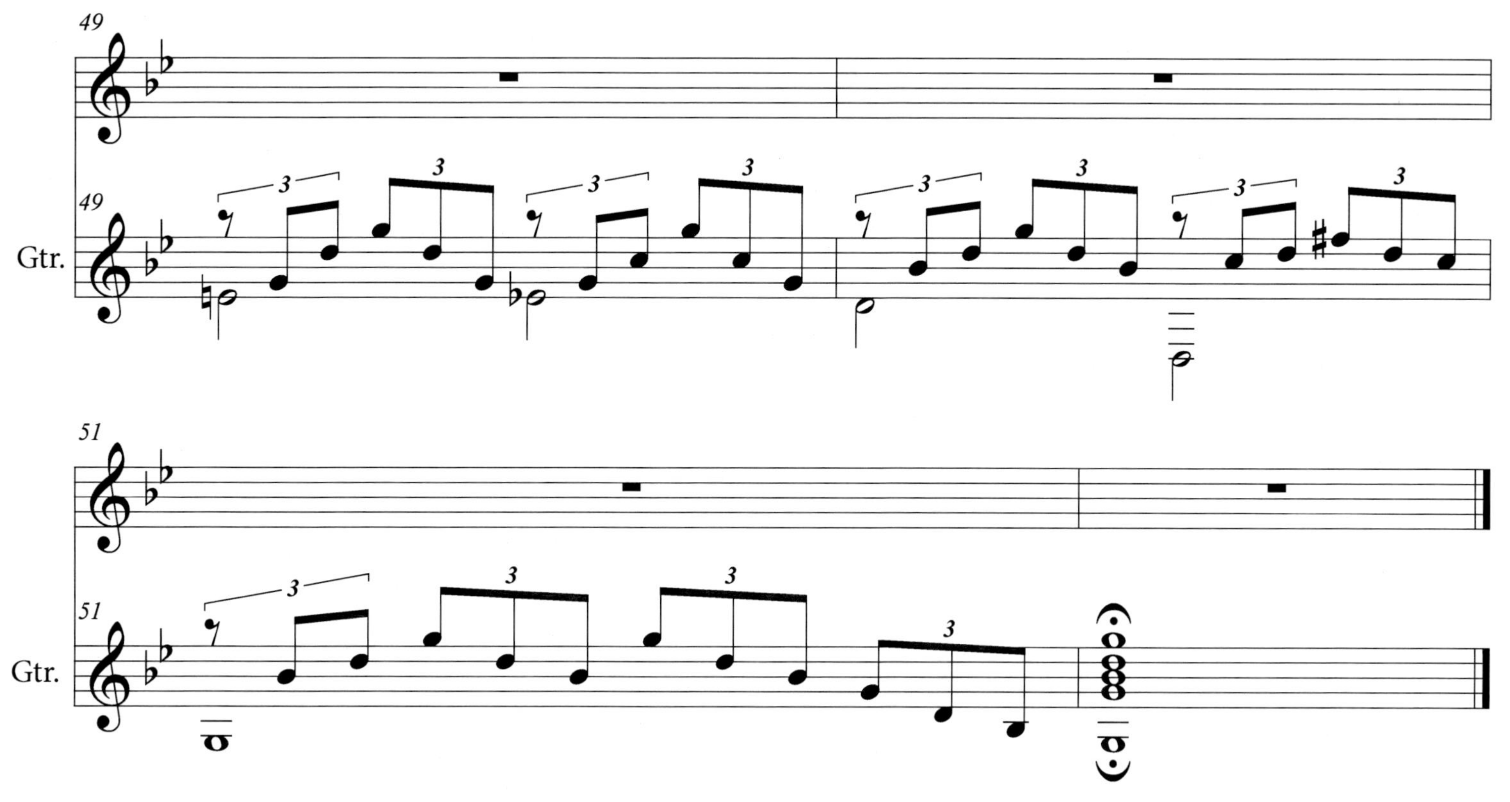
49
Gtr.
51
Gtr.

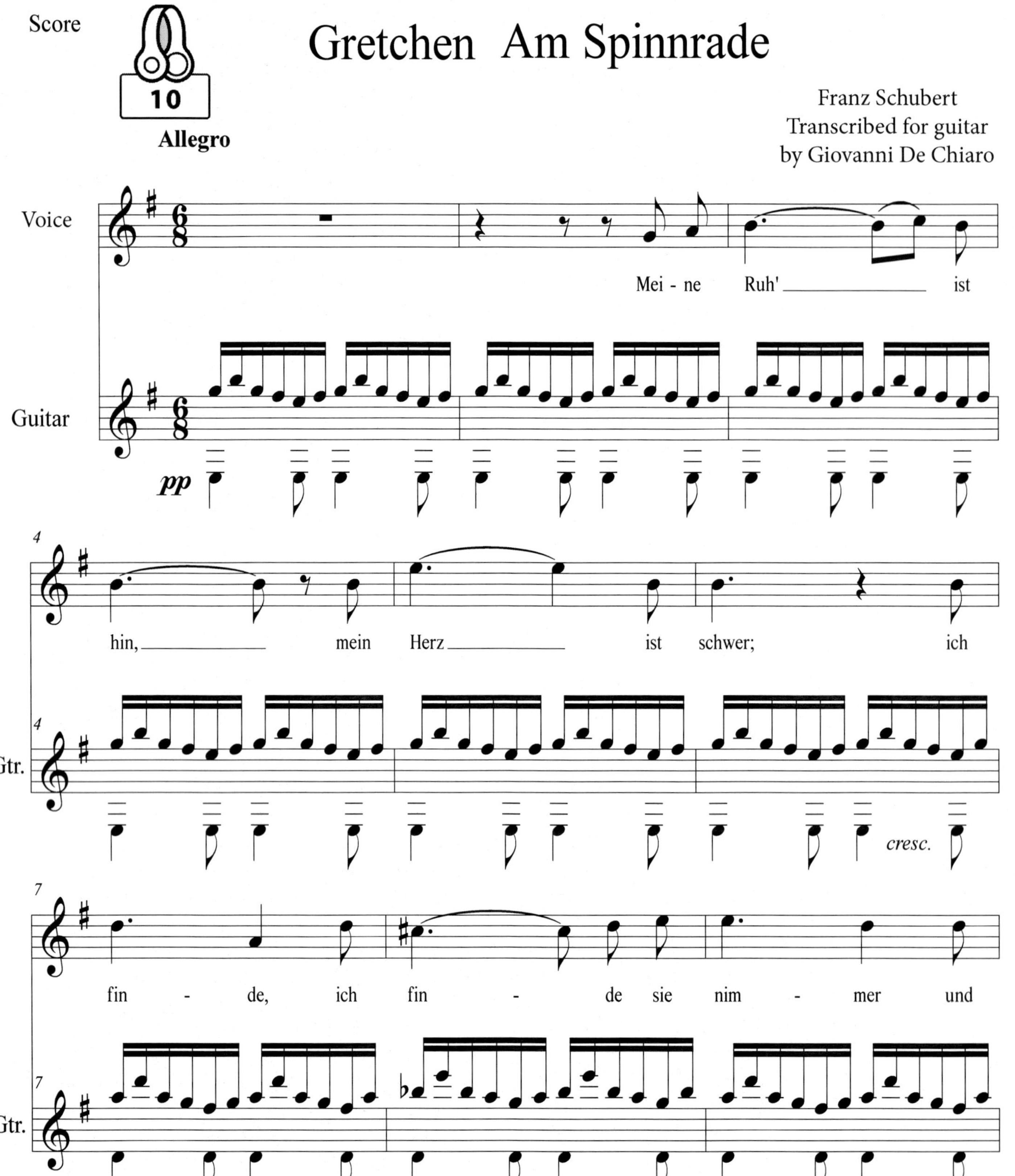
Score
10
Gretchen Am Spinnrade
Allegro
Franz Schubert
Transcribed for guitar
by Giovanni De Chiaro
Voice
Guitar
pp
Mei - ne Ruh' ist
hin, mein Herz ist schwer; ich
Gtr.
cresc.
fin - de, ich fin - de sie nim - mer und
f

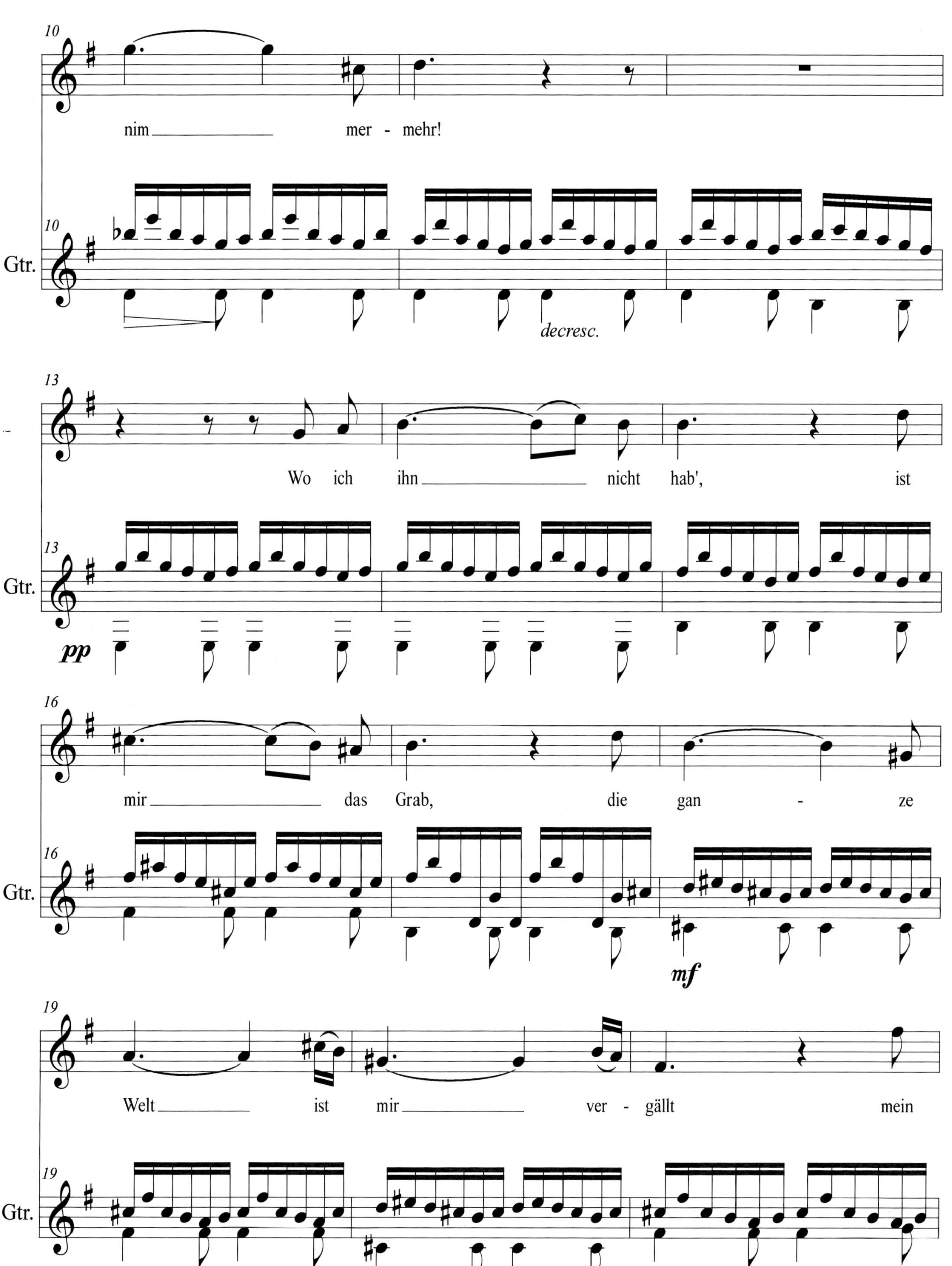
nim mer - mehr!
Gtr.
decresc.
Wo ich ihn nicht hab', ist
pp
mir das Grab, die gan - ze
mf
Welt ist mir ver - gällt mein

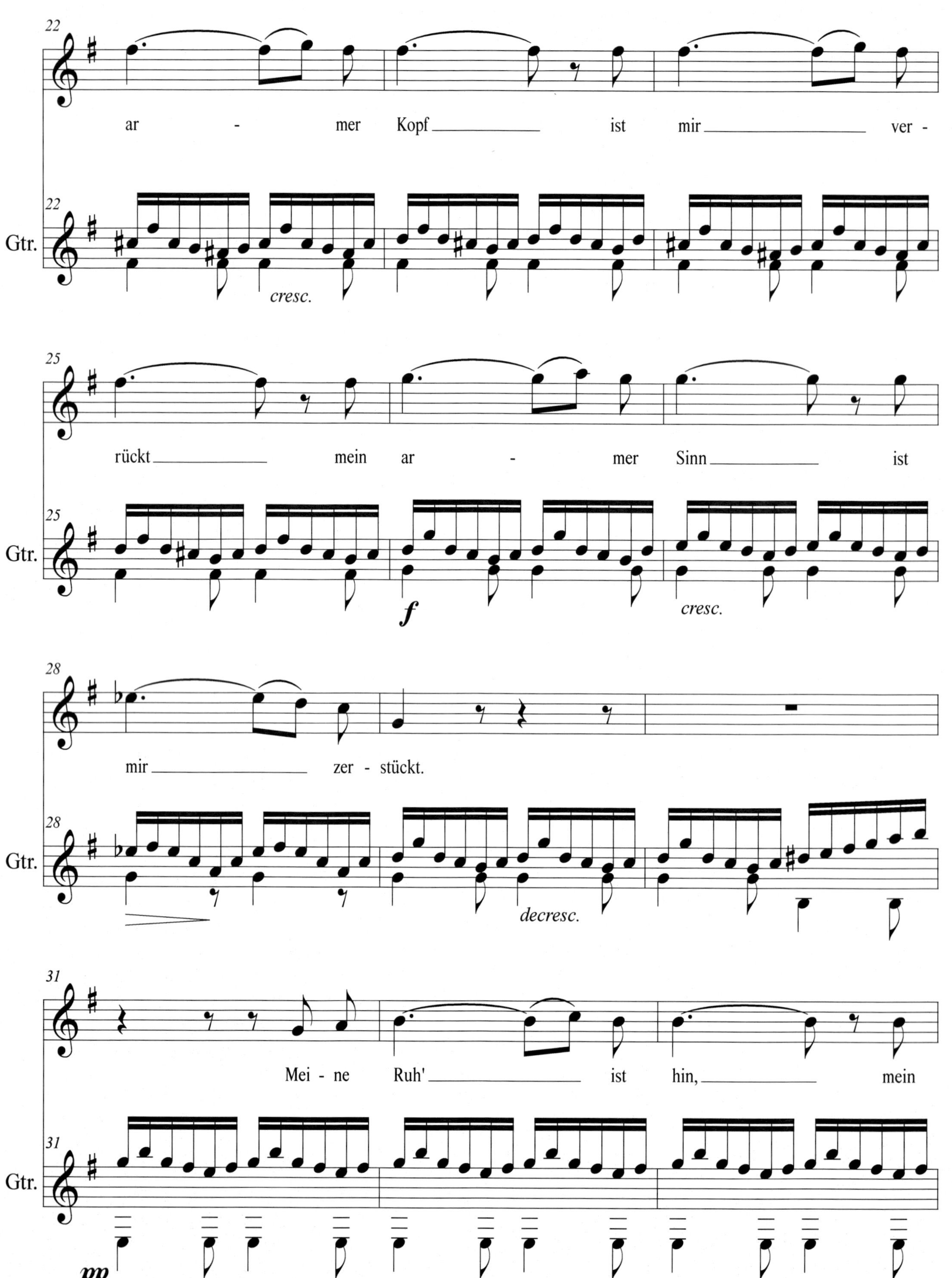
22
ar - mer Kopf ist mir ver -
Gtr.
cresc.
25
rückt mein ar - mer Sinn ist
Gtr.
f
cresc.
28
mir zer - stückt.
Gtr.
decresc.
31
Mei - ne Ruh' ist hin, mein
Gtr.
pp

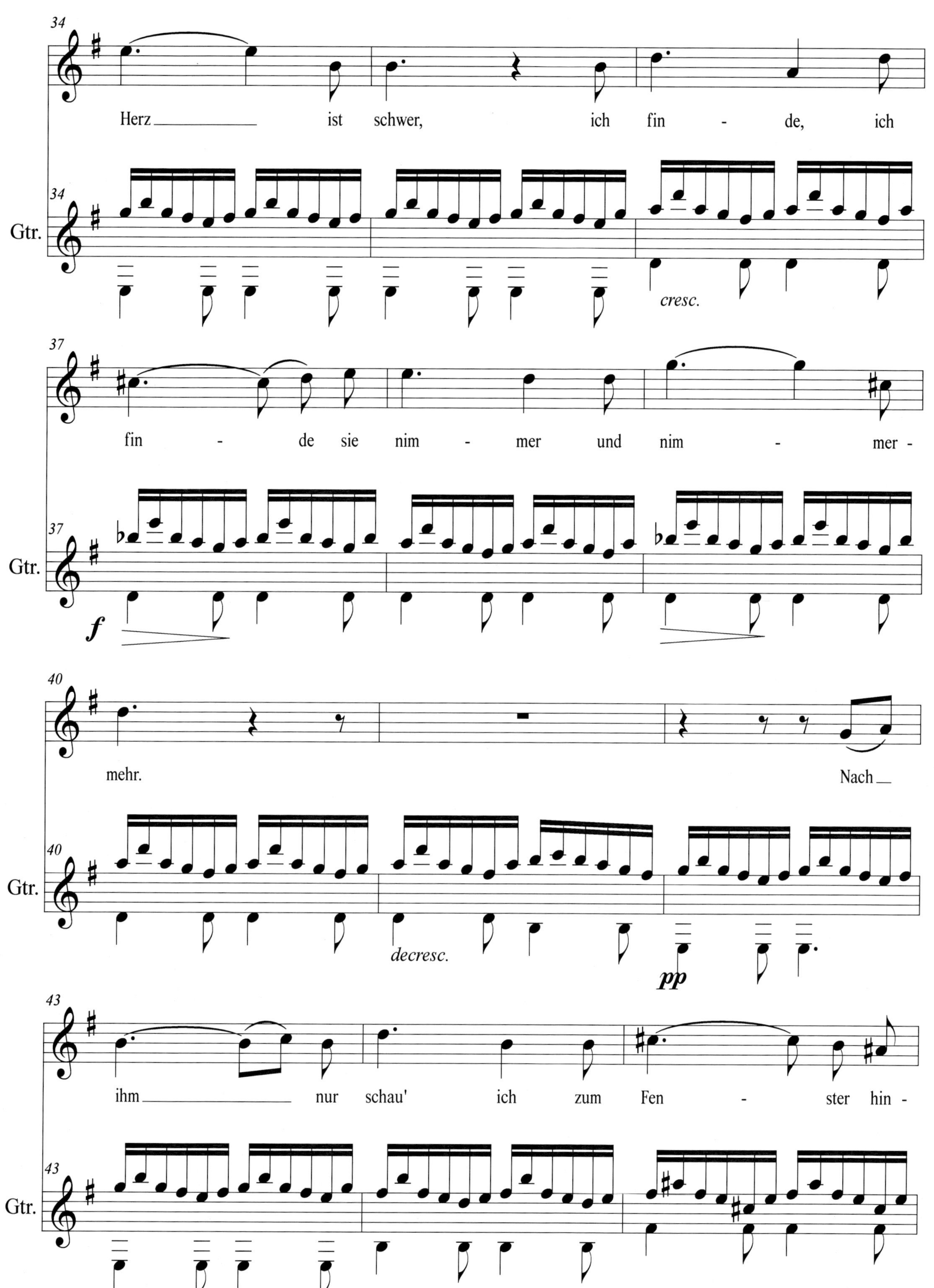
34
Herz ist schwer, ich fin - de, ich
Gtr.
cresc.
37
fin - de sie nim - mer und nim - mer -
Gtr.
f
40
mehr. Nach
Gtr.
decresc.
pp
43
ihm nur schau' ich zum Fen - ster hin -
Gtr.

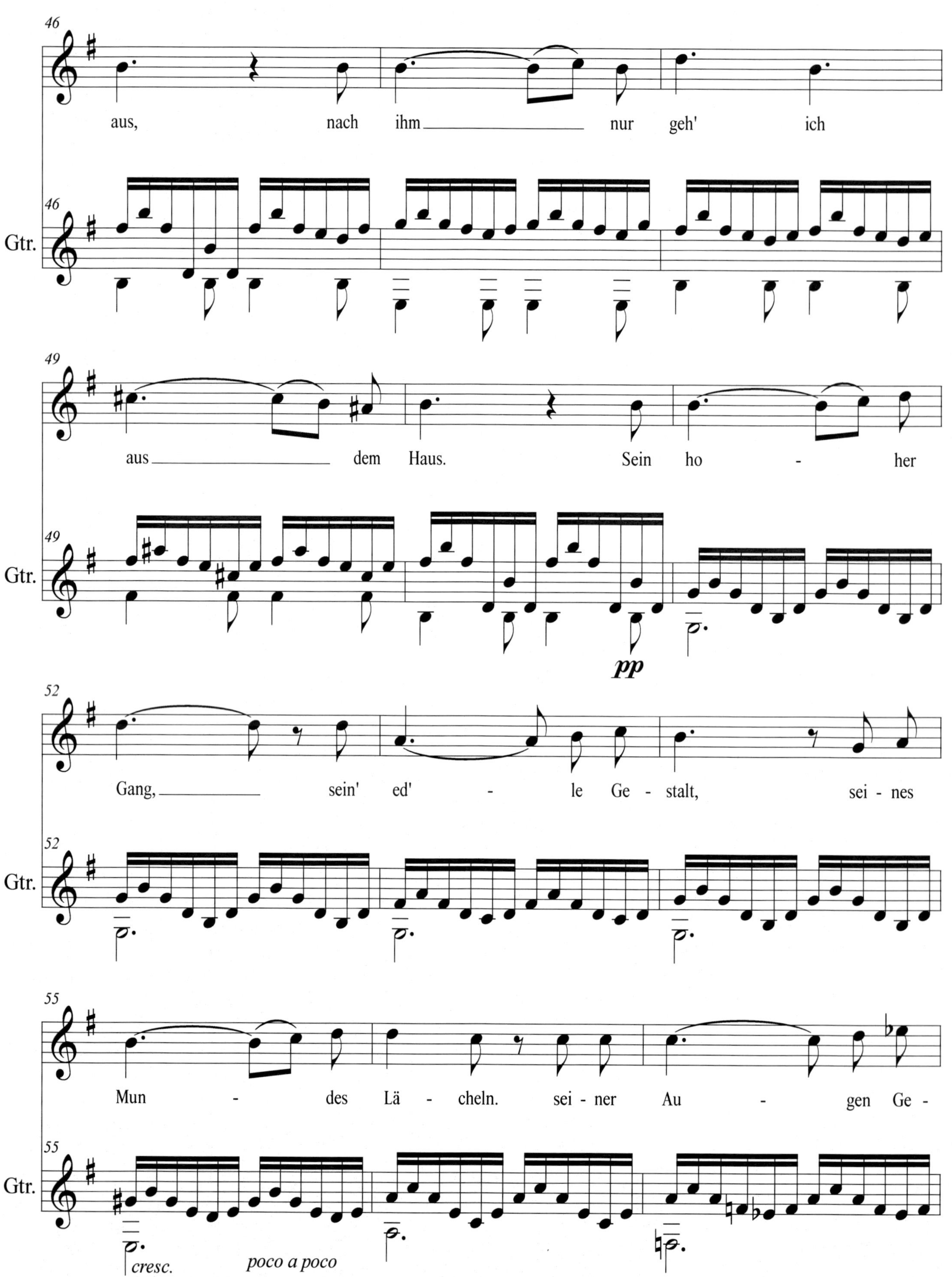
46
aus, nach ihm nur geh' ich
Gtr.
49
aus dem Haus. Sein ho - her
Gtr.
pp
52
Gang, sein' ed' - le Ge - stalt, sei - nes
Gtr.
55
Mun - des Lä - cheln. sei - ner Au - gen Ge -
Gtr.
cresc. poco a poco

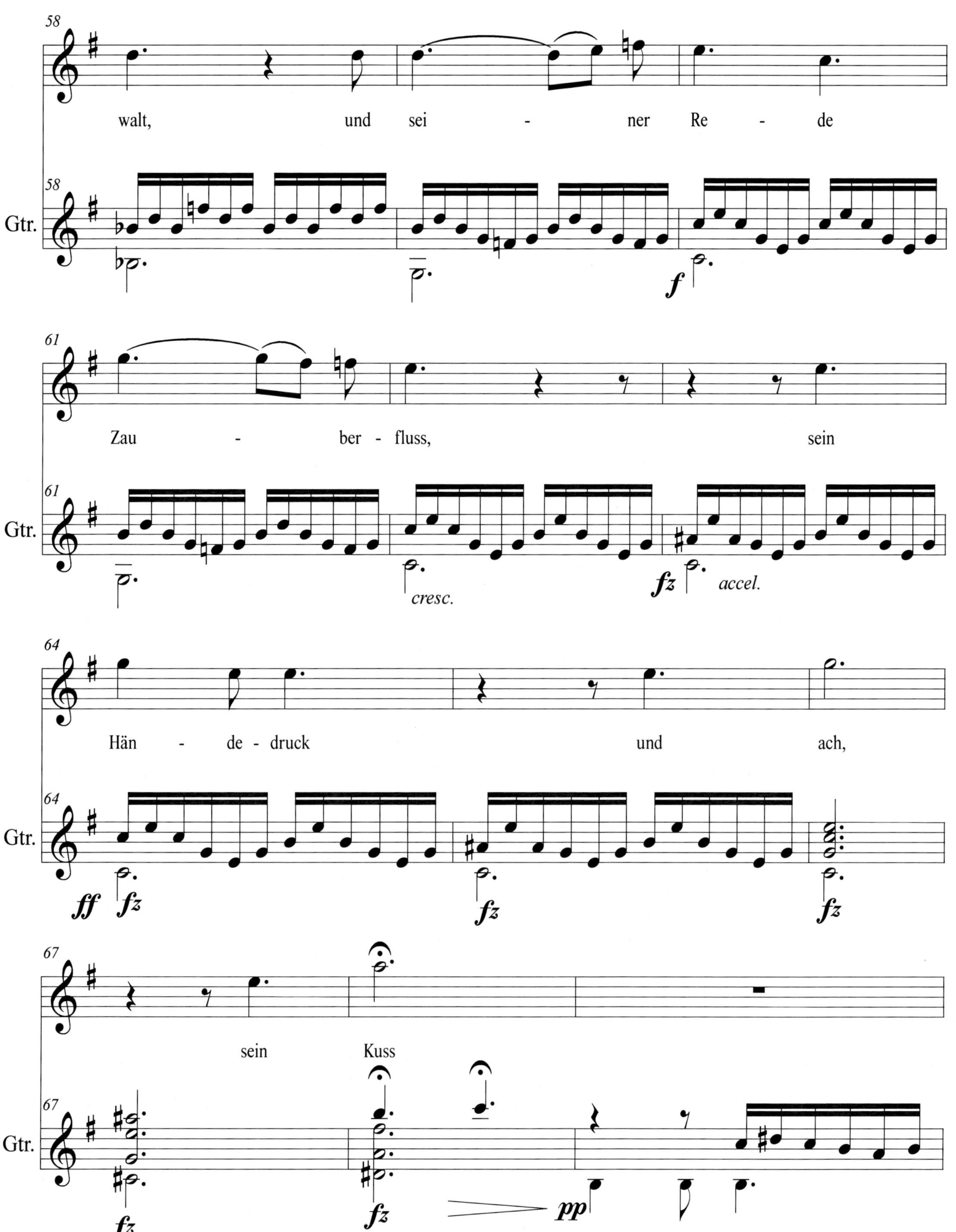
58
walt, und sei - ner Re - de
Gtr.
f
61
Zau - ber - fluss, sein
Gtr.
cresc.
fz
accel.
64
Hän - de - druck und ach,
Gtr.
ff
fz
67
sein Kuss
Gtr.
pp

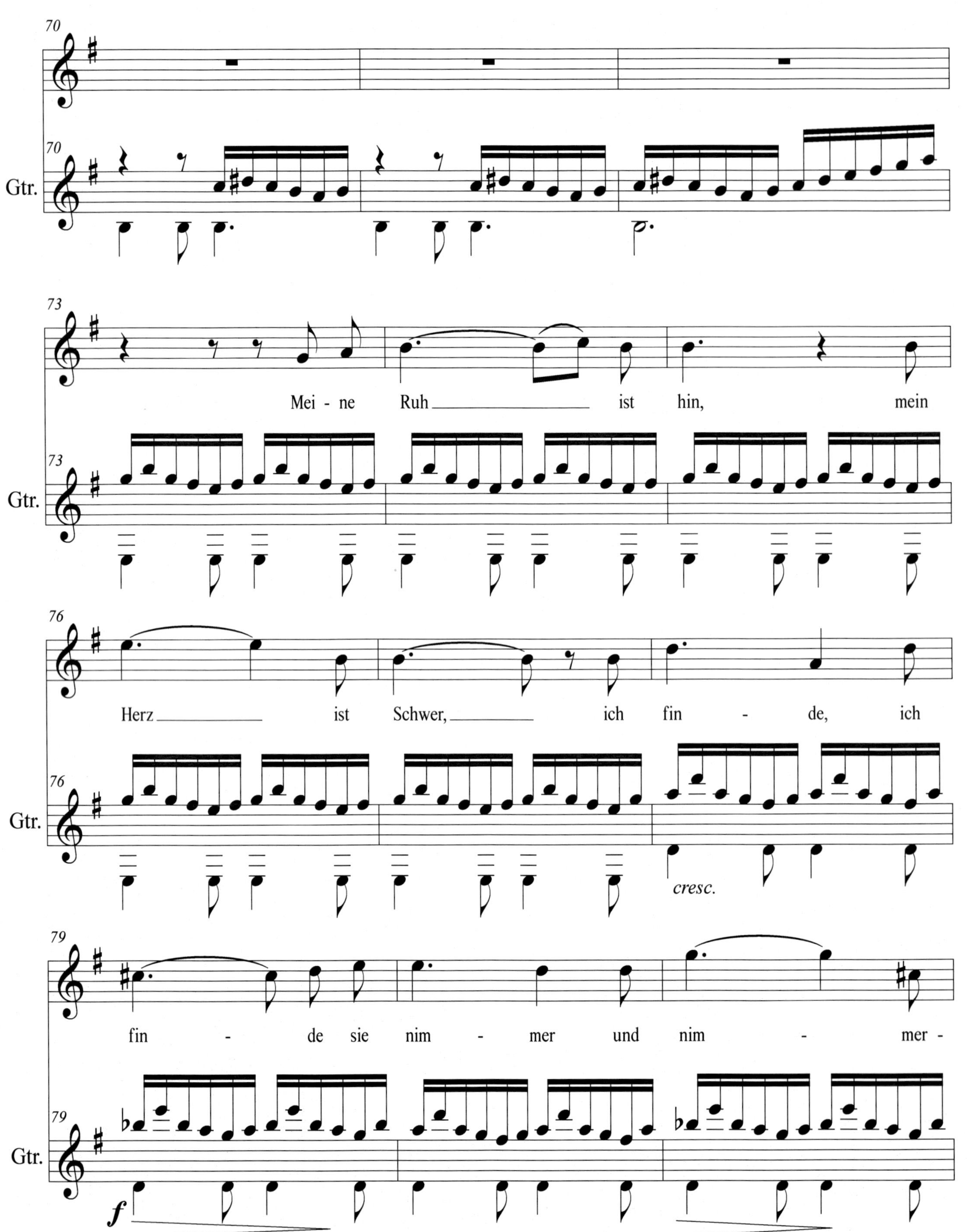
70
Gtr.
73
Mei - ne Ruh ist hin, mein
Herz ist Schwer, ich fin - de, ich
cresc.
79
fin - de sie nim - mer und nim - mer -
f

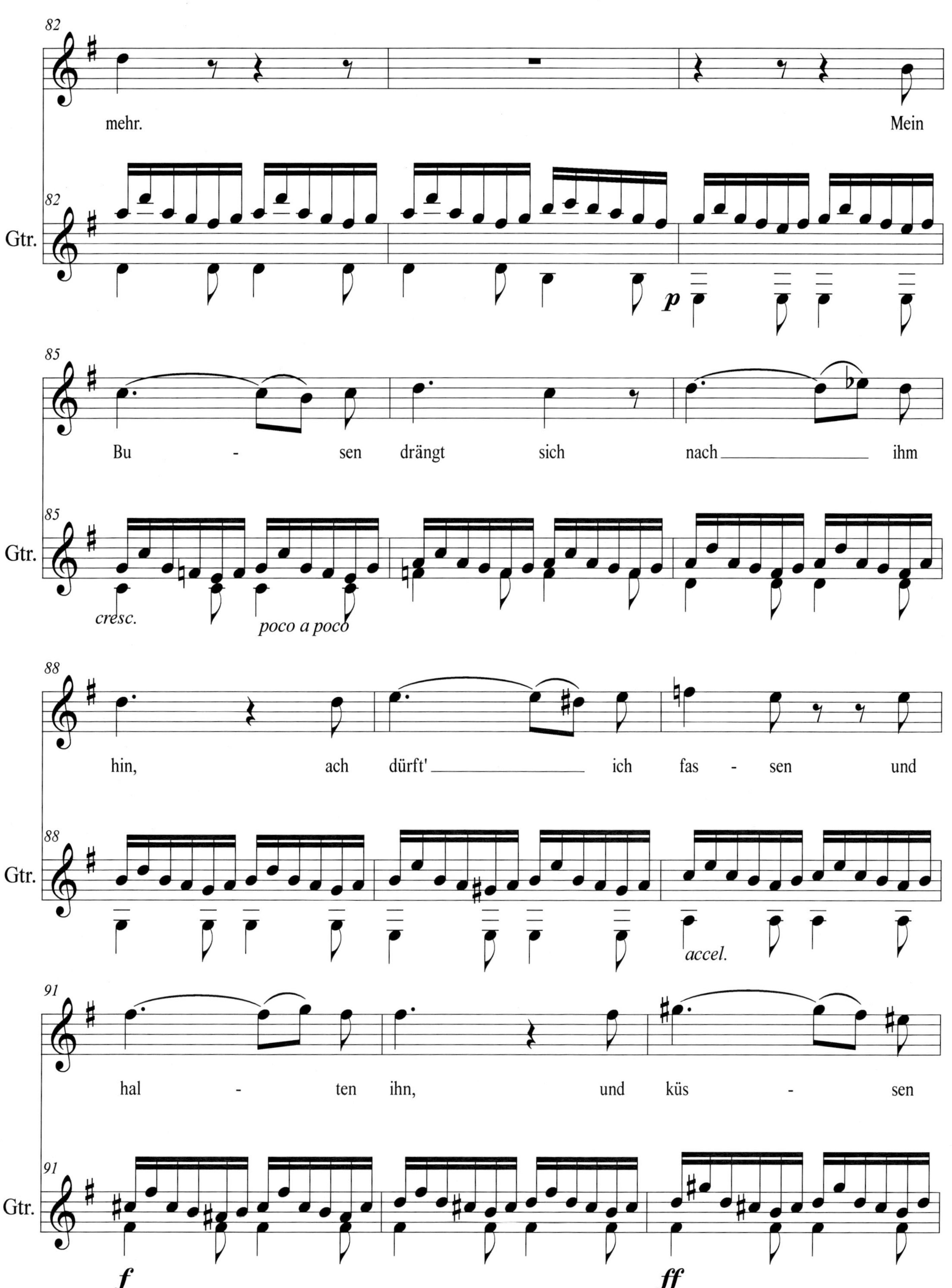
82
mehr. Mein
82
Gtr.
p
85
Bu - sen drängt sich nach ihm
85
Gtr.
cresc.
poco a poco
88
hin, ach dürft' ich fas - sen und
88
Gtr.
accel.
91
hal - ten ihn, und küs - sen
91
Gtr.
f
ff

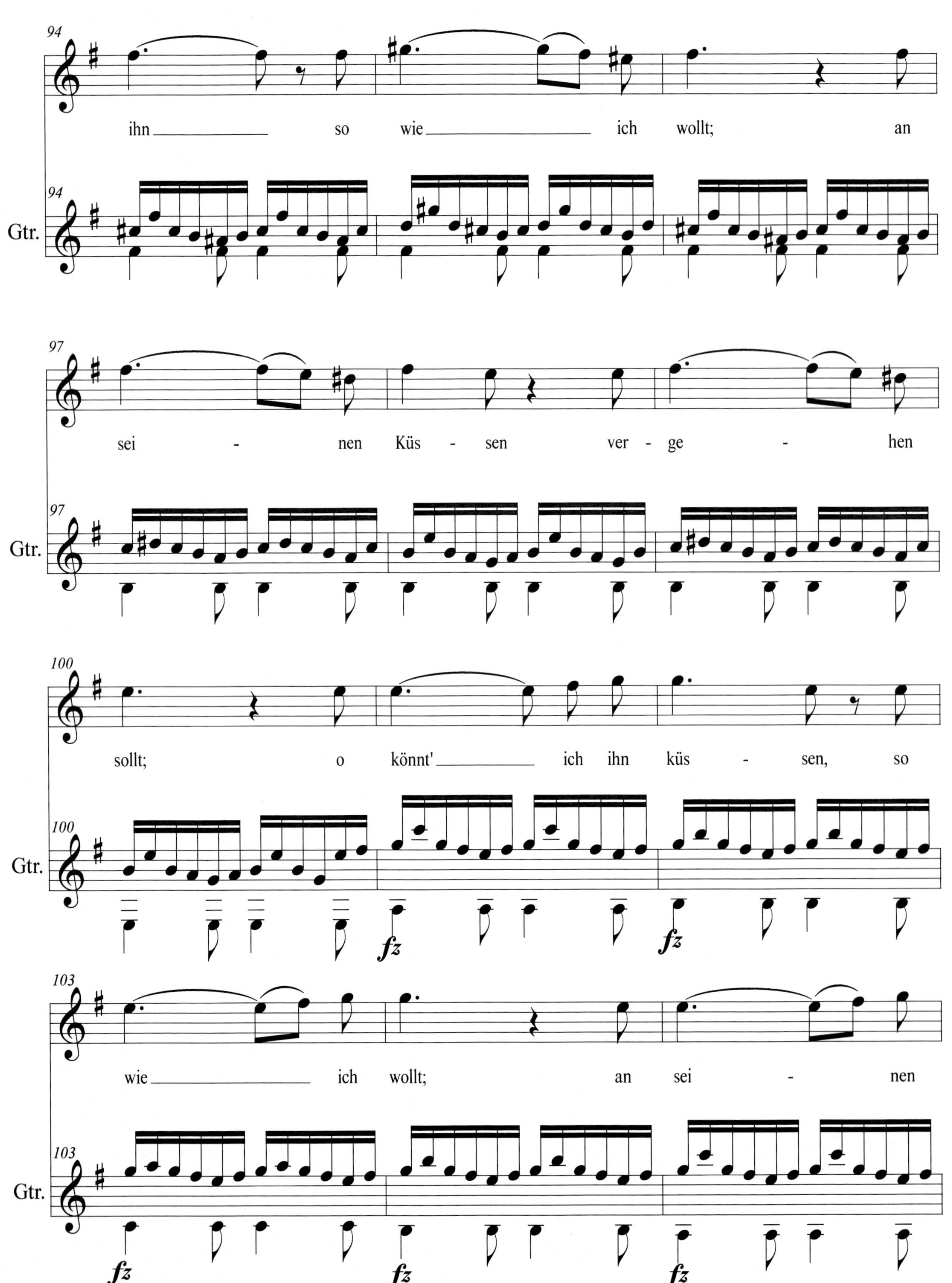
94
ihn so wie ich wollt; an
Gtr.
97
sei - nen Küs - sen ver - ge - hen
Gtr.
100
sollt; o könnt' ich ihn küs - sen, so
Gtr.
fz
103
wie ich wollt; an sei - nen
Gtr.
fz

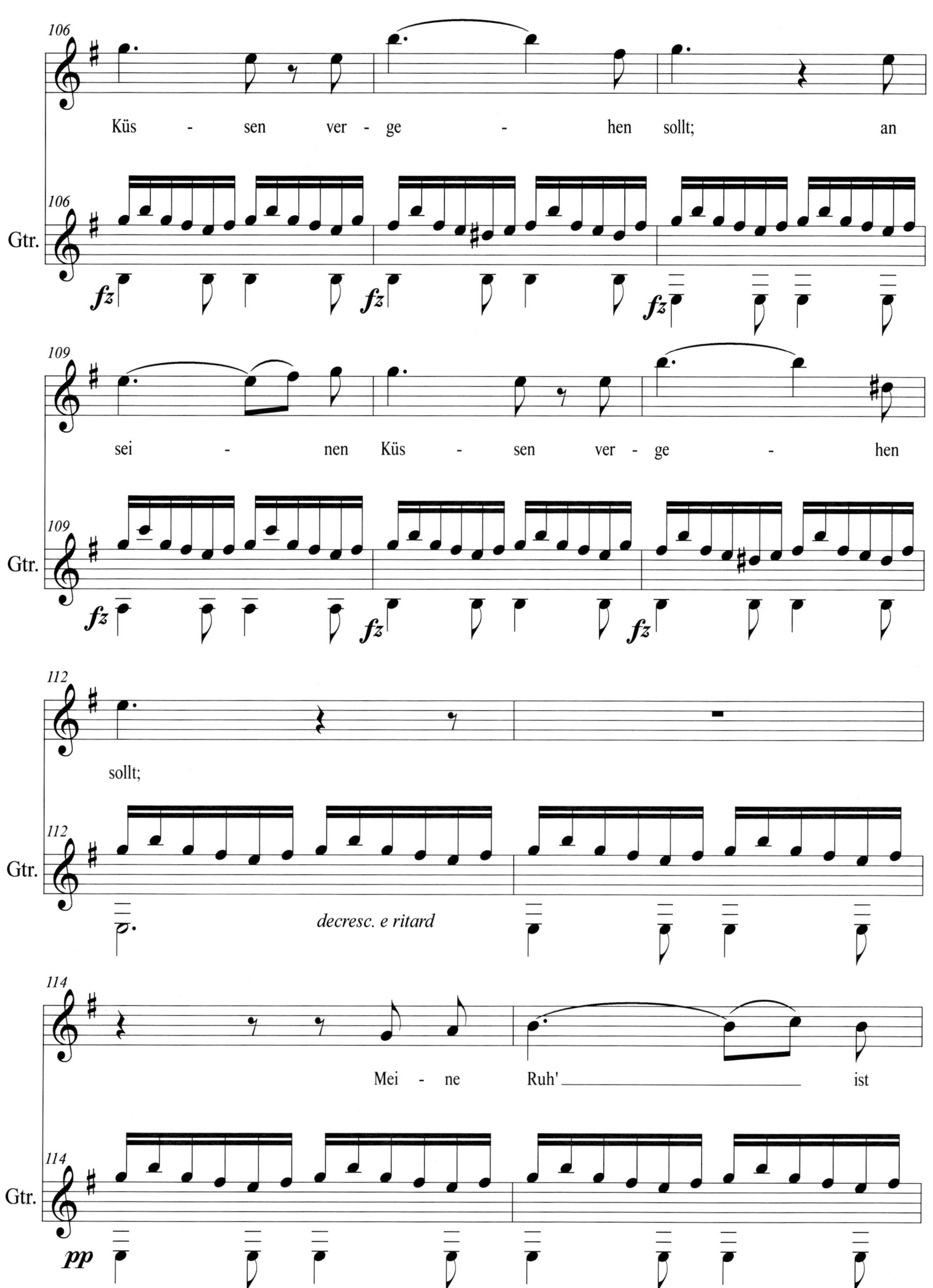
106
Küs - sen ver - ge - hen sollt; an
Gtr.
fz
109
sei - nen Küs - sen ver - ge - hen
112
sollt;
decresc. e ritard
114
Mei - ne Ruh' ist
pp

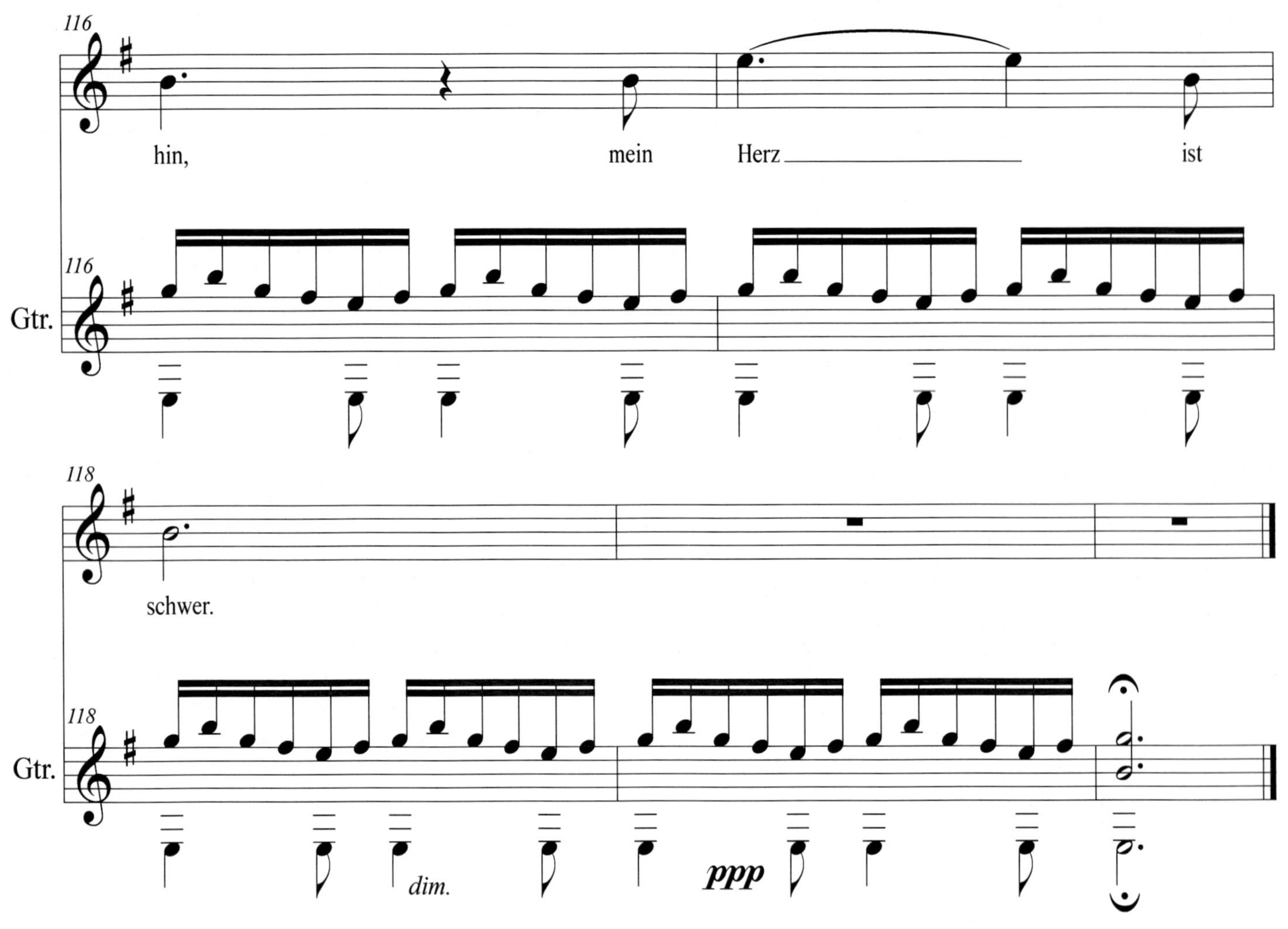
116
hin,
mein
Herz
ist
116
Gtr.
118
schwer.
118
Gtr.
dim.
ppp

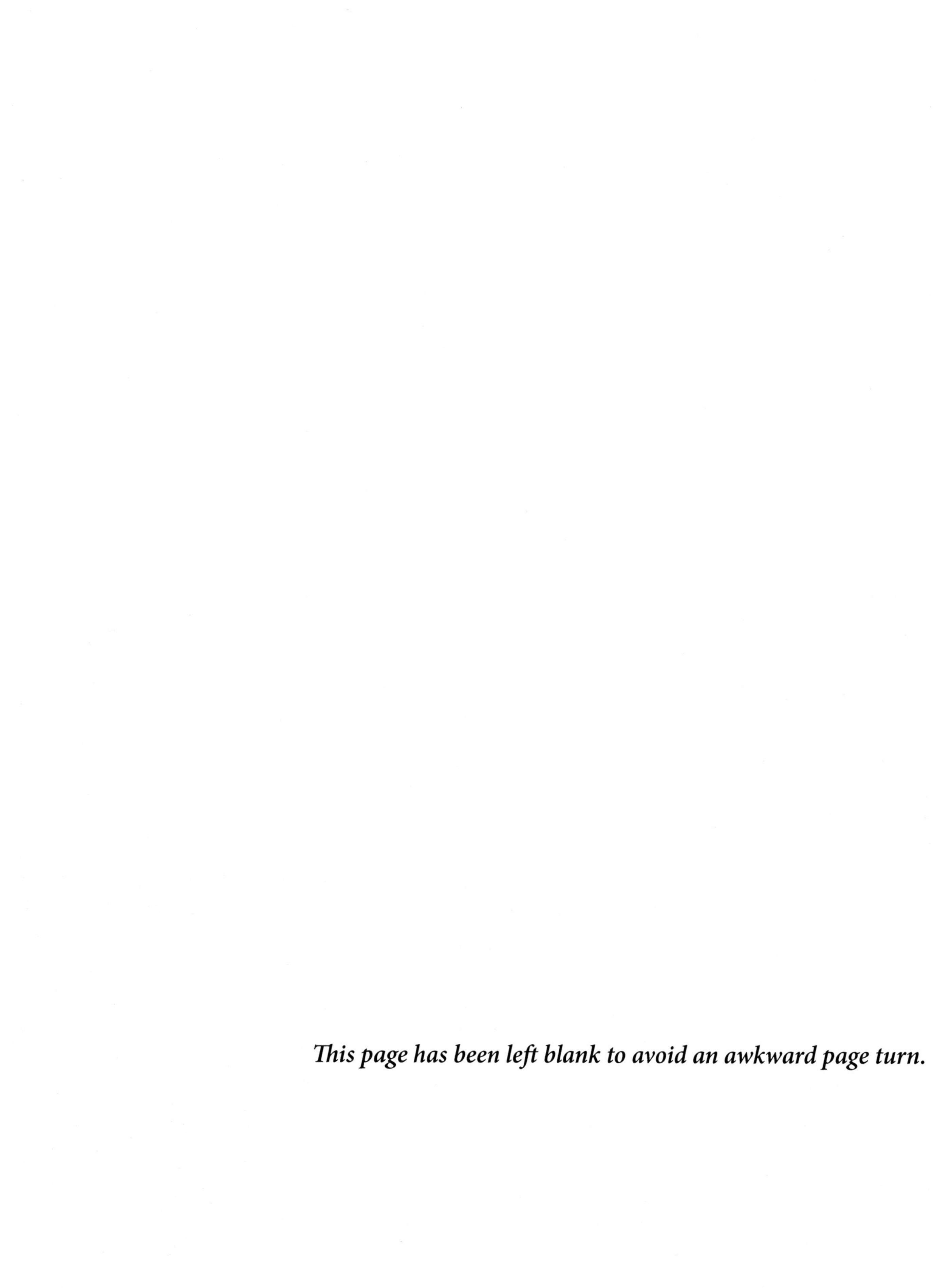

This page has been left blank to avoid an awkward page turn.

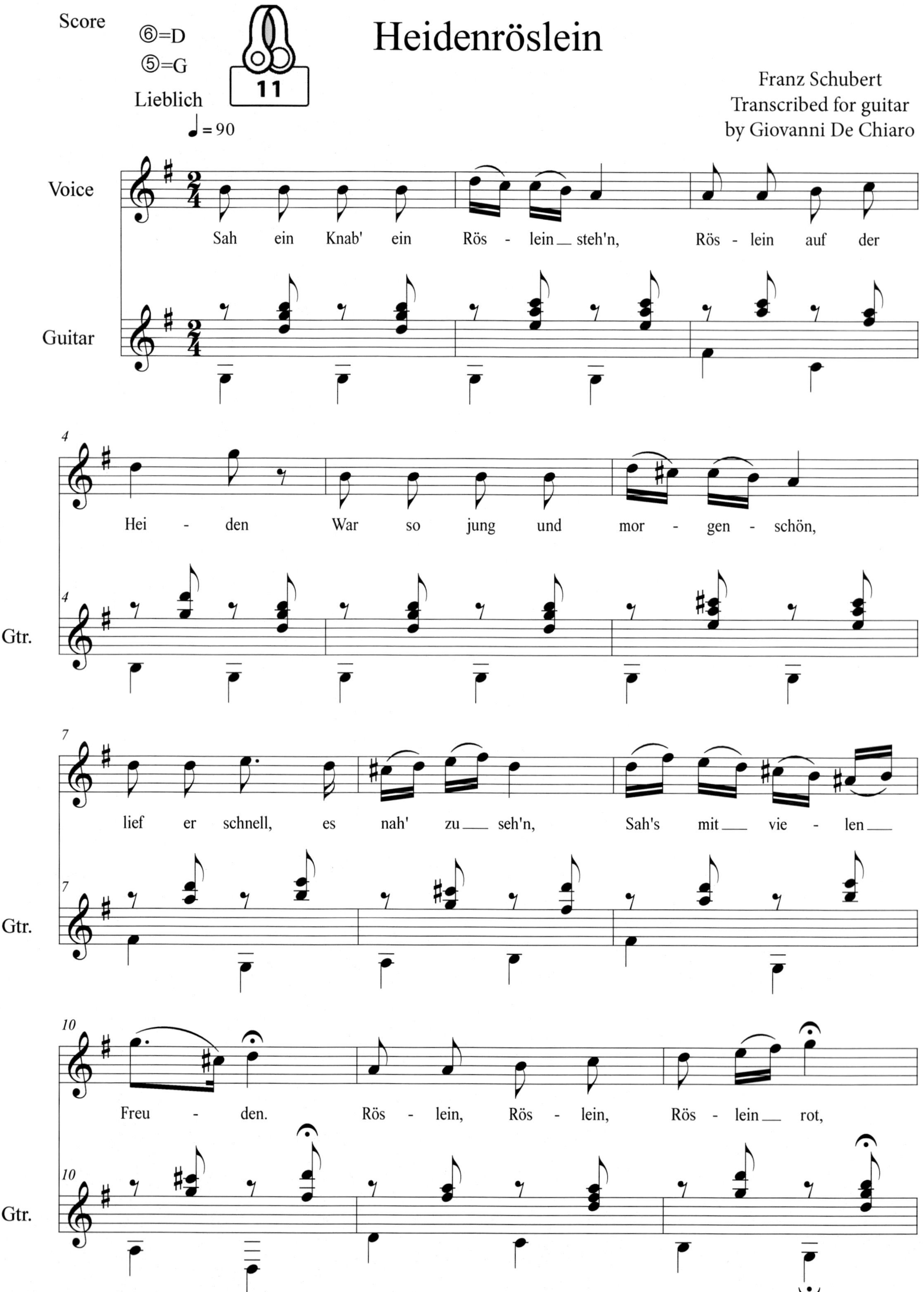
Score
⑥=D
⑤=G
Lieblich
♩ = 90
11
Heidenröslein
Franz Schubert
Transcribed for guitar
by Giovanni De Chiaro
Voice
Guitar
Sah ein Knab' ein Rös - lein steh'n, Rös - lein auf der
Hei - den War so jung und mor - gen - schön,
Gtr.
lief er schnell, es nah' zu seh'n, Sah's mit vie - len
Gtr.
Freu - den. Rös - lein, Rös - lein, Rös - lein rot,
Gtr.

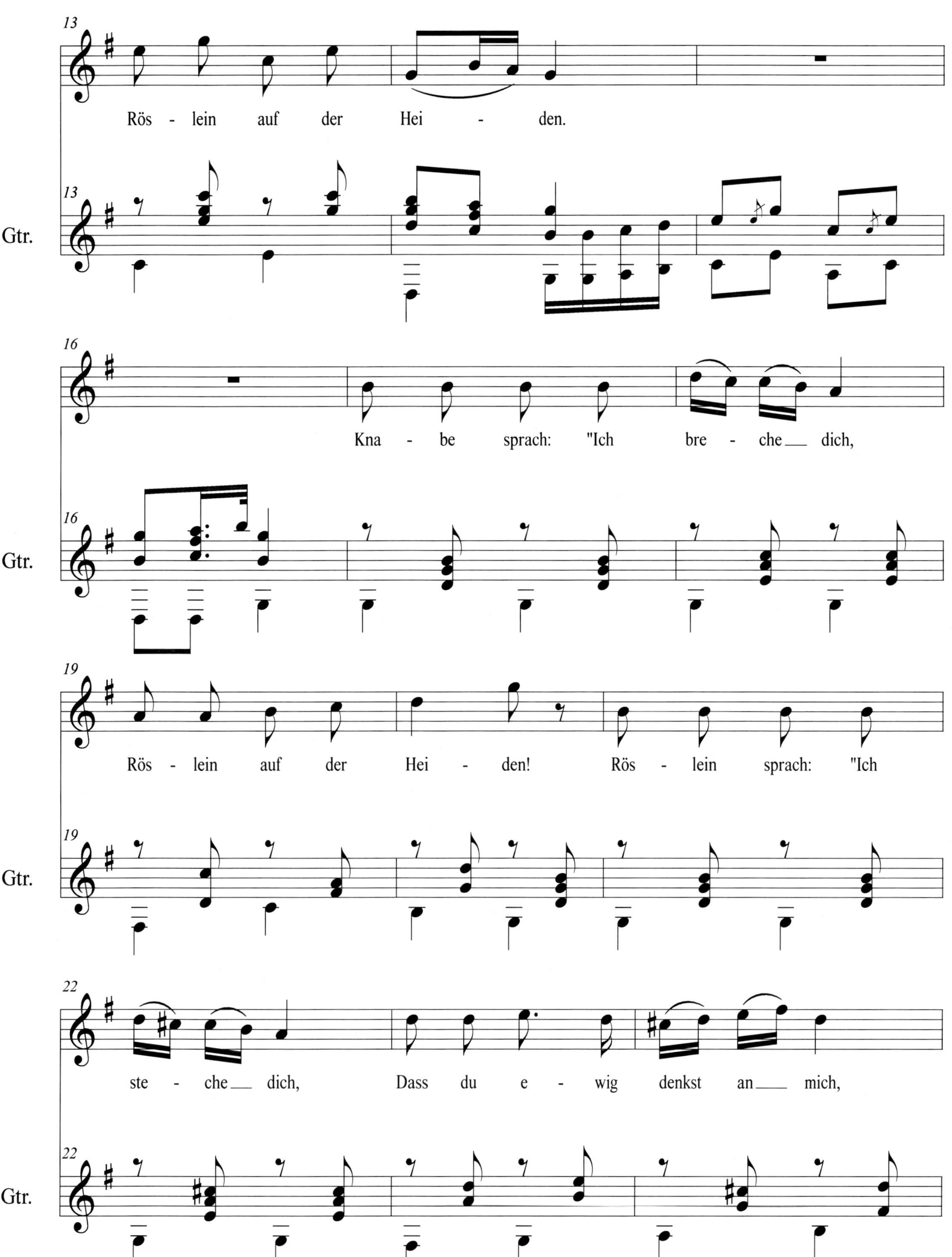
13
Rös - lein auf der Hei - den.
Gtr.
16
Kna - be sprach: "Ich bre - che dich,
19
Rös - lein auf der Hei - den! Rös - lein sprach: "Ich
22
ste - che dich, Dass du e - wig denkst an mich,

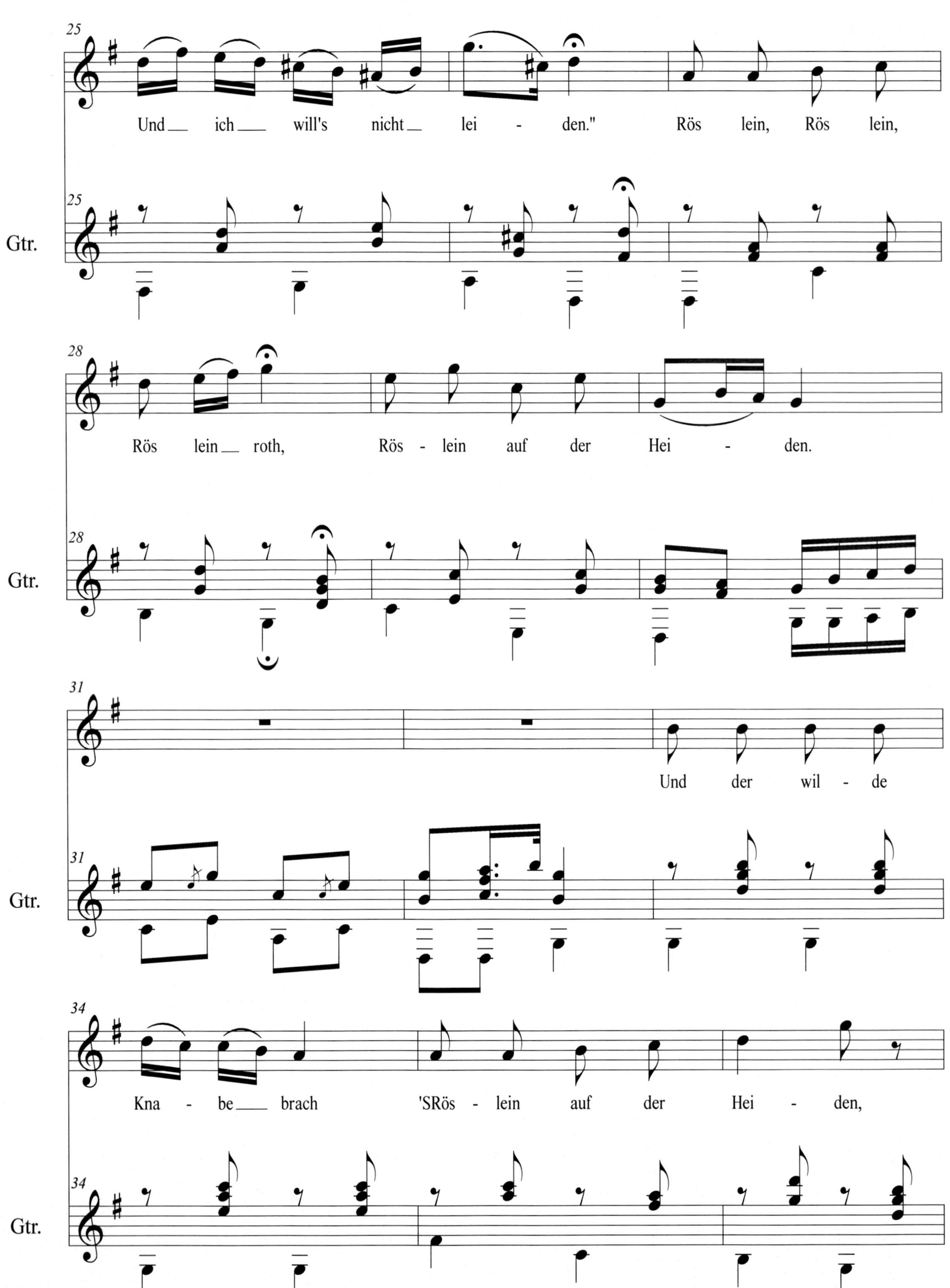
25
Und ich will's nicht lei - den." Rös lein, Rös lein,
Gtr.
28
Rös lein roth, Rös - lein auf der Hei - den.
31
Und der wil - de
34
Kna - be brach 'SRös - lein auf der Hei - den,

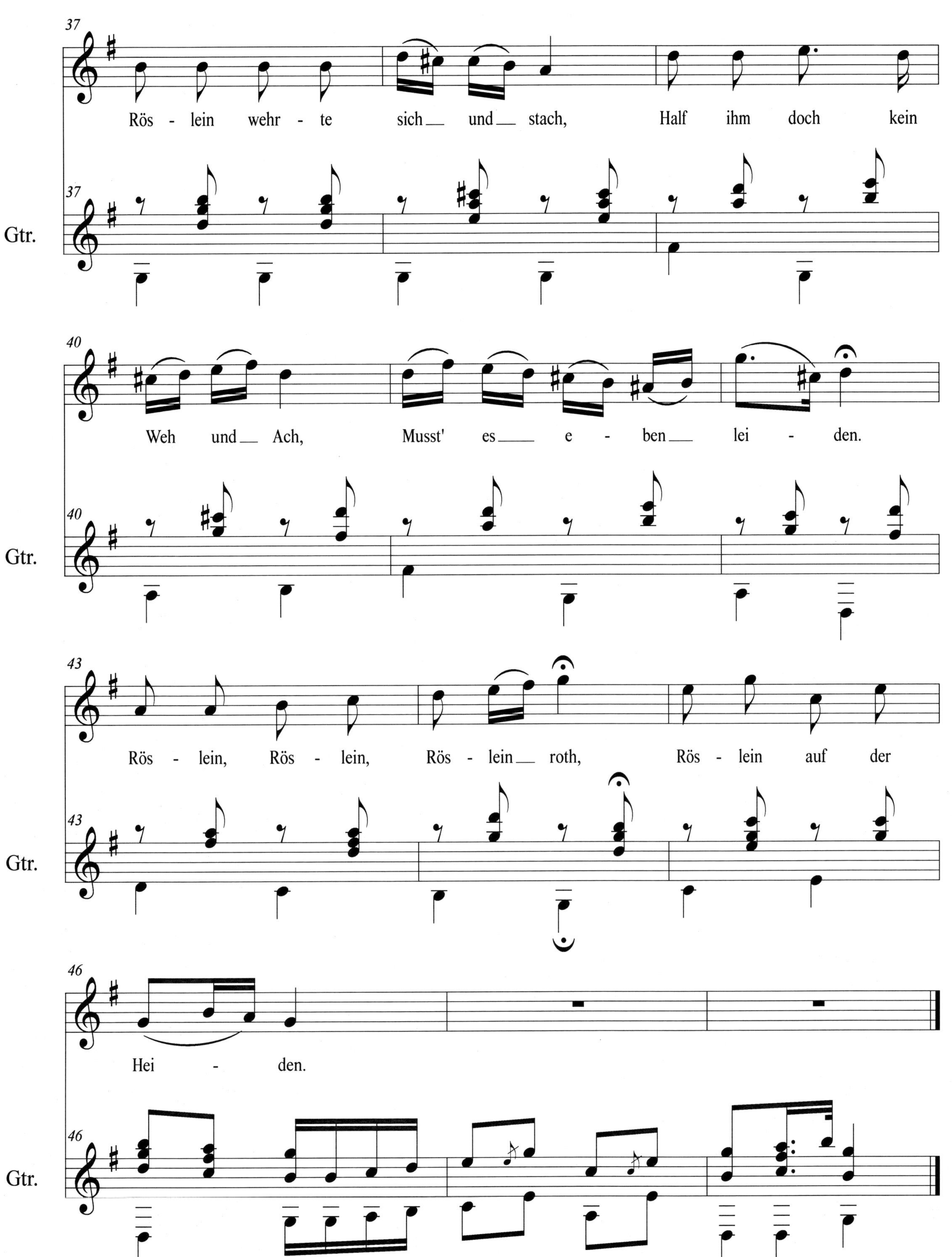
37
Rös - lein wehr - te sich und stach, Half ihm doch kein
Gtr.
40
Weh und Ach, Musst' es e - ben lei - den.
Gtr.
43
Rös - lein, Rös - lein, Rös - lein roth, Rös - lein auf der
Gtr.
46
Hei - den.
Gtr.

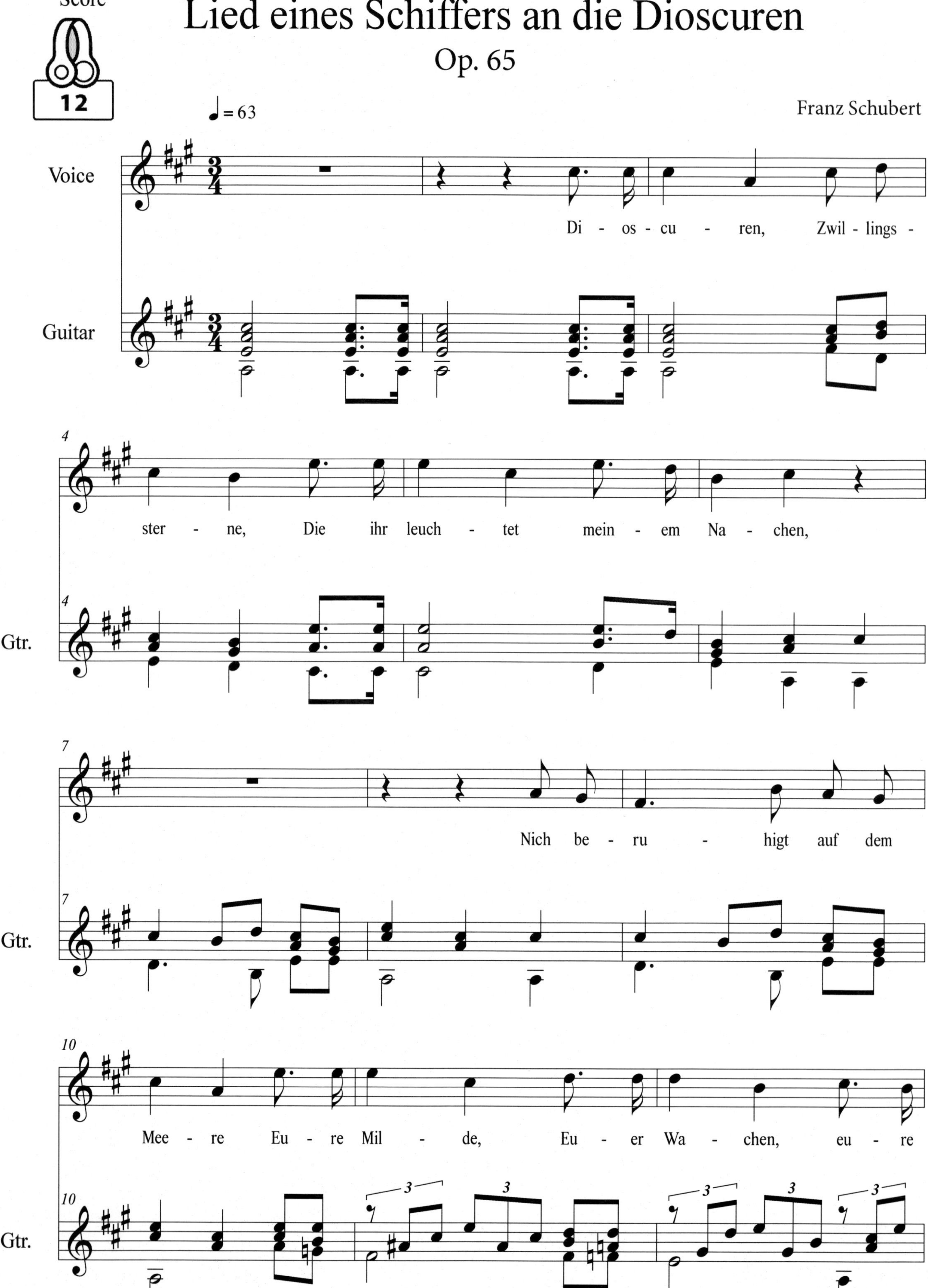
Score
12
Lied eines Schiffers an die Dioscuren
Op. 65
♩= 63
Franz Schubert
Voice
Guitar
Di - os - cu - ren, Zwil - lings -
Gtr.
ster - ne, Die ihr leuch - tet mein - em Na - chen,
Nich be - ru - higt auf dem
Mee - re Eu - re Mil - de, Eu - er Wa - chen, eu - re

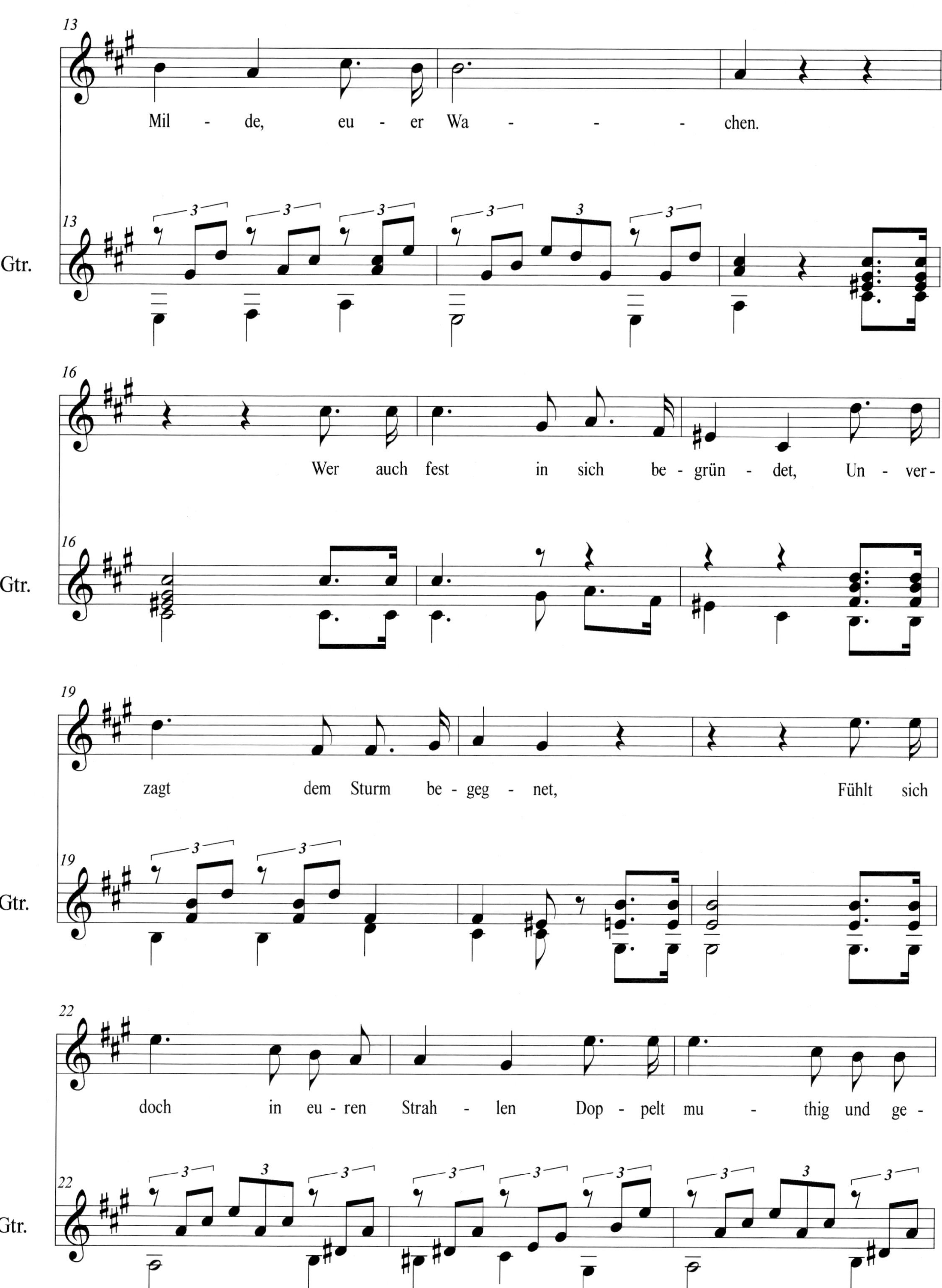
13
Mil - de, eu - er Wa - - - chen.
13
Gtr.
16
Wer auch fest in sich be - grün - det, Un - ver -
16
Gtr.
19
zagt dem Sturm be - geg - net, Fühlt sich
19
Gtr.
22
doch in eu - ren Strah - len Dop - pelt mu - thig und ge -
22
Gtr.

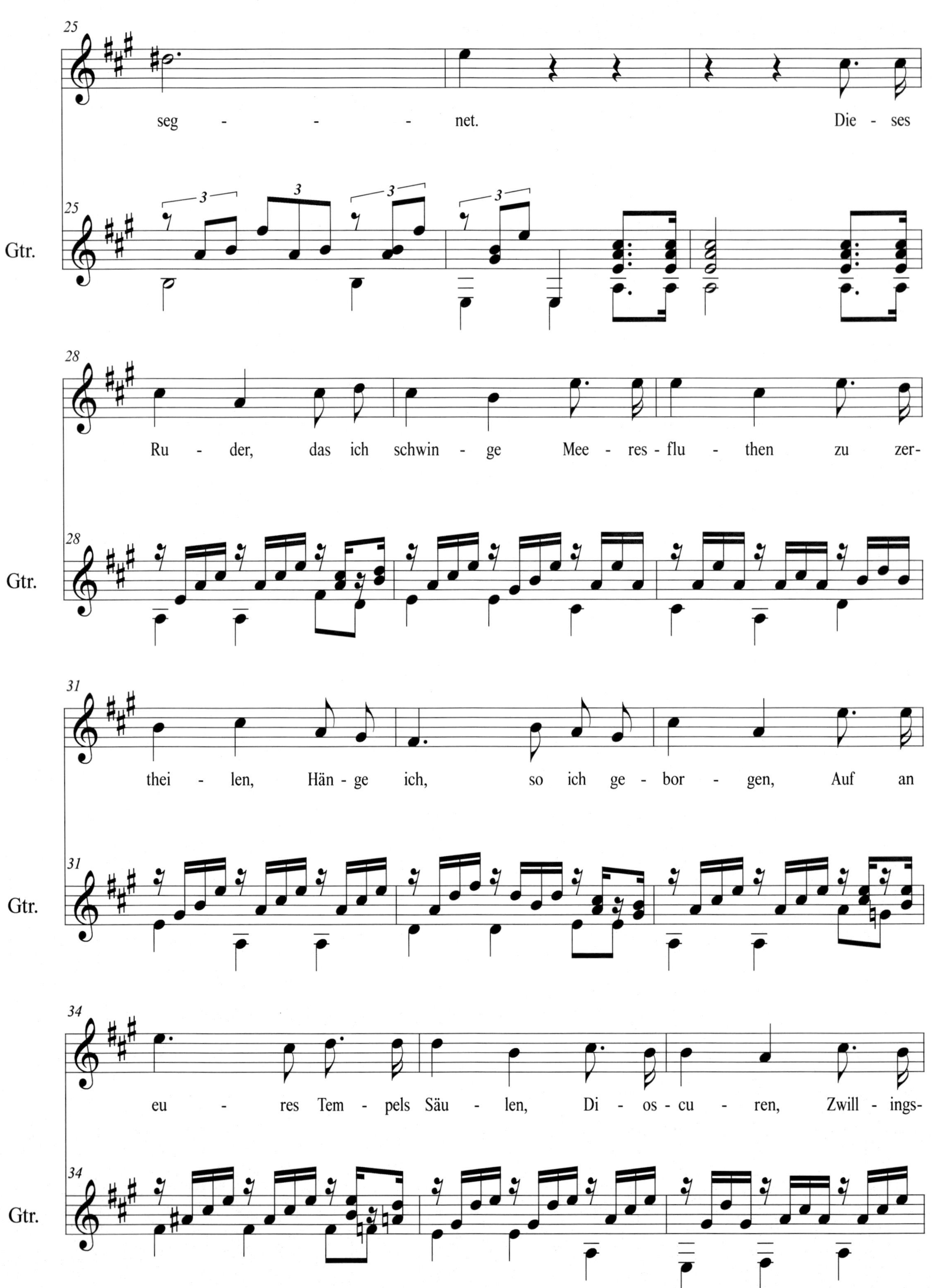
25
seg - - - net. Die - ses
25
Gtr.
28
Ru - der, das ich schwin - ge Mee - res - flu - then zu zer-
28
Gtr.
31
thei - len, Hän - ge ich, so ich ge - bor - gen, Auf an
31
Gtr.
34
eu - res Tem - pels Säu - len, Di - os - cu - ren, Zwill - ings-
34
Gtr.

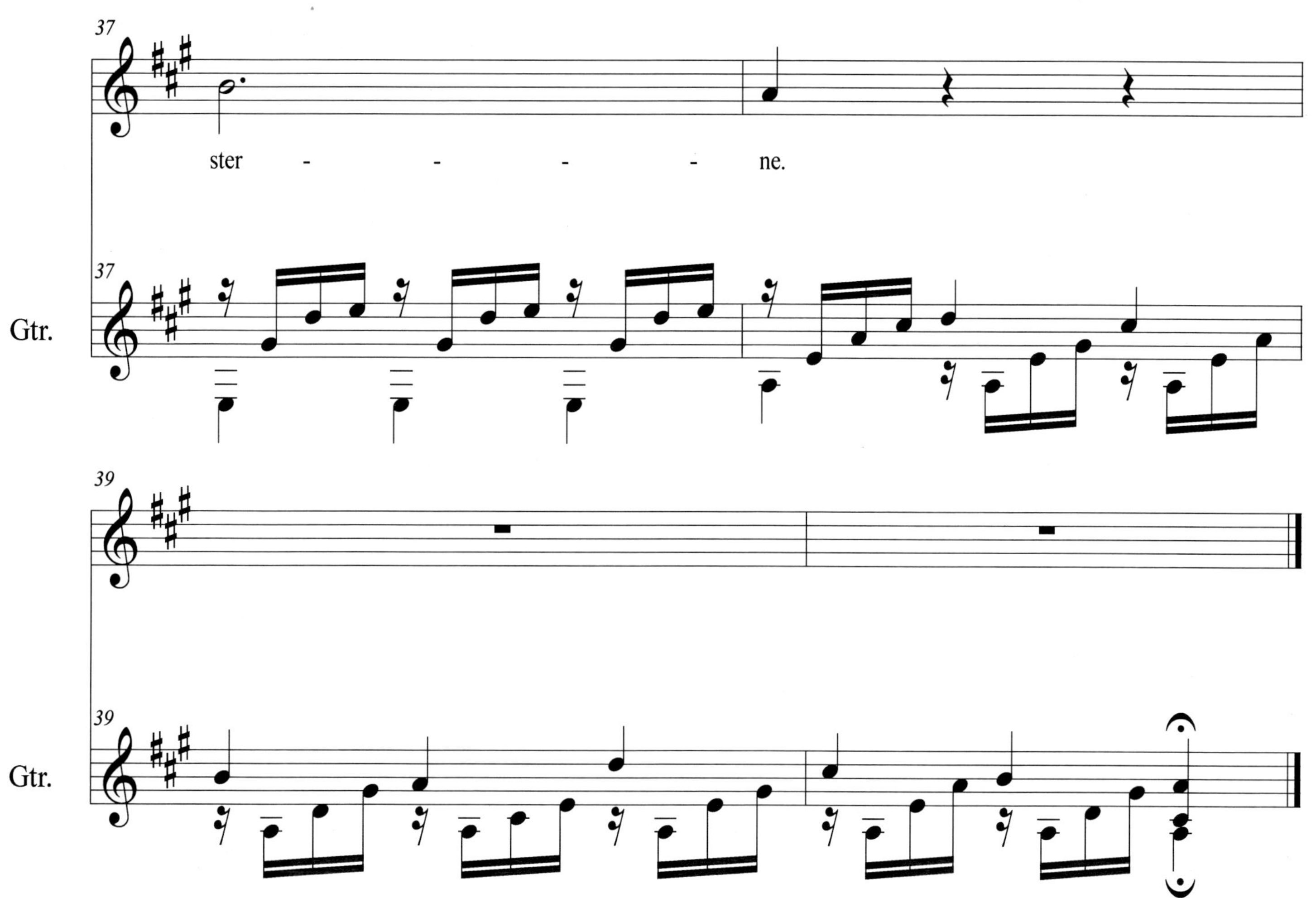
37
ster - - - - ne.
Gtr.
39
Gtr.

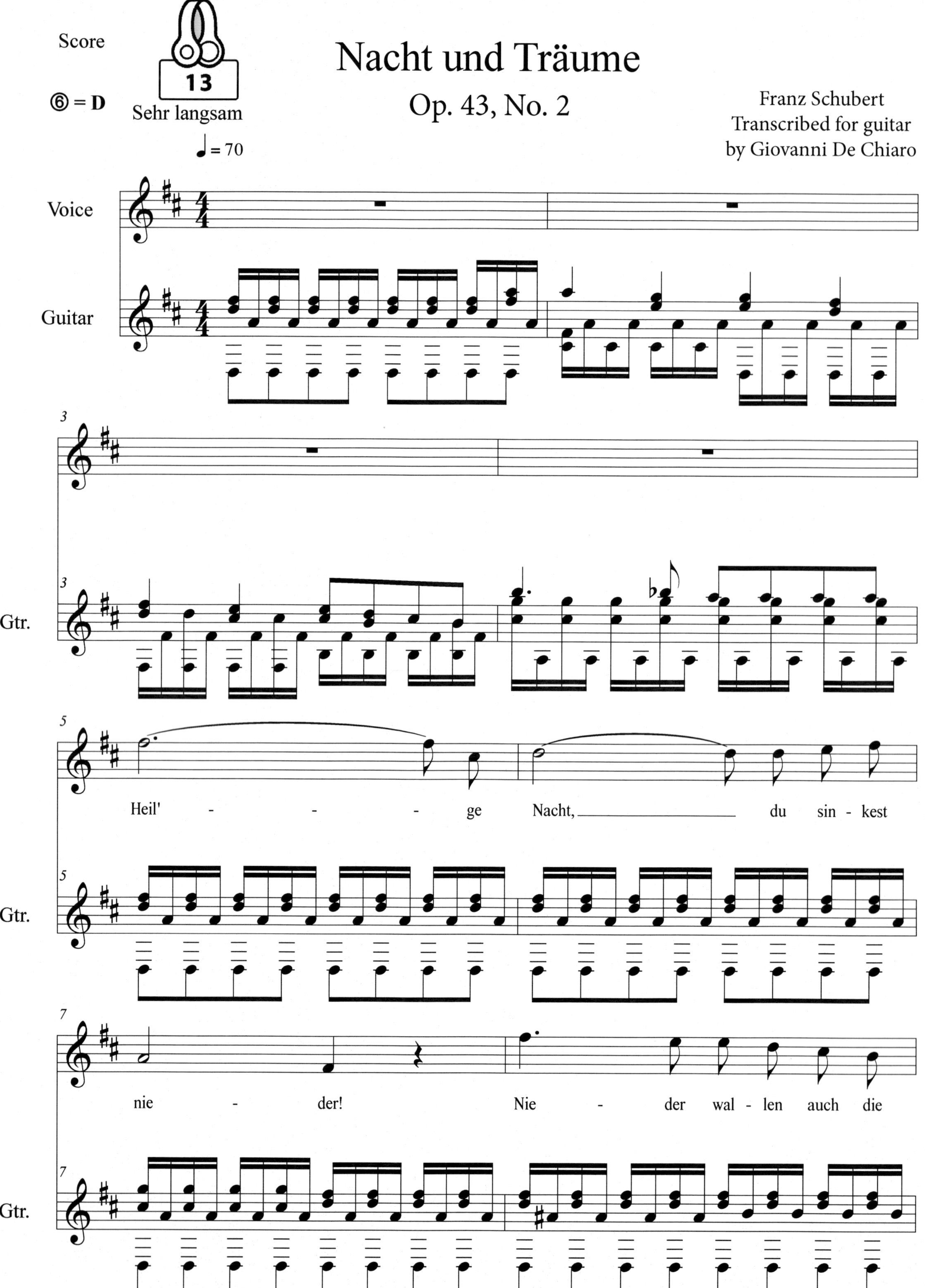
Score
13
⑥ = D
Sehr langsam
♩= 70
Nacht und Träume
Op. 43, No. 2
Franz Schubert
Transcribed for guitar
by Giovanni De Chiaro
Voice
Guitar
Gtr.
Heil' - - - ge Nacht, du sin - kest
nie - der! Nie - der wal - len auch die

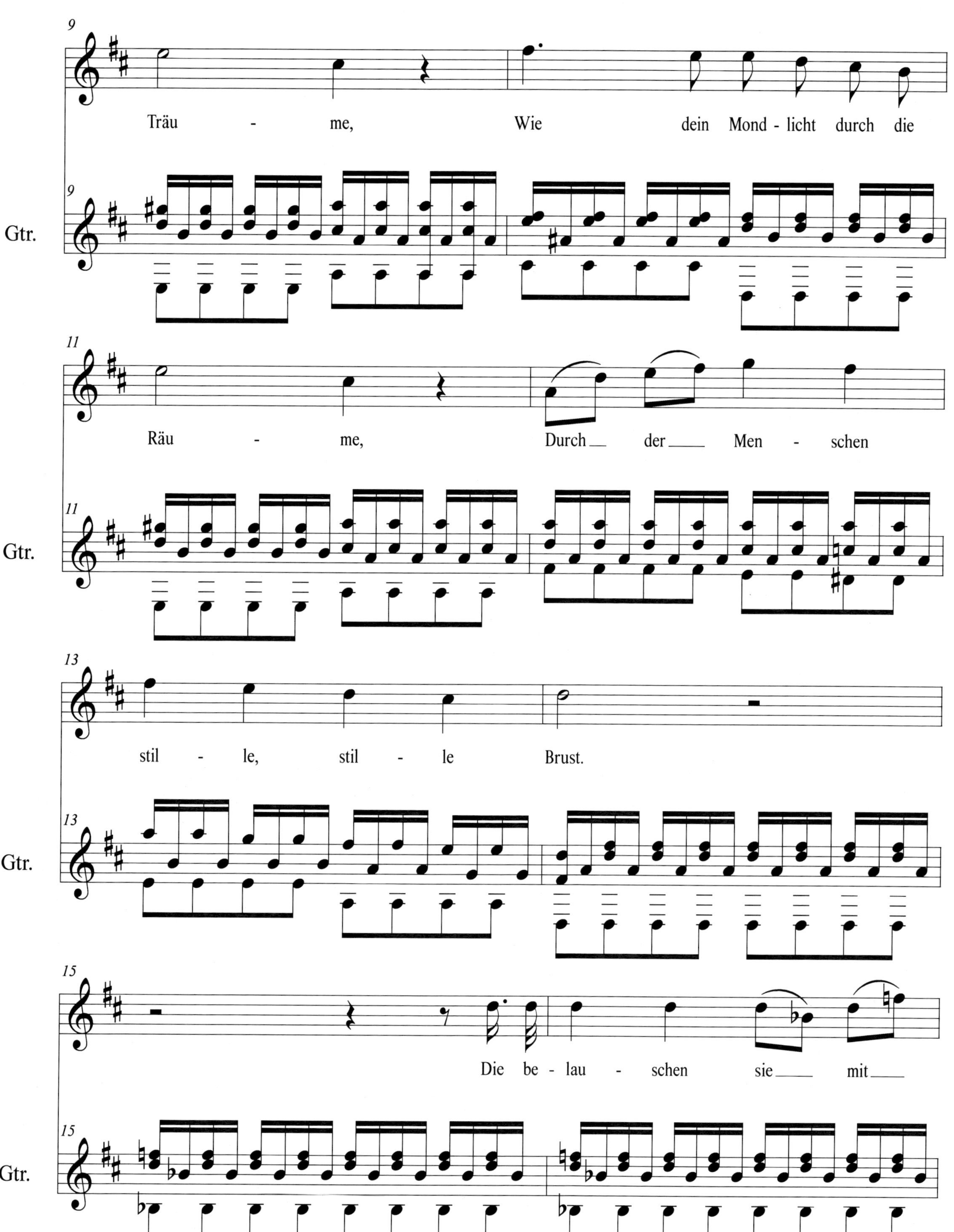
9
Träu - me, Wie dein Mond - licht durch die
9
Gtr.
11
Räu - me, Durch der Men - schen
11
Gtr.
13
stil - le, stil - le Brust.
13
Gtr.
15
Die be - lau - schen sie mit
15
Gtr.

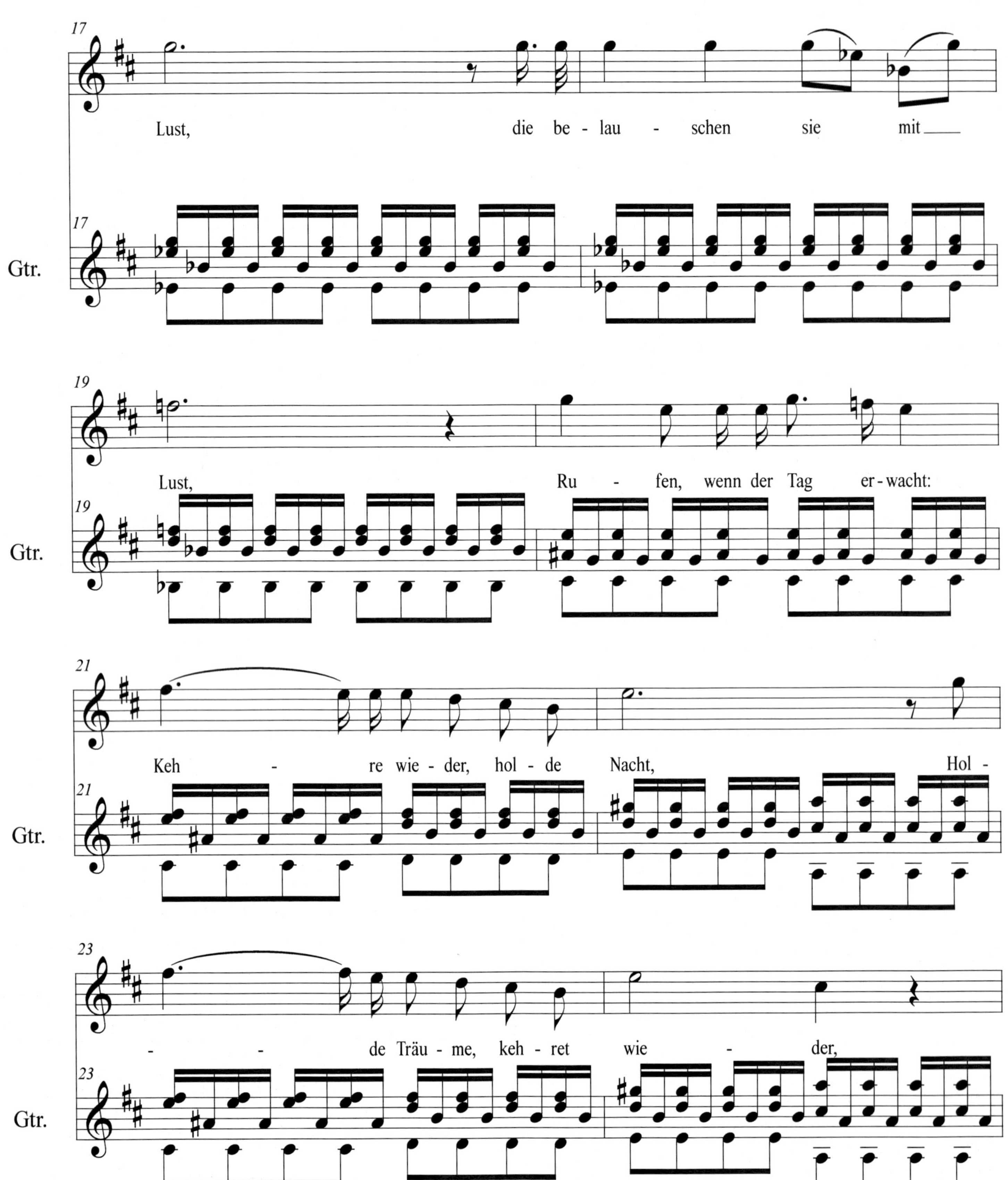
17
Lust, die be - lau - schen sie mit
17
Gtr.
19
Lust, Ru - fen, wenn der Tag er - wacht:
19
Gtr.
21
Keh - re wie - der, hol - de Nacht, Hol -
21
Gtr.
23
- - de Träu - me, keh - ret wie - der,
23
Gtr.

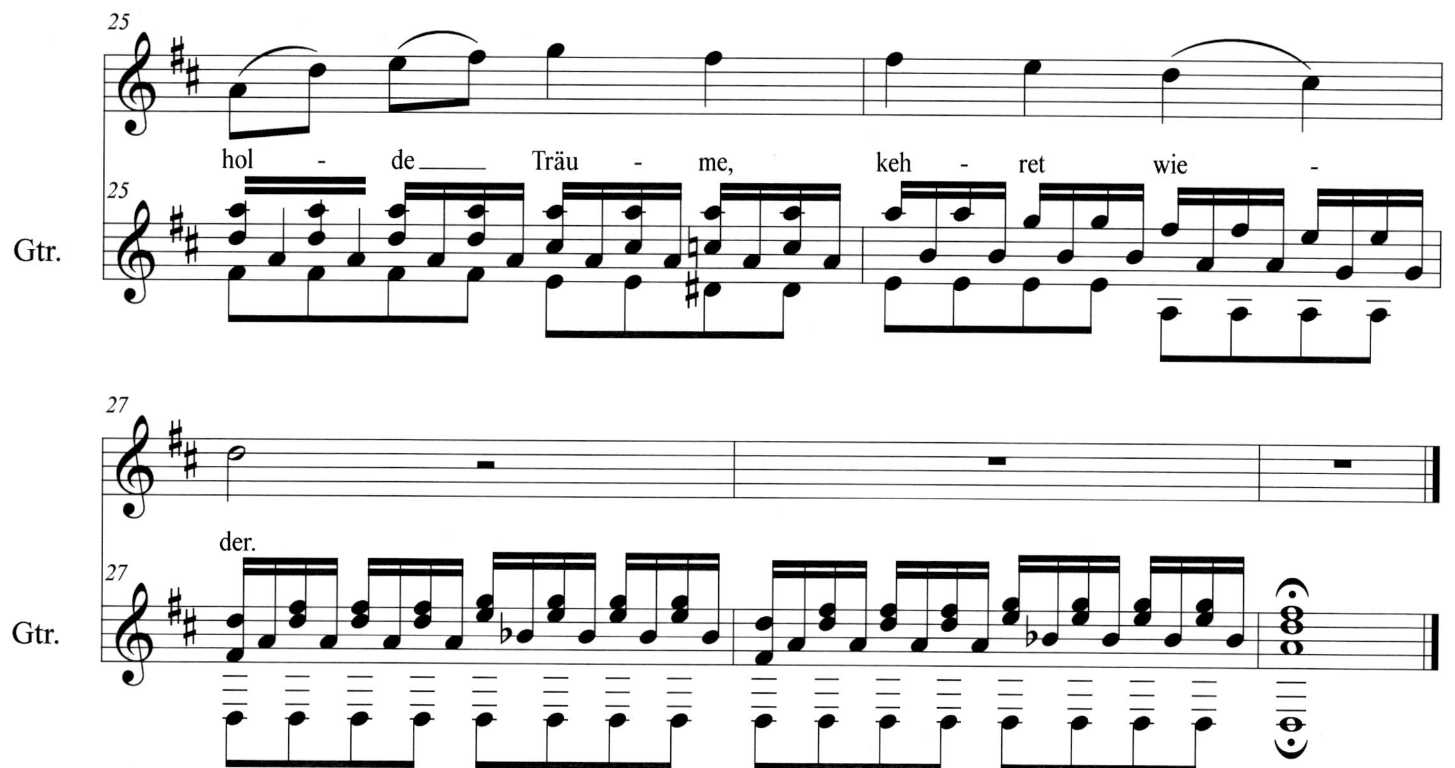
25
hol - de Träu - me, keh - ret wie -
Gtr.
27
der.
Gtr.

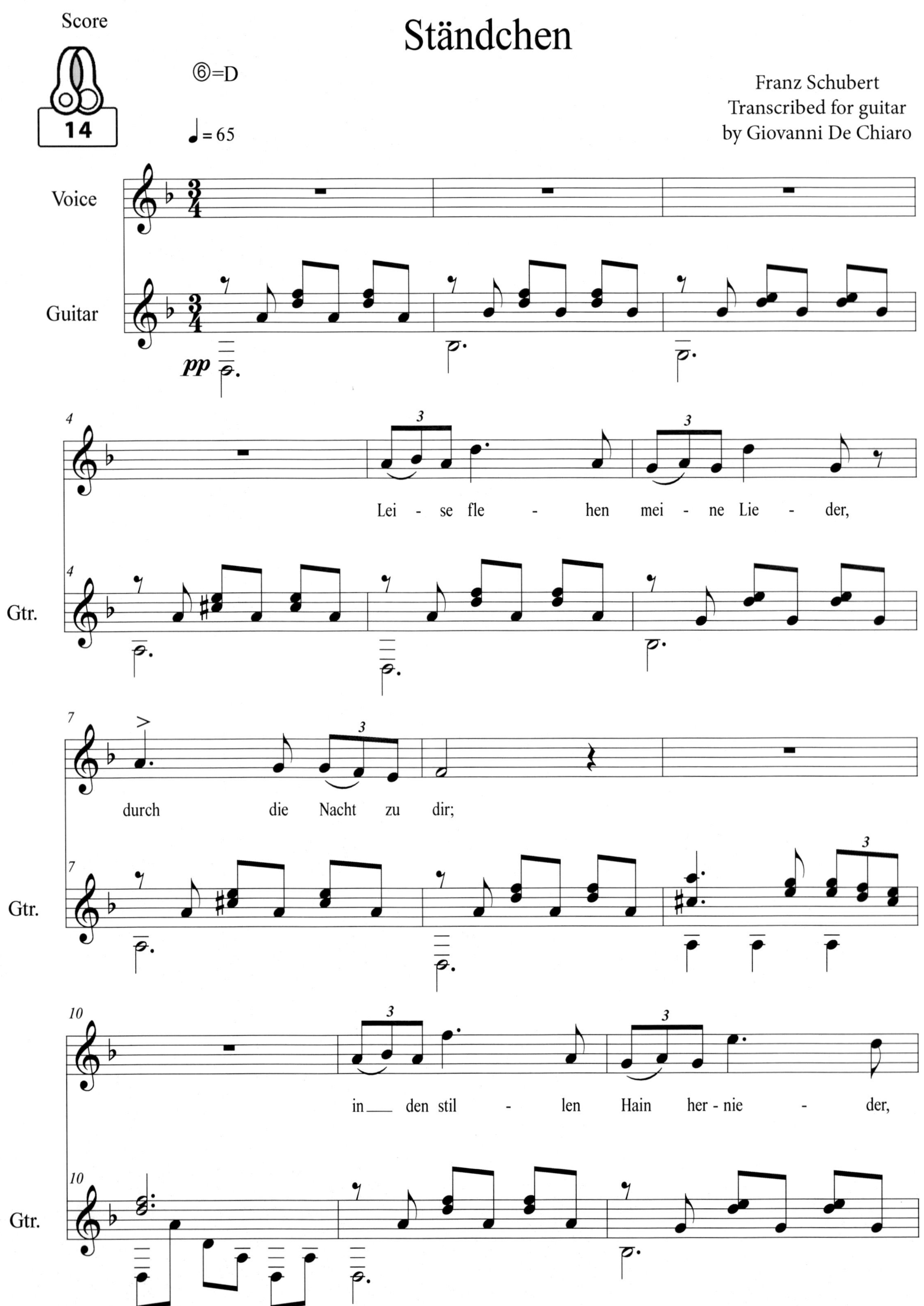
Score
14
Ständchen
⑥=D
♩= 65
Franz Schubert
Transcribed for guitar
by Giovanni De Chiaro
Voice
Guitar
pp
Lei - se fle - hen mei - ne Lie - der,
Gtr.
durch die Nacht zu dir;
in den stil - len Hain her - nie - der,

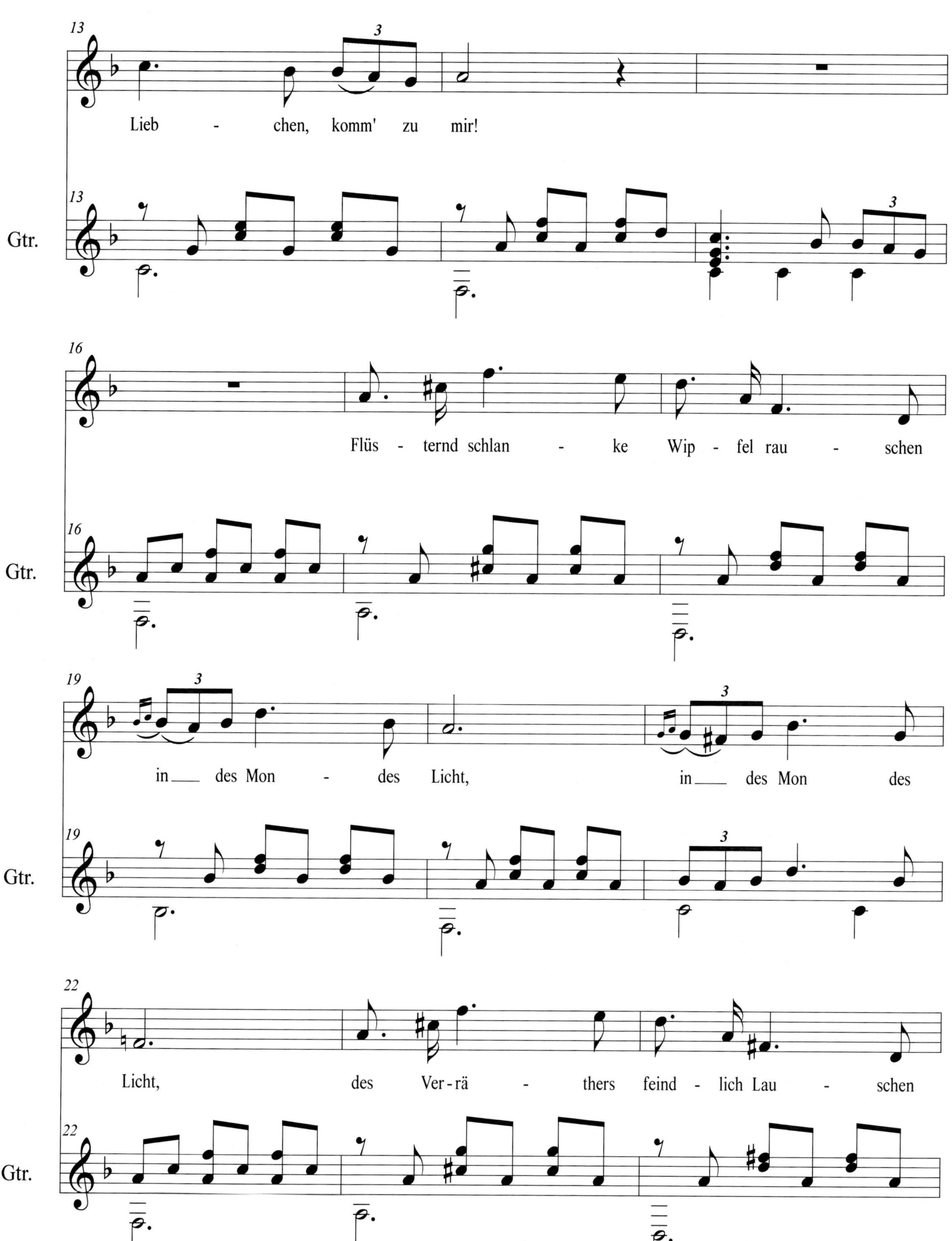
13
Lieb - chen, komm' zu mir!
Gtr.
16
Flüs - ternd schlan - ke Wip - fel rau - schen
Gtr.
19
in des Mon - des Licht, in des Mon des
Gtr.
22
Licht, des Ver-rä - thers feind - lich Lau - schen
Gtr.

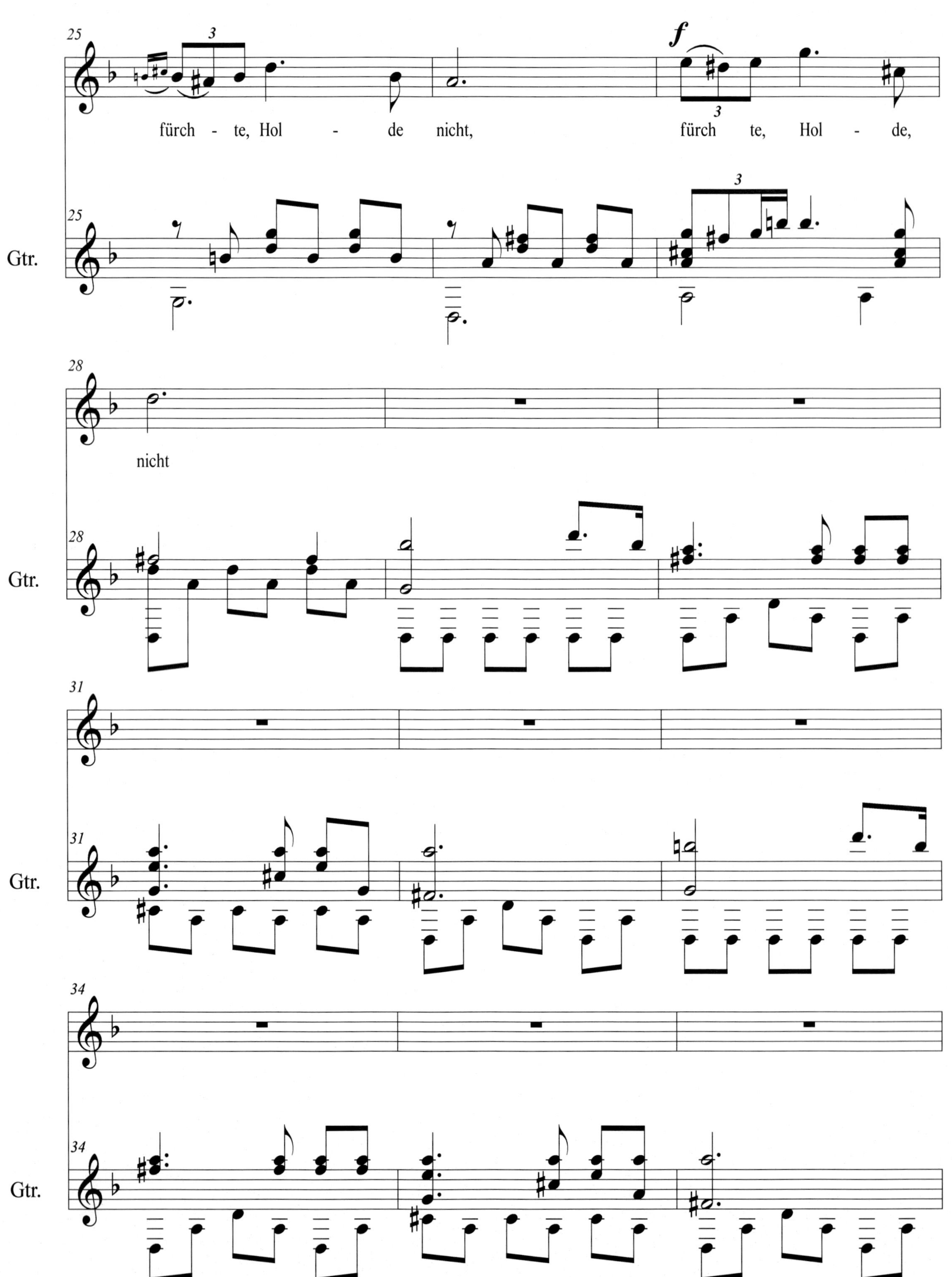
25
f
fürch - te, Hol - de nicht,
fürch te, Hol - de,
Gtr.
28
nicht
Gtr.
31
Gtr.
34
Gtr.

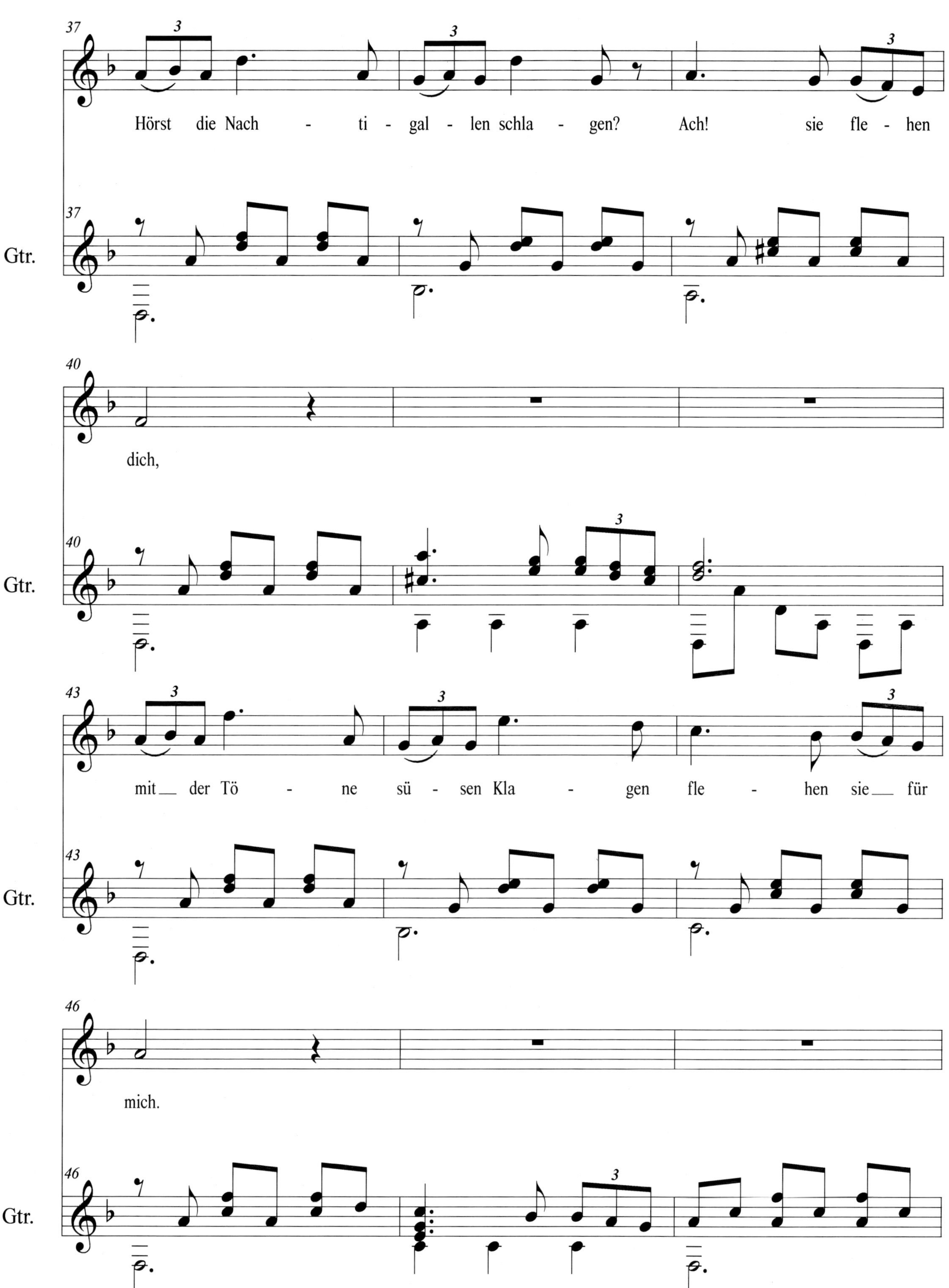
37
Hörst die Nach - ti - gal - len schla - gen? Ach! sie fle - hen
37
Gtr.
40
dich,
40
Gtr.
43
mit der Tö - ne sü - sen Kla - gen fle - hen sie für
43
Gtr.
46
mich.
46
Gtr.

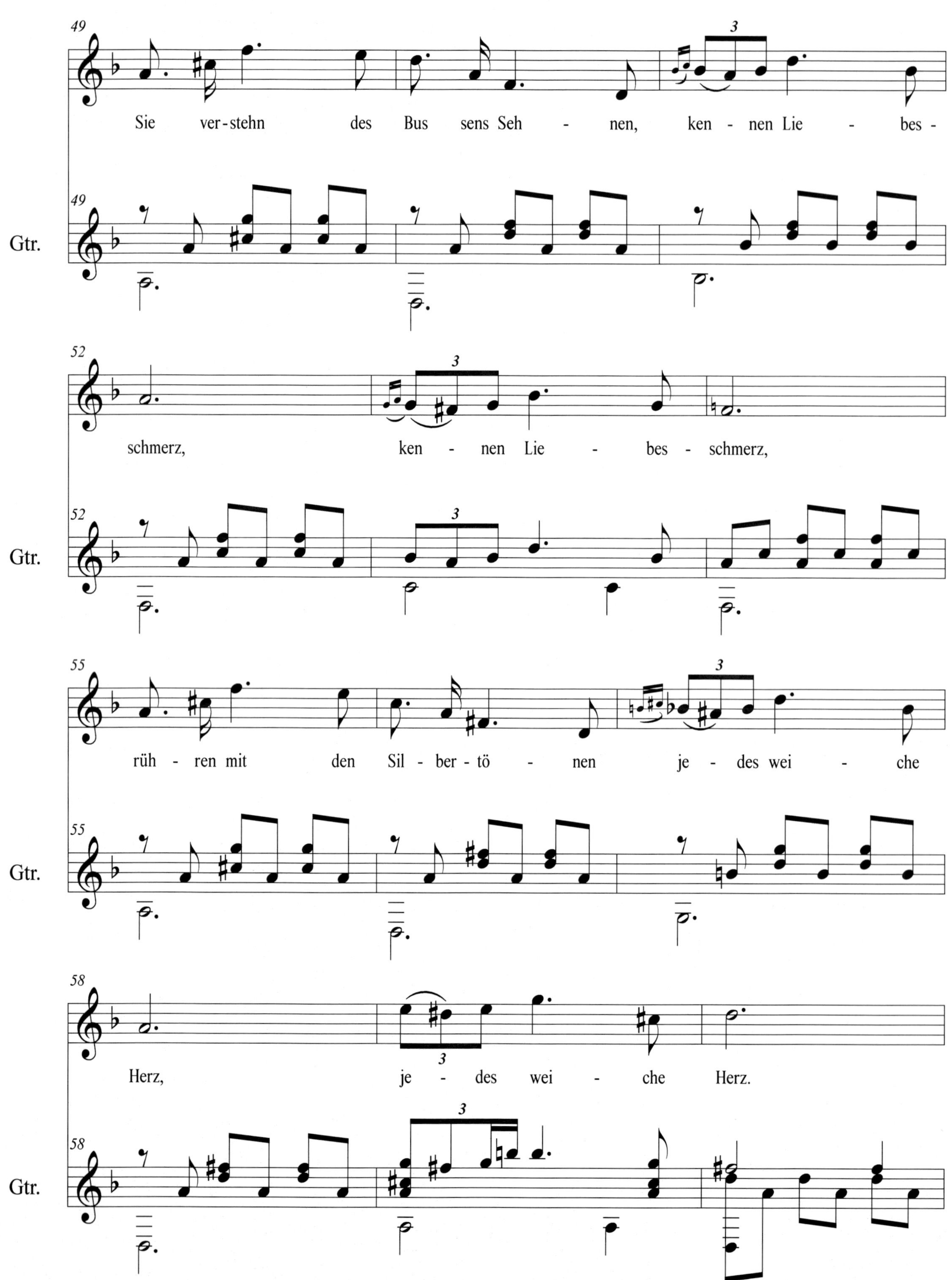
49
Sie ver-stehn des Bus sens Seh - nen, ken - nen Lie - bes -
3
Gtr.
52
schmerz, ken - nen Lie - bes - schmerz,
Gtr.
55
rüh - ren mit den Sil - ber - tö - nen je - des wei - che
Gtr.
58
Herz, je - des wei - che Herz.
Gtr.

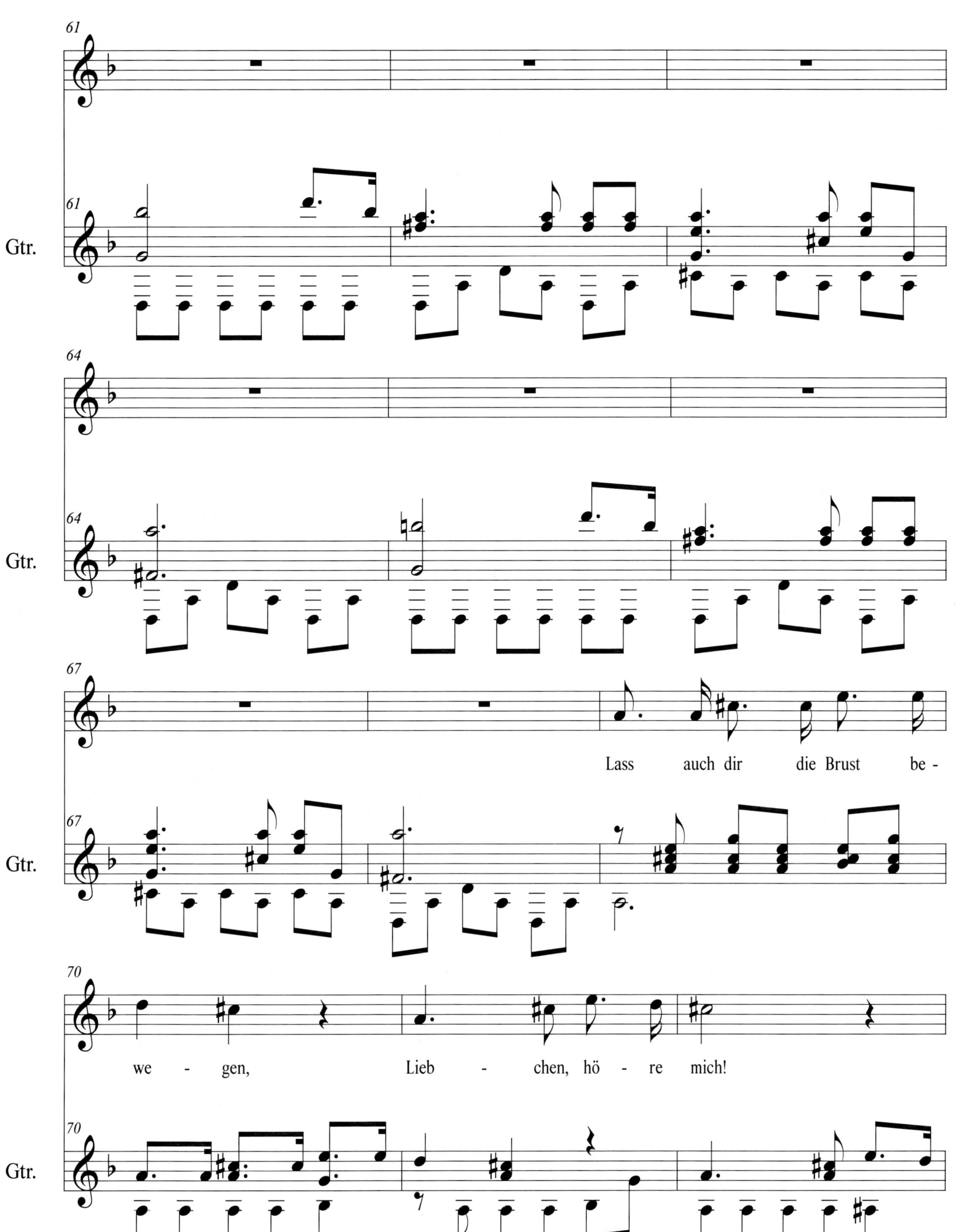
Gtr.
Lass auch dir die Brust be-
we - gen, Lieb - chen, hö - re mich!

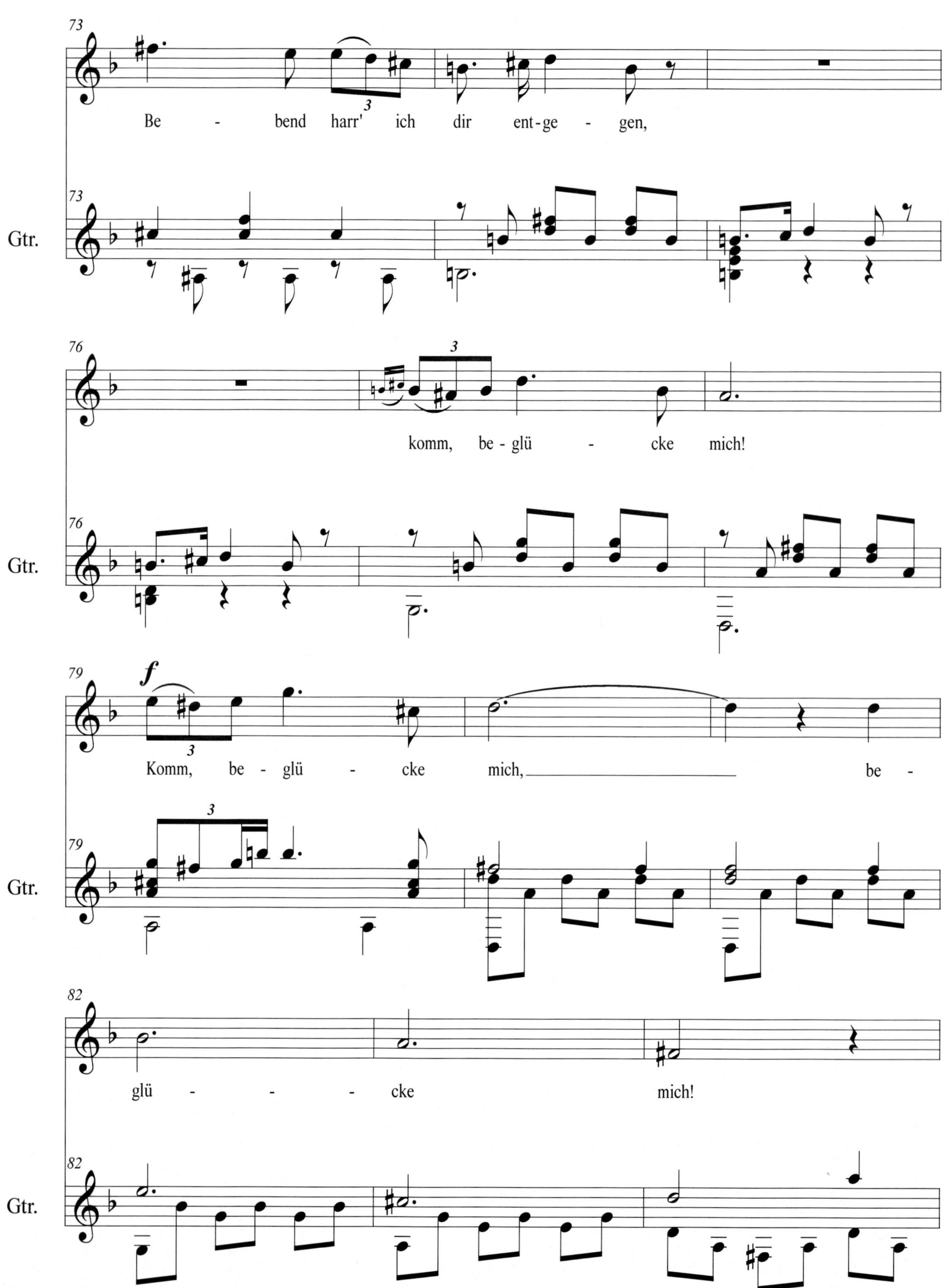
73
Be - bend harr' ich dir ent-ge - gen,
Gtr.
76
komm, be-glü - cke mich!
79
Komm, be - glü - cke mich, be -
82
glü - - - cke mich!

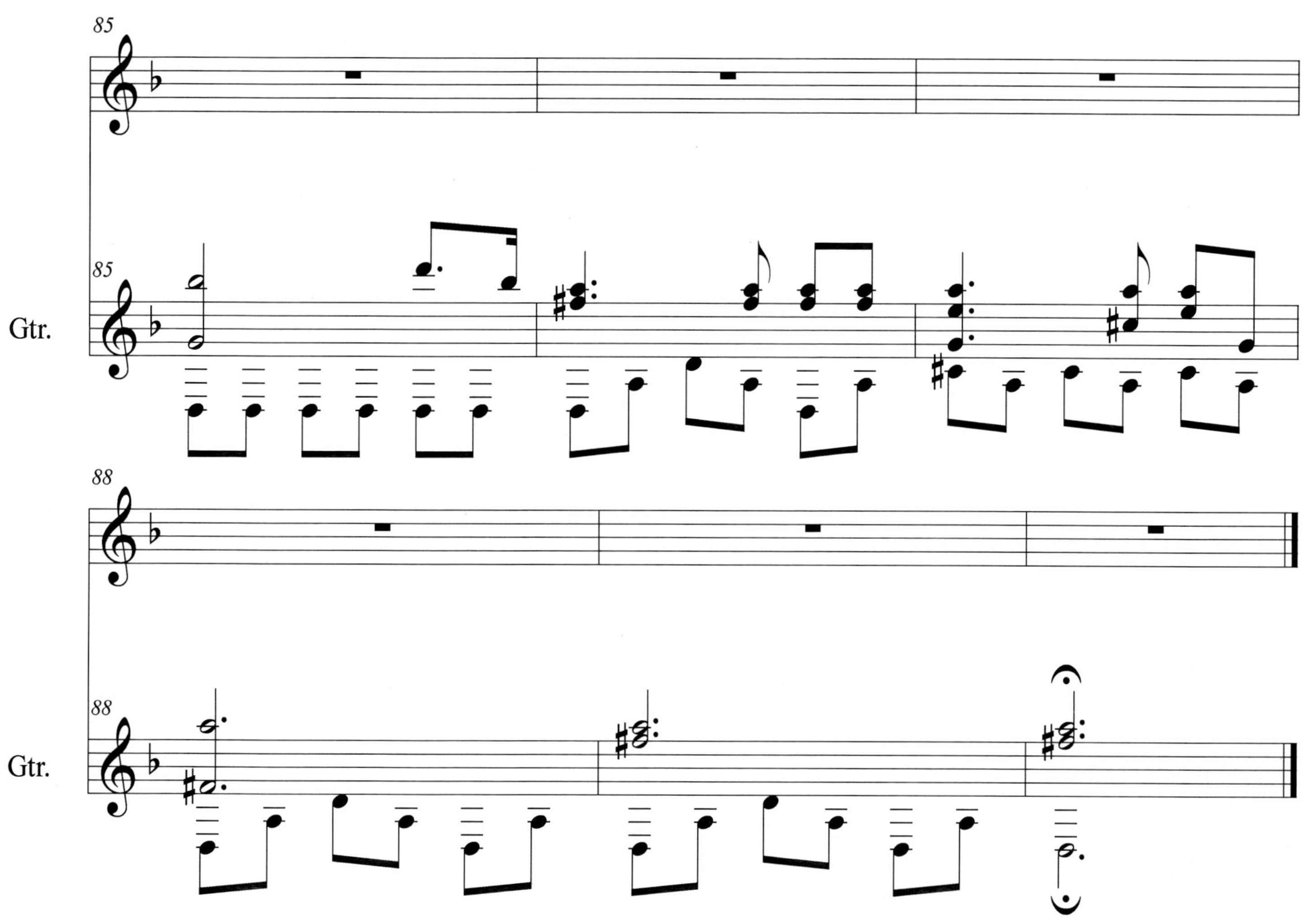
85
Gtr.
88
Gtr.

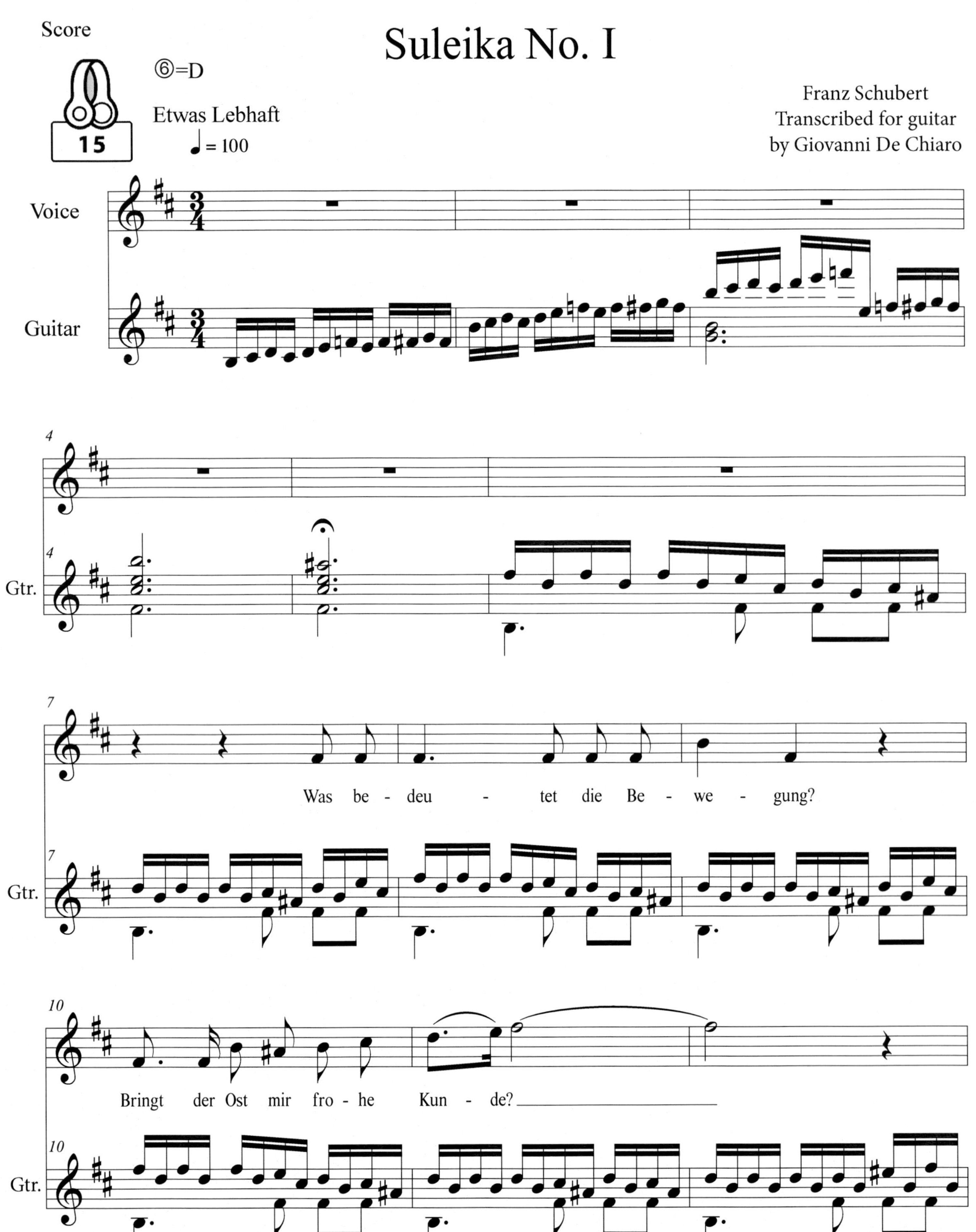
Score
15
⑥=D
Suleika No. I
Etwas Lebhaft
♩ = 100
Franz Schubert
Transcribed for guitar
by Giovanni De Chiaro
Voice
Guitar
Gtr.
Was be - deu - tet die Be - we - gung?
Bringt der Ost mir fro - he Kun - de?

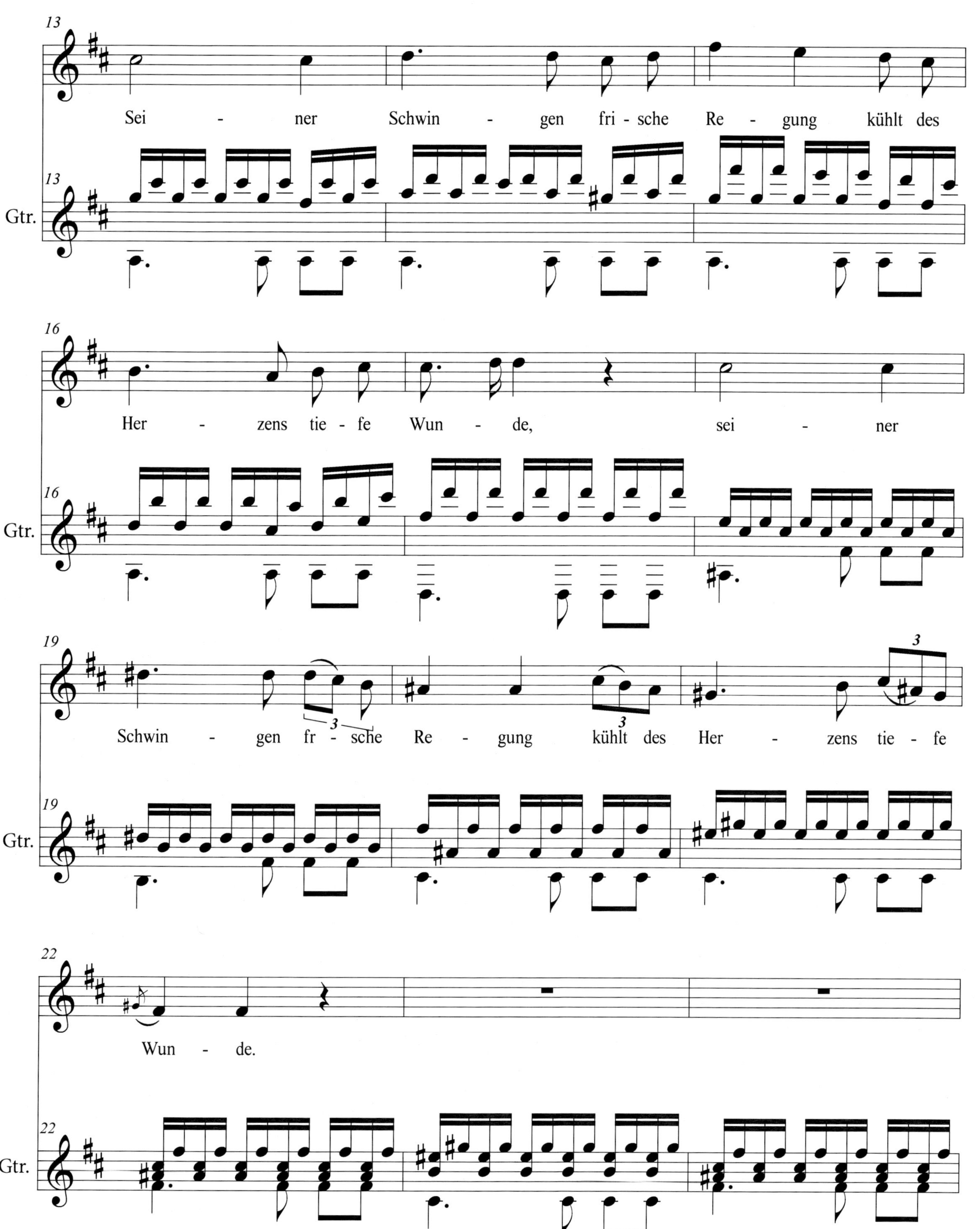
13
Sei - ner Schwin - gen fri - sche Re - gung kühlt des
Gtr.
16
Her - zens tie - fe Wun - de, sei - ner
Gtr.
19
Schwin - gen fr - sche Re - gung kühlt des Her - zens tie - fe
Gtr.
22
Wun - de.
Gtr.

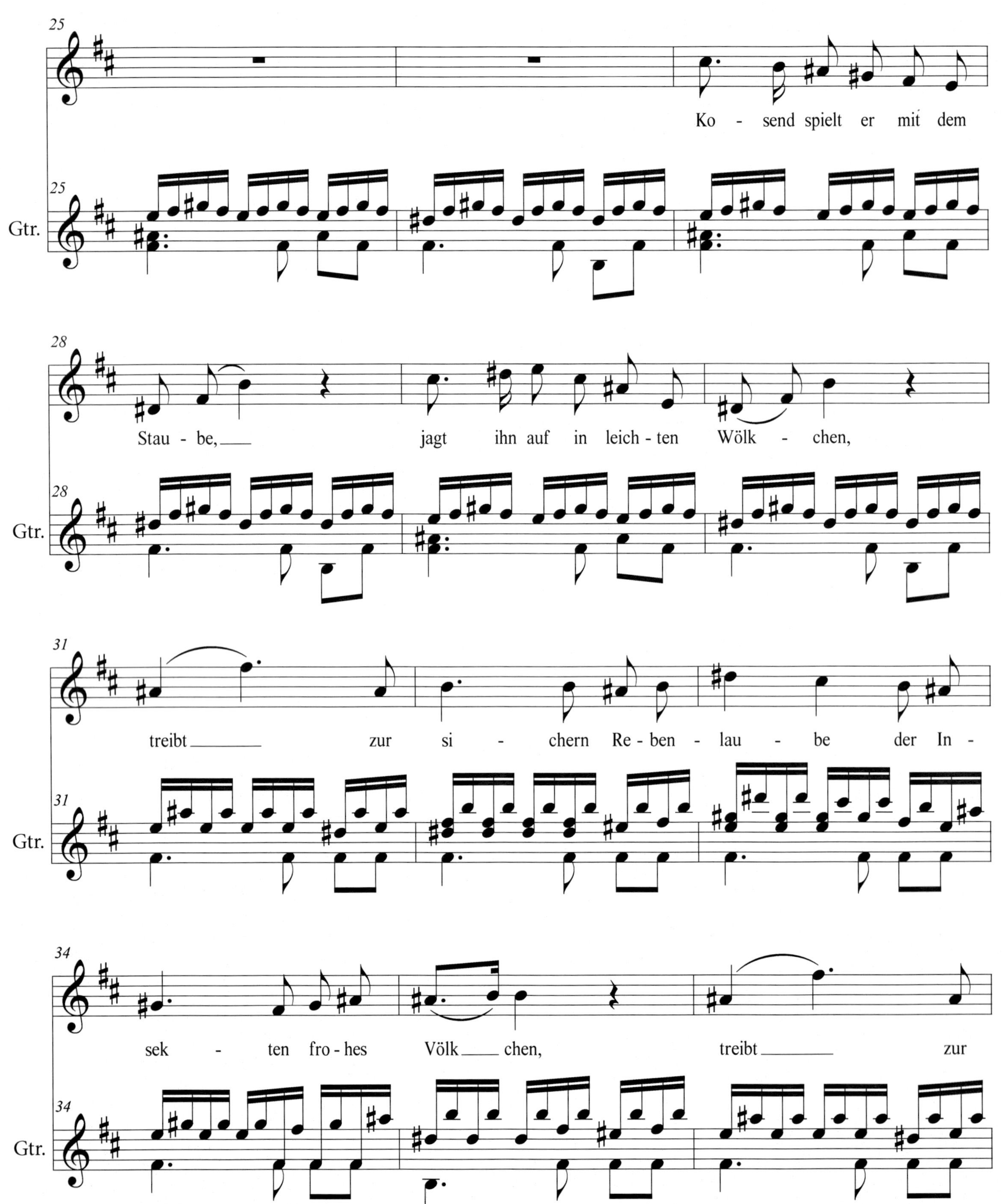
25
Ko - send spielt er mit dem
25
Gtr.
28
Stau - be,
jagt ihn auf in leich - ten Wölk - chen,
28
Gtr.
31
treibt zur si - chern Re - ben - lau - be der In -
31
Gtr.
34
sek - ten fro - hes Völk chen, treibt zur
34
Gtr.

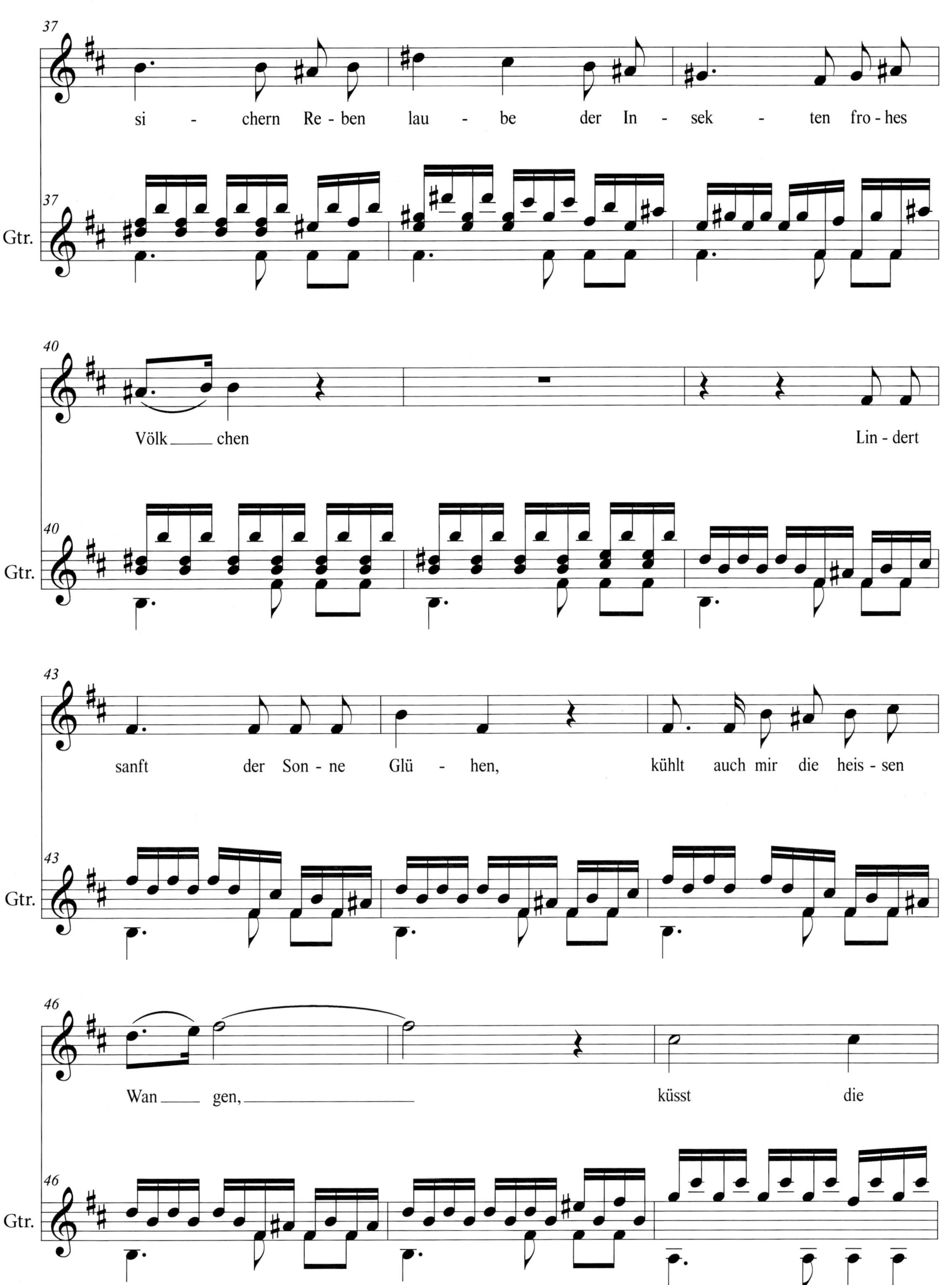
37
si - chern Re - ben lau - be der In - sek - ten fro - hes
Gtr.
40
Völk chen
Lin - dert
43
sanft der Son - ne Glü - hen, kühlt auch mir die heis - sen
46
Wan gen,
küsst die

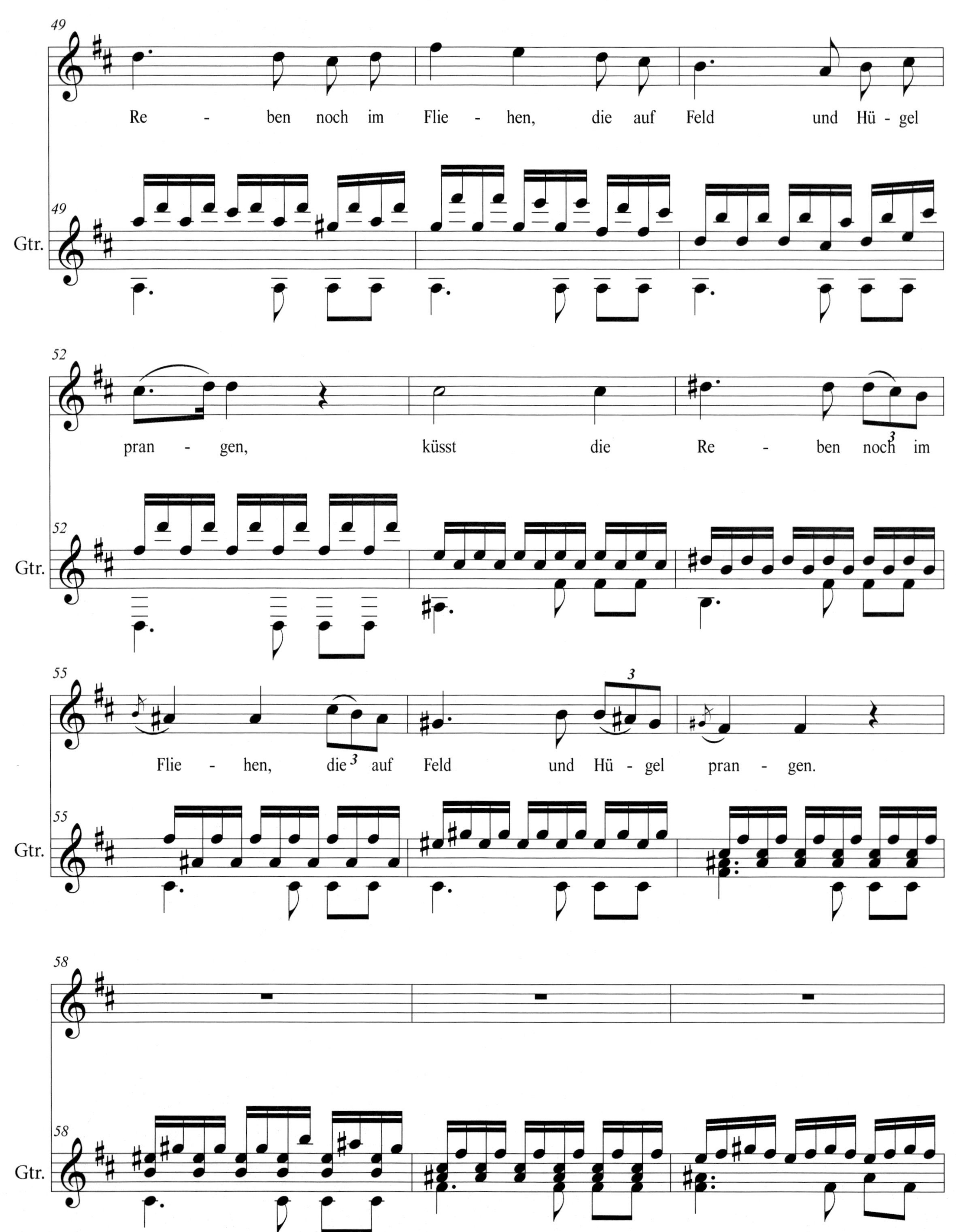
49
Re - ben noch im Flie - hen, die auf Feld und Hü - gel
Gtr.
52
pran - gen, küsst die Re - ben noch im
3
Gtr.
55
Flie - hen, die auf Feld und Hü - gel pran - gen.
3
3
Gtr.
58
Gtr.

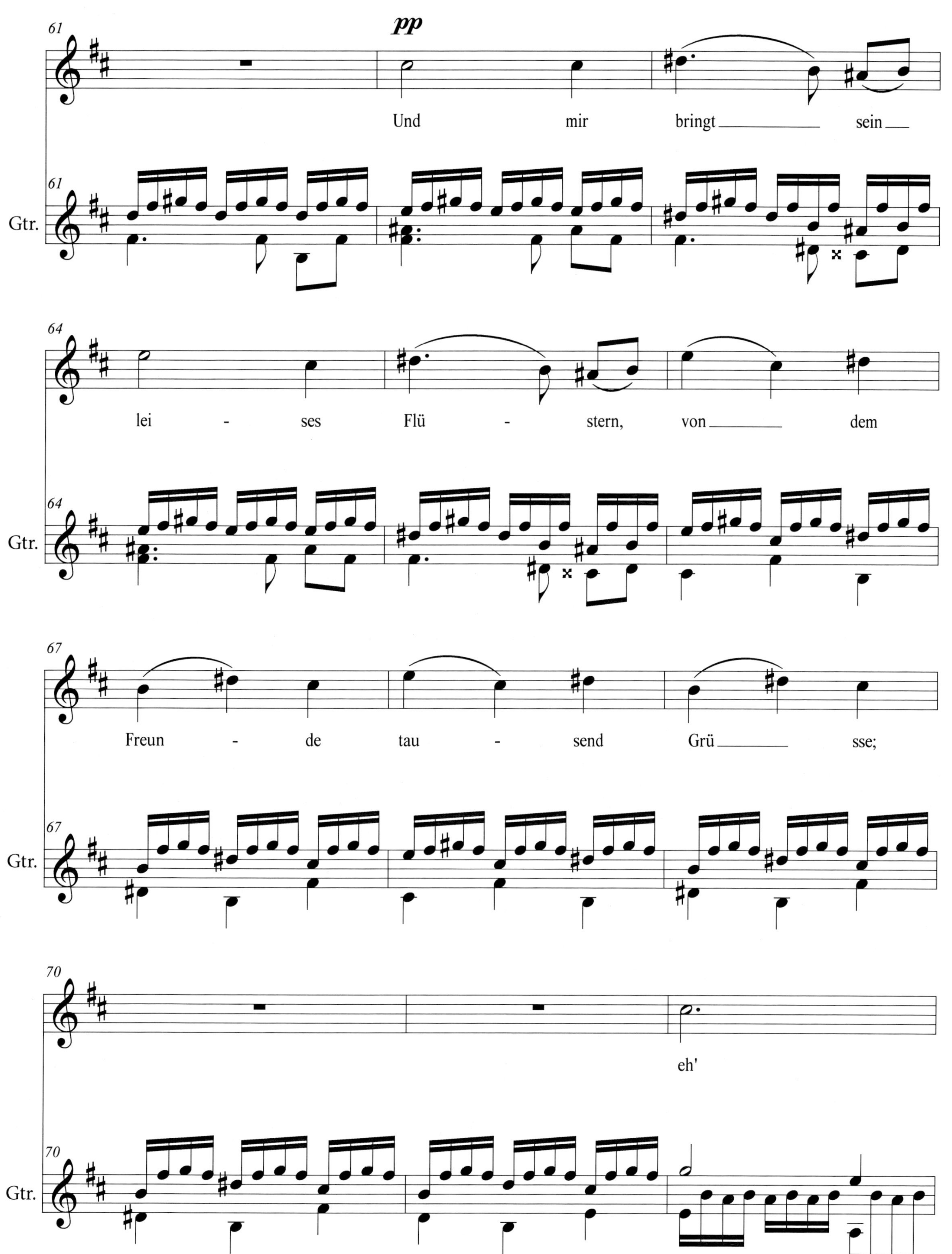
61
pp
Und mir bringt sein
61
Gtr.
64
lei - ses Flü - stern, von dem
64
Gtr.
67
Freun - de tau - send Grü sse;
67
Gtr.
70
eh'
70
Gtr.

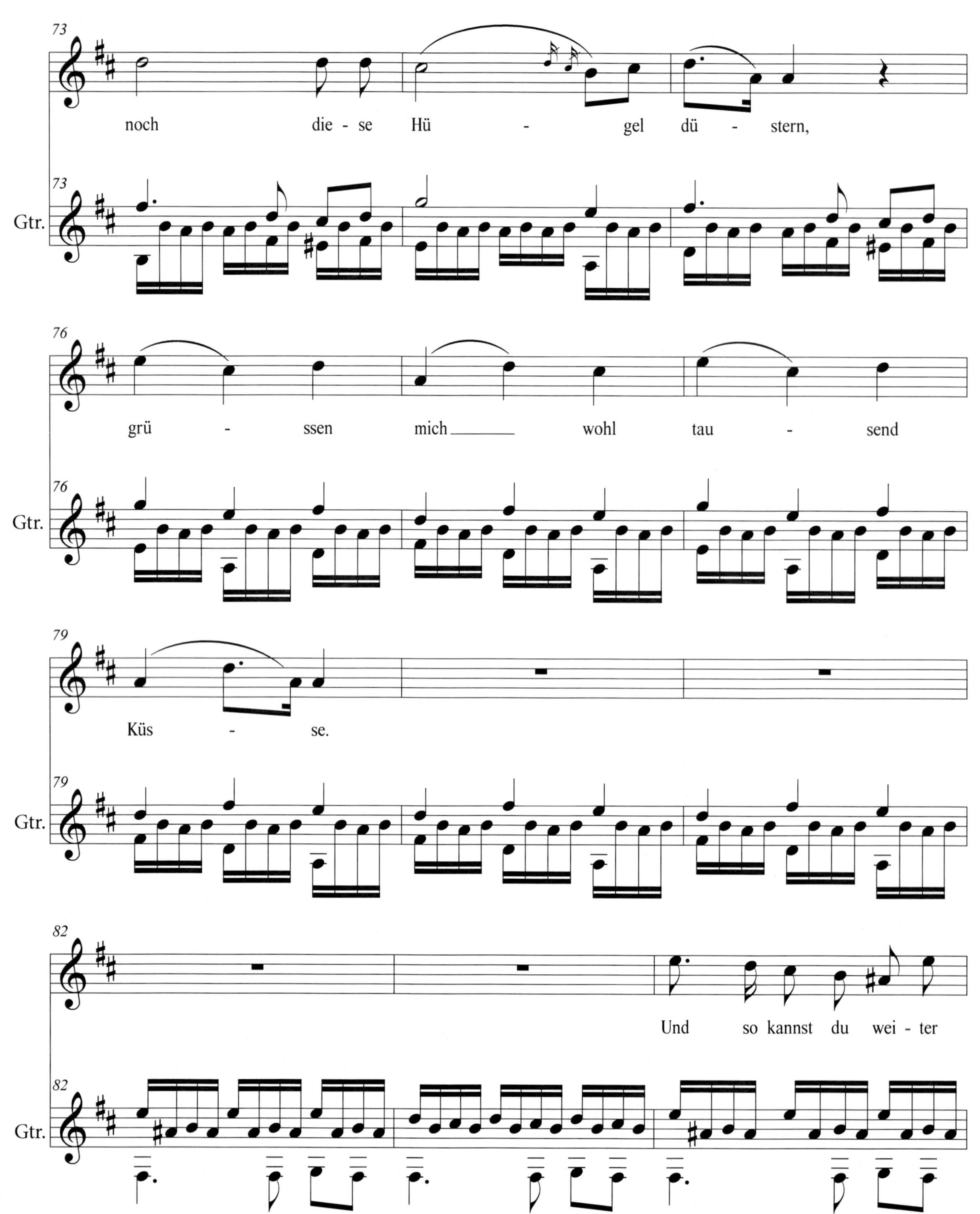
noch die - se Hü - gel dü - stern,
Gtr.
grü - ssen mich wohl tau - send
Gtr.
Küs - se.
Gtr.
Und so kannst du wei - ter
Gtr.

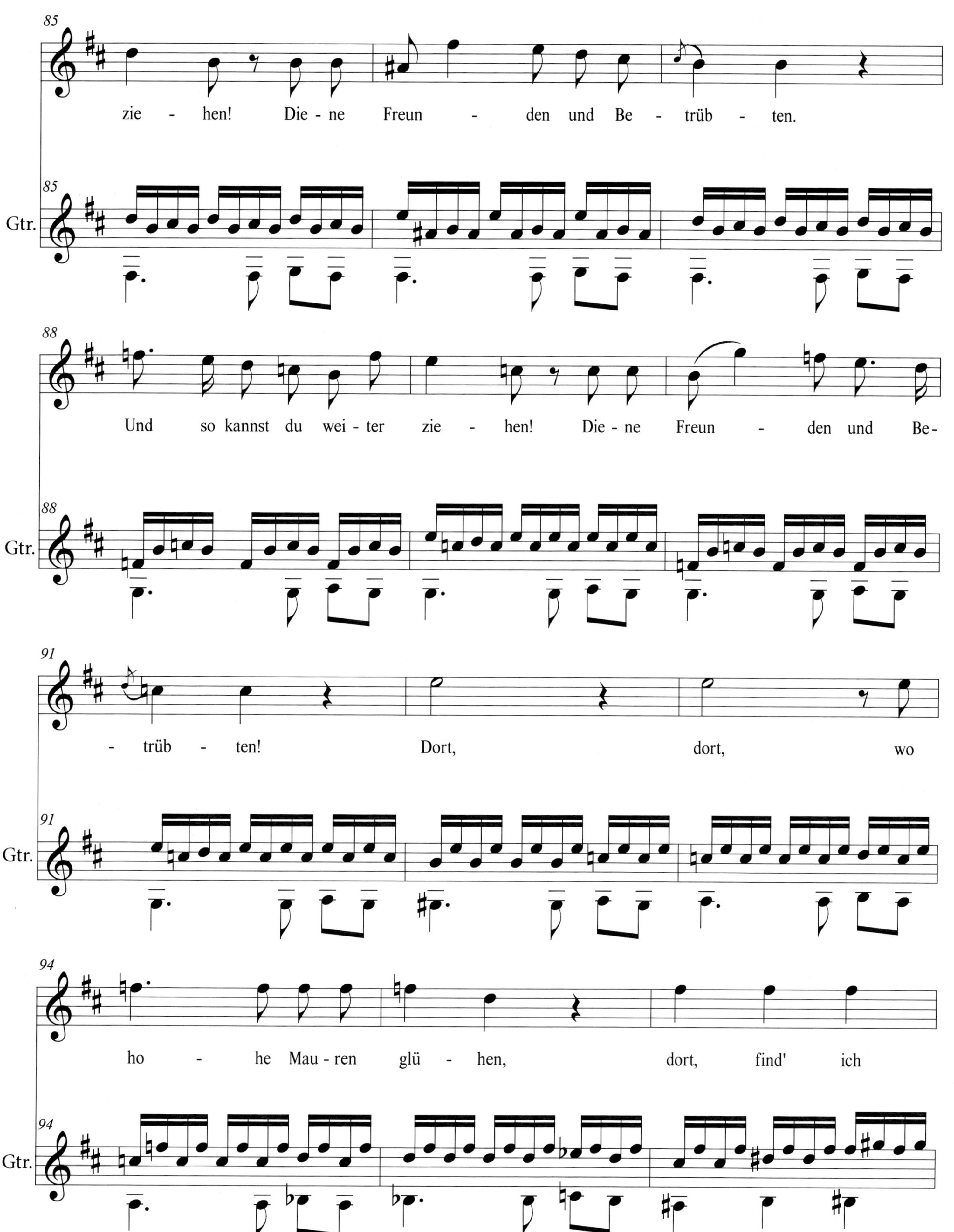
85
zie - hen! Die - ne Freun - den und Be - trüb - ten.
85
Gtr.
88
Und so kannst du wei - ter zie - hen! Die - ne Freun - den und Be-
88
Gtr.
91
- trüb - ten! Dort, dort, wo
91
Gtr.
94
ho - he Mau - ren glü - hen, dort, find' ich
94
Gtr.

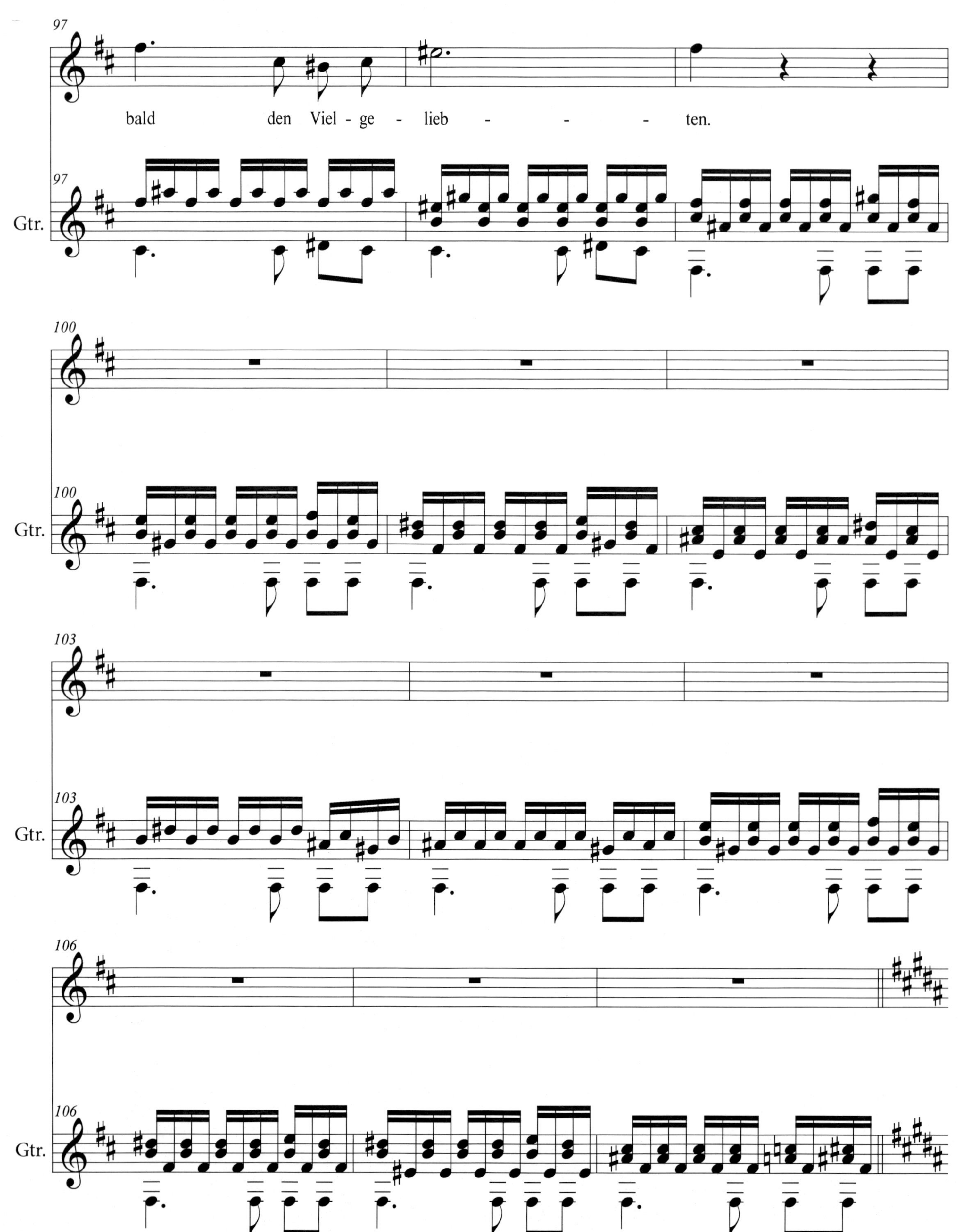
97
bald den Viel - ge - lieb - - - ten.
97
Gtr.
100
100
Gtr.
103
103
Gtr.
106
106
Gtr.

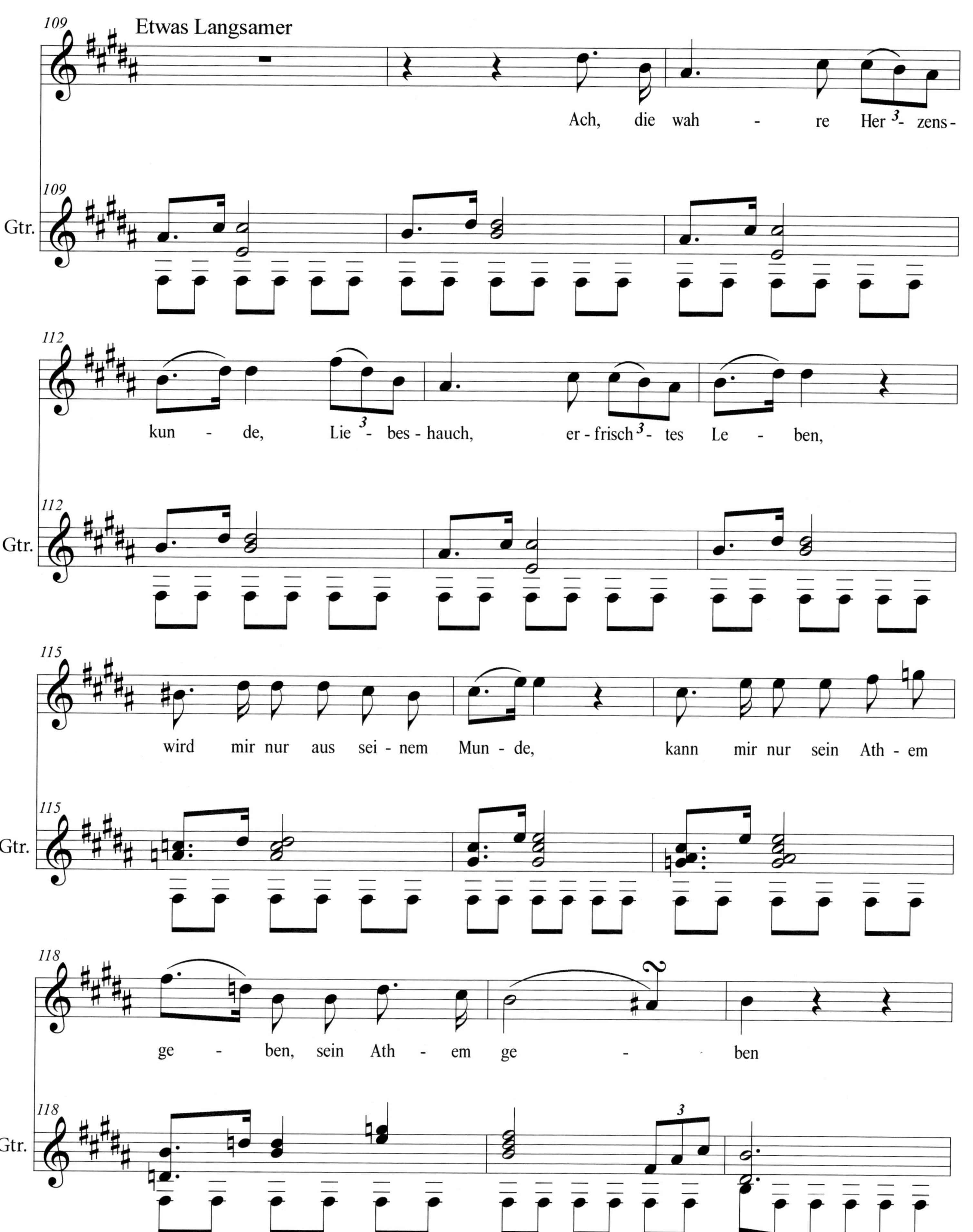
Etwas Langsamer
Ach, die wah - re Her - zens-
Gtr.
kun - de, Lie - bes - hauch, er - frisch - tes Le - ben,
Gtr.
wird mir nur aus sei - nem Mun - de, kann mir nur sein Ath - em
Gtr.
ge - ben, sein Ath - em ge - ben
Gtr.

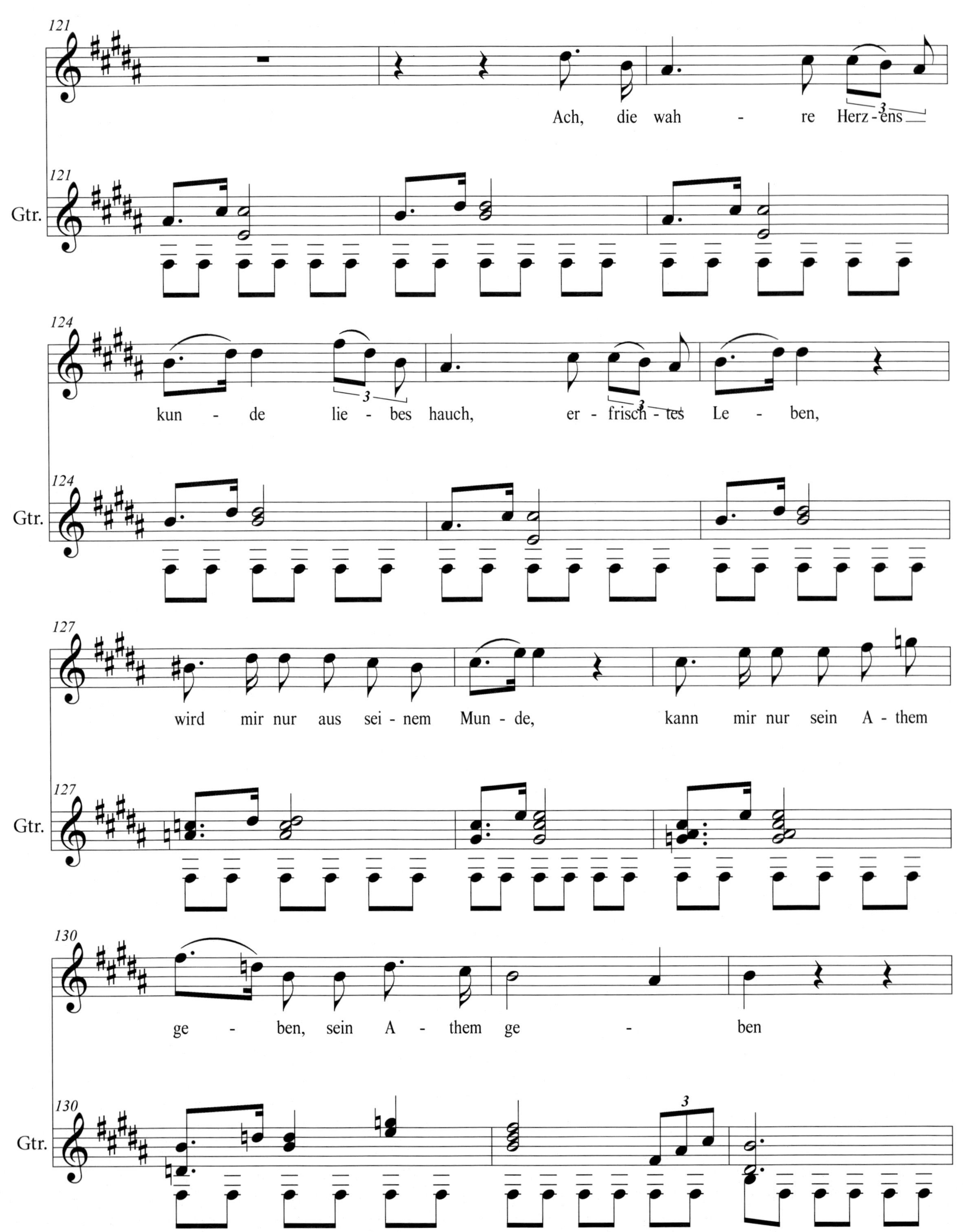
121
Ach, die wah - re Herz - ens
Gtr.
124
kun - de lie - bes hauch, er - frisch - tes Le - ben,
127
wird mir nur aus sei - nem Mun - de, kann mir nur sein A - them
130
ge - ben, sein A - them ge - ben

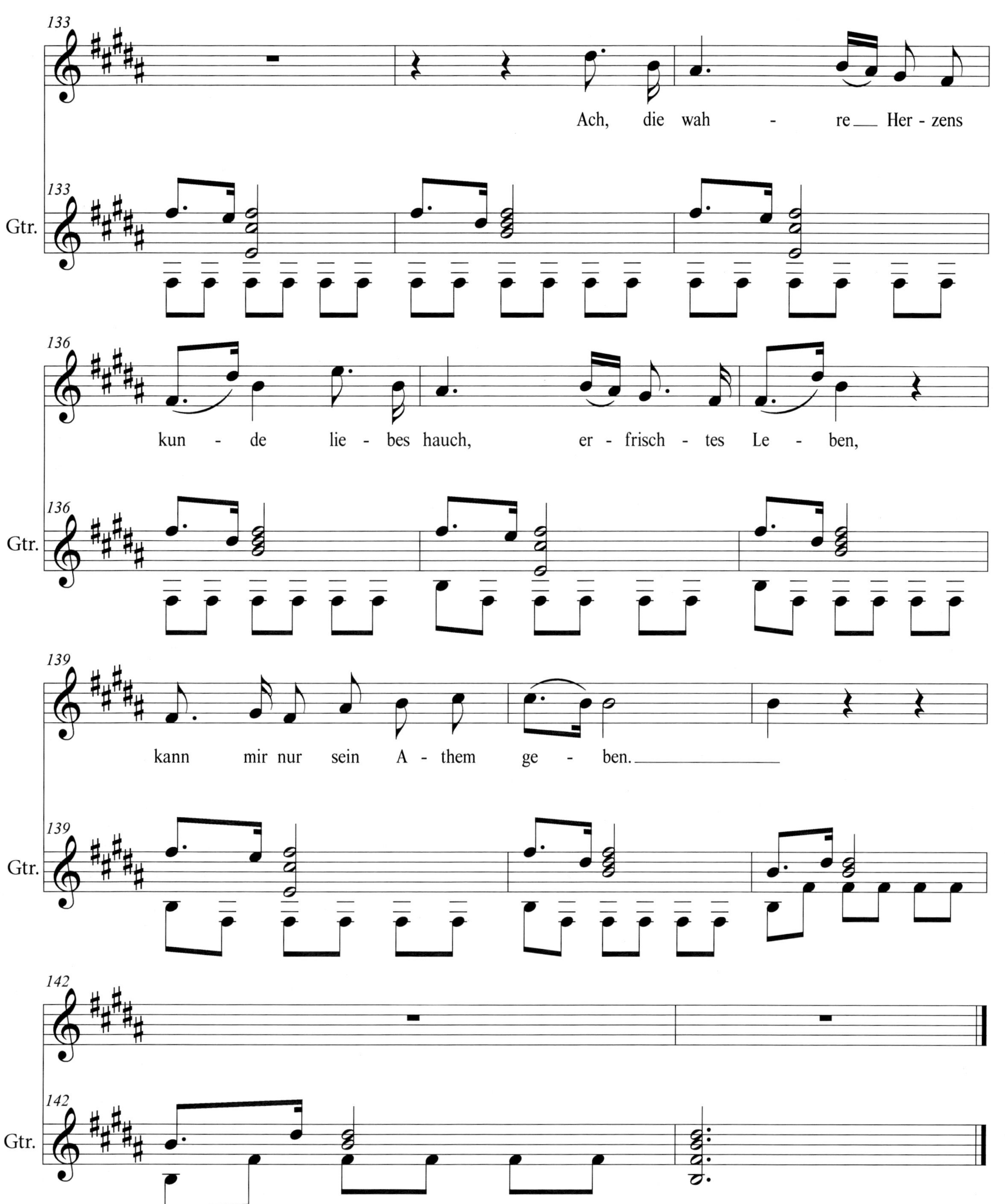
133
Ach, die wah - re Her - zens
Gtr.
136
kun - de lie - bes hauch, er - frisch - tes Le - ben,
Gtr.
139
kann mir nur sein A - them ge - ben.
Gtr.
142
Gtr.

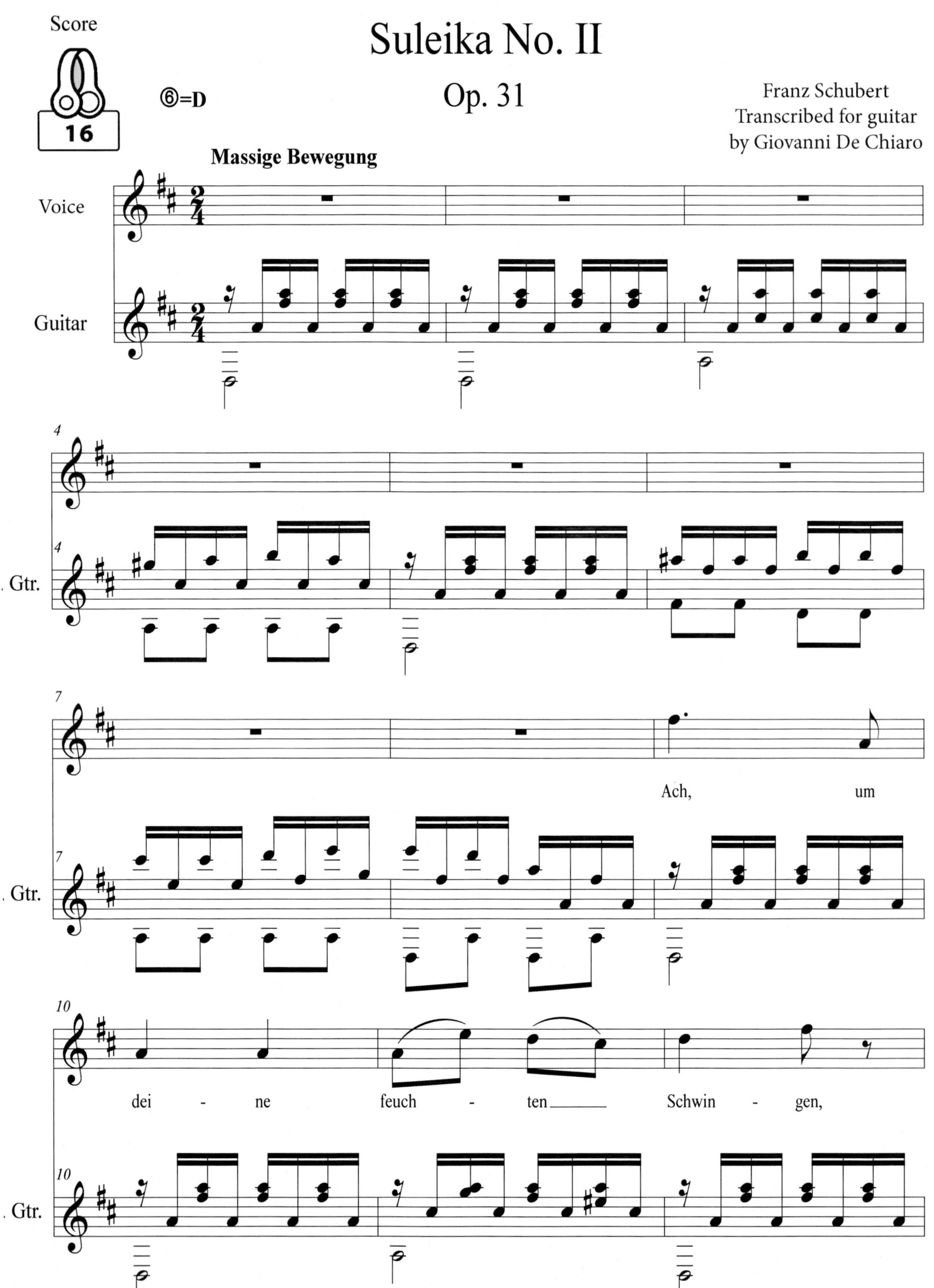
Score
16
Suleika No. II
Op. 31
⑥=D
Franz Schubert
Transcribed for guitar
by Giovanni De Chiaro
Massige Bewegung
Voice
Guitar
Gtr.
Ach, um
dei - ne feuch - ten Schwin - gen,

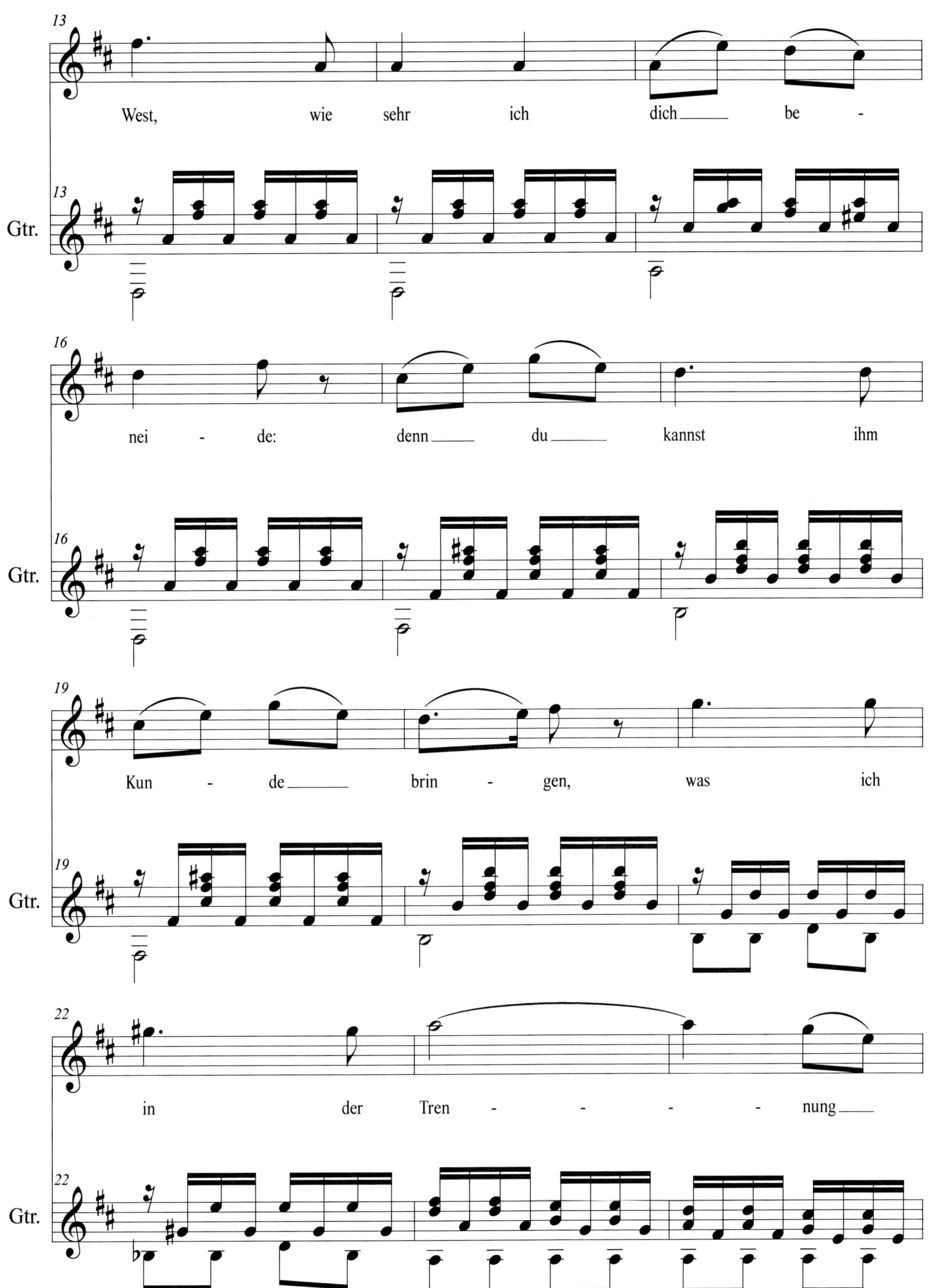
13
West, wie sehr ich dich be -
13
Gtr.
16
nei - de: denn du kannst ihm
16
Gtr.
19
Kun - de brin - gen, was ich
19
Gtr.
22
in der Tren - - - - nung
22
Gtr.

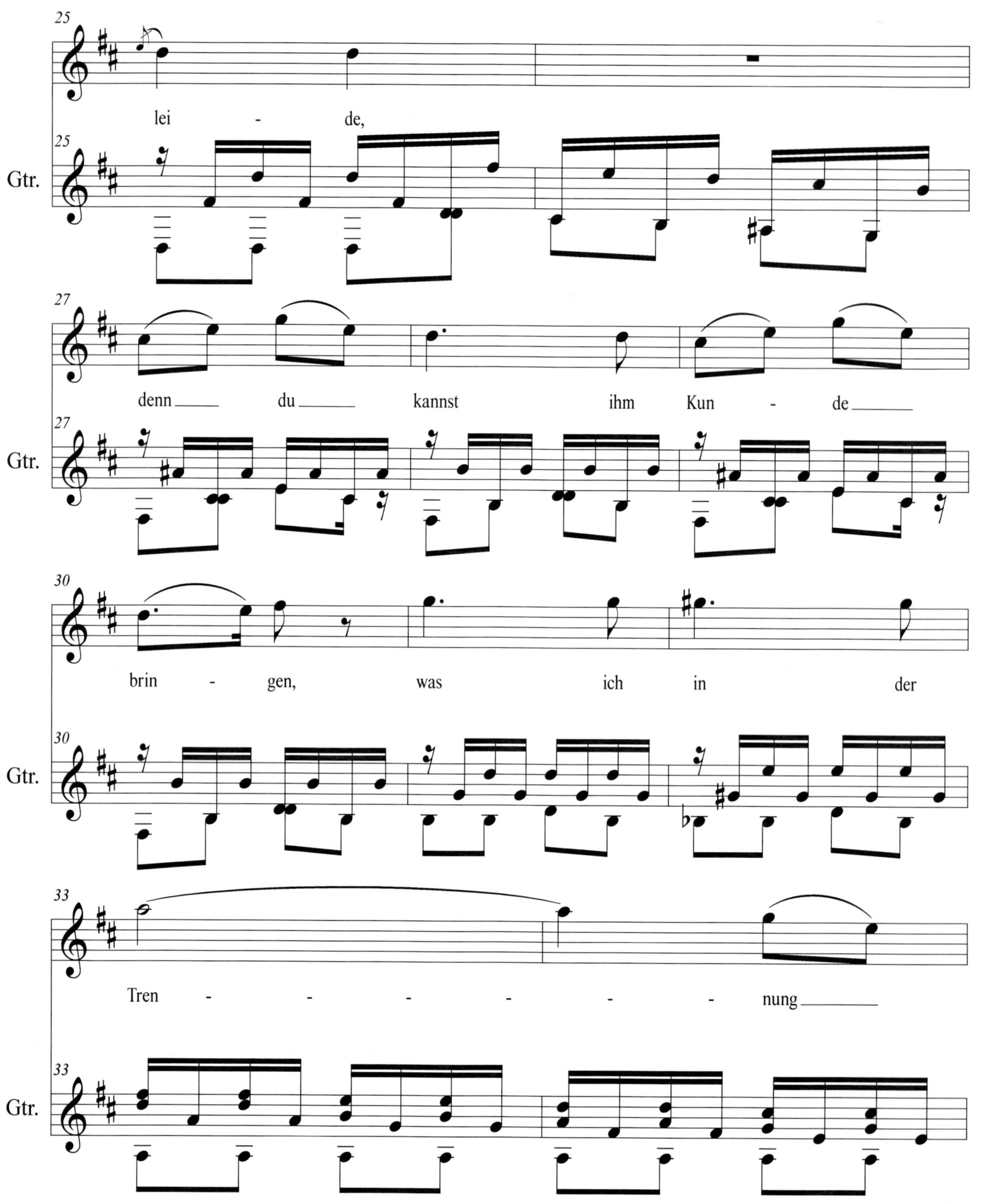
25
lei - de,
Gtr.
27
denn du kannst ihm Kun - de
Gtr.
30
brin - gen, was ich in der
Gtr.
33
Tren - - - - - - nung
Gtr.

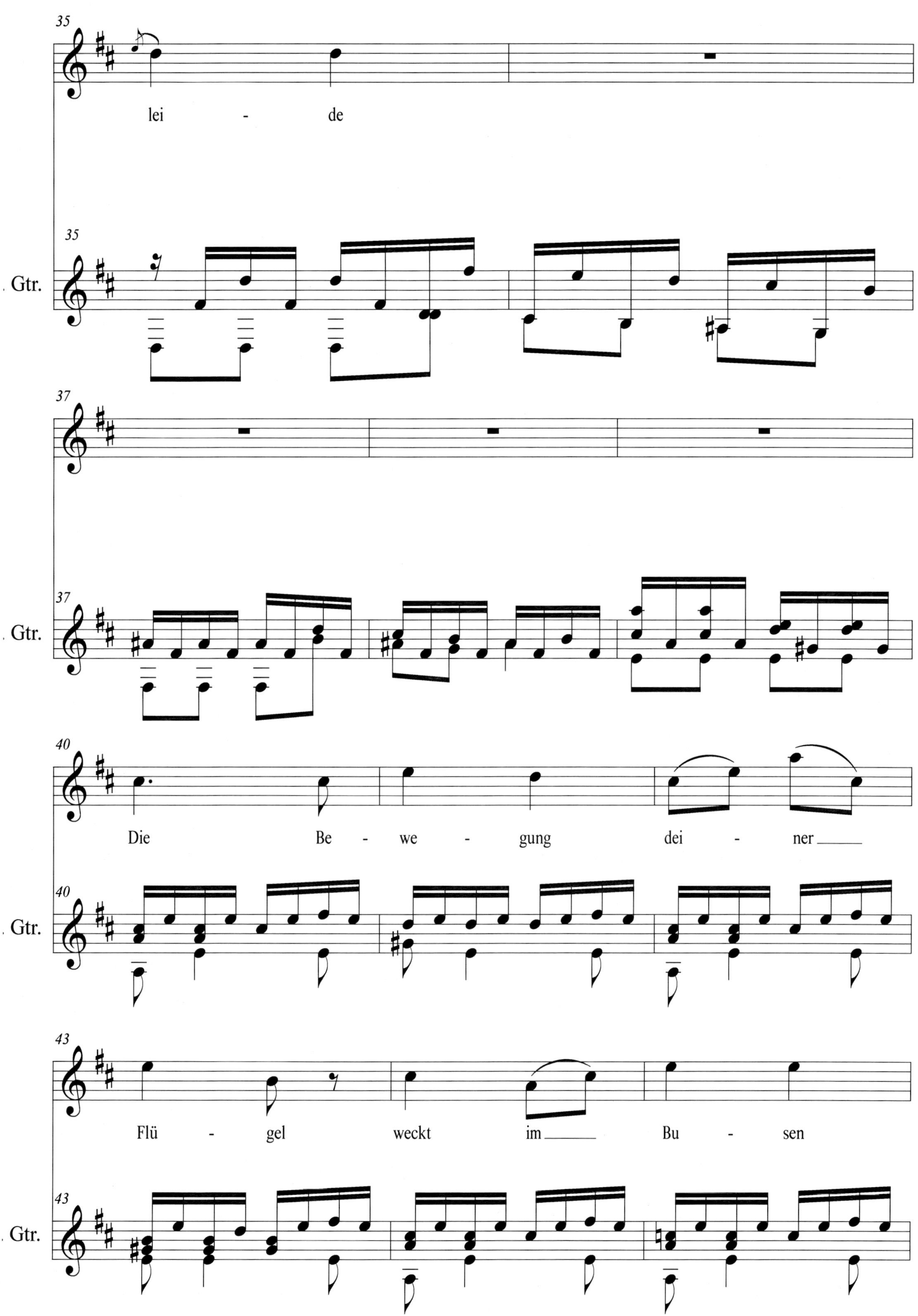
35
lei - de
35
Gtr.
37
37
Gtr.
40
Die Be - we - gung dei - ner
40
Gtr.
43
Flü - gel weckt im Bu - sen
43
Gtr.

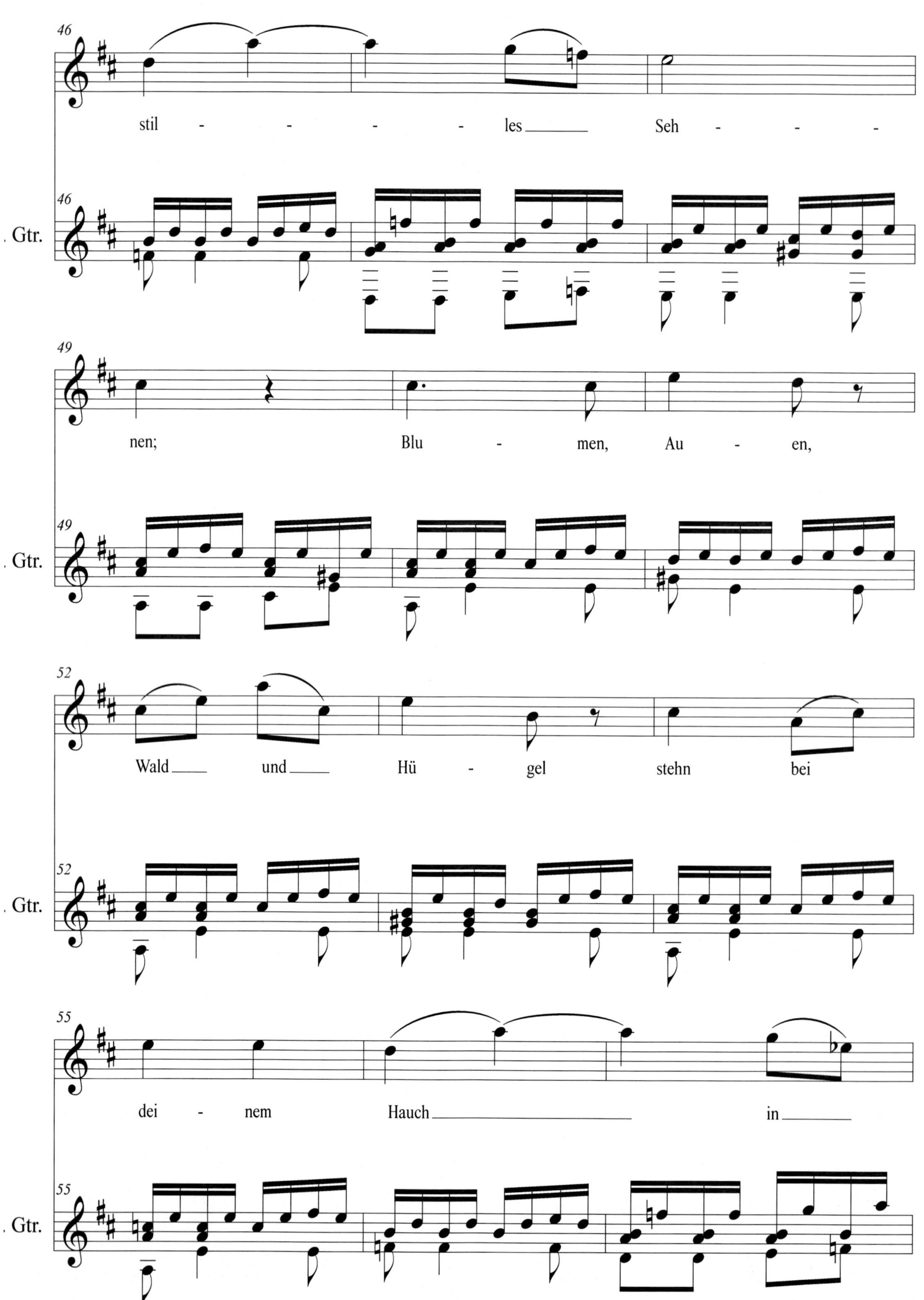
46
stil - - - - les Seh - - -
. Gtr.
49
nen; Blu - men, Au - en,
. Gtr.
52
Wald und Hü - gel stehn bei
. Gtr.
55
dei - nem Hauch in
. Gtr.

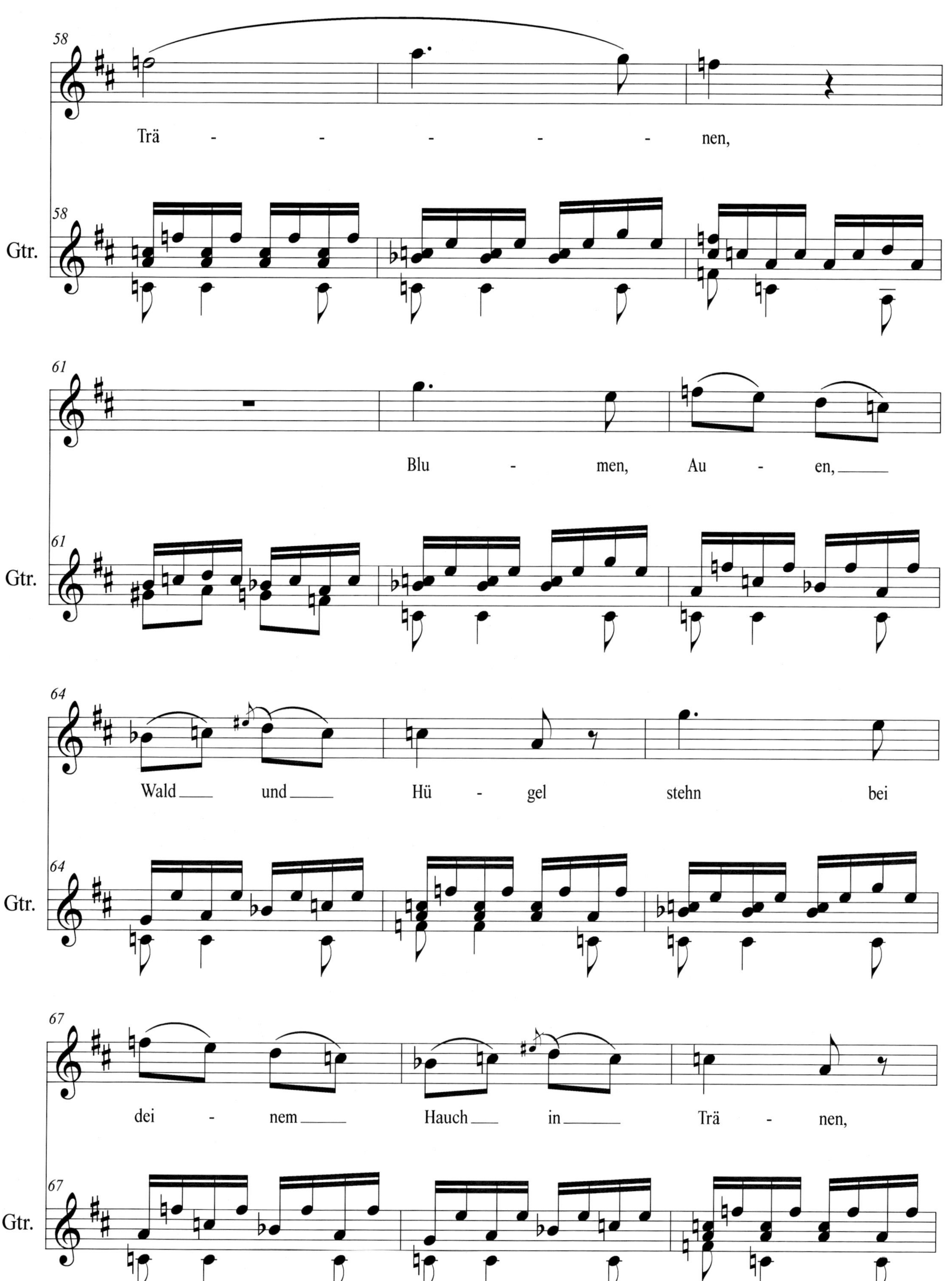
58
Trä - - - - - nen,
58
Gtr.
61
Blu - men, Au - en,
61
Gtr.
64
Wald und Hü - gel stehn bei
64
Gtr.
67
dei - nem Hauch in Trä - nen,
67
Gtr.

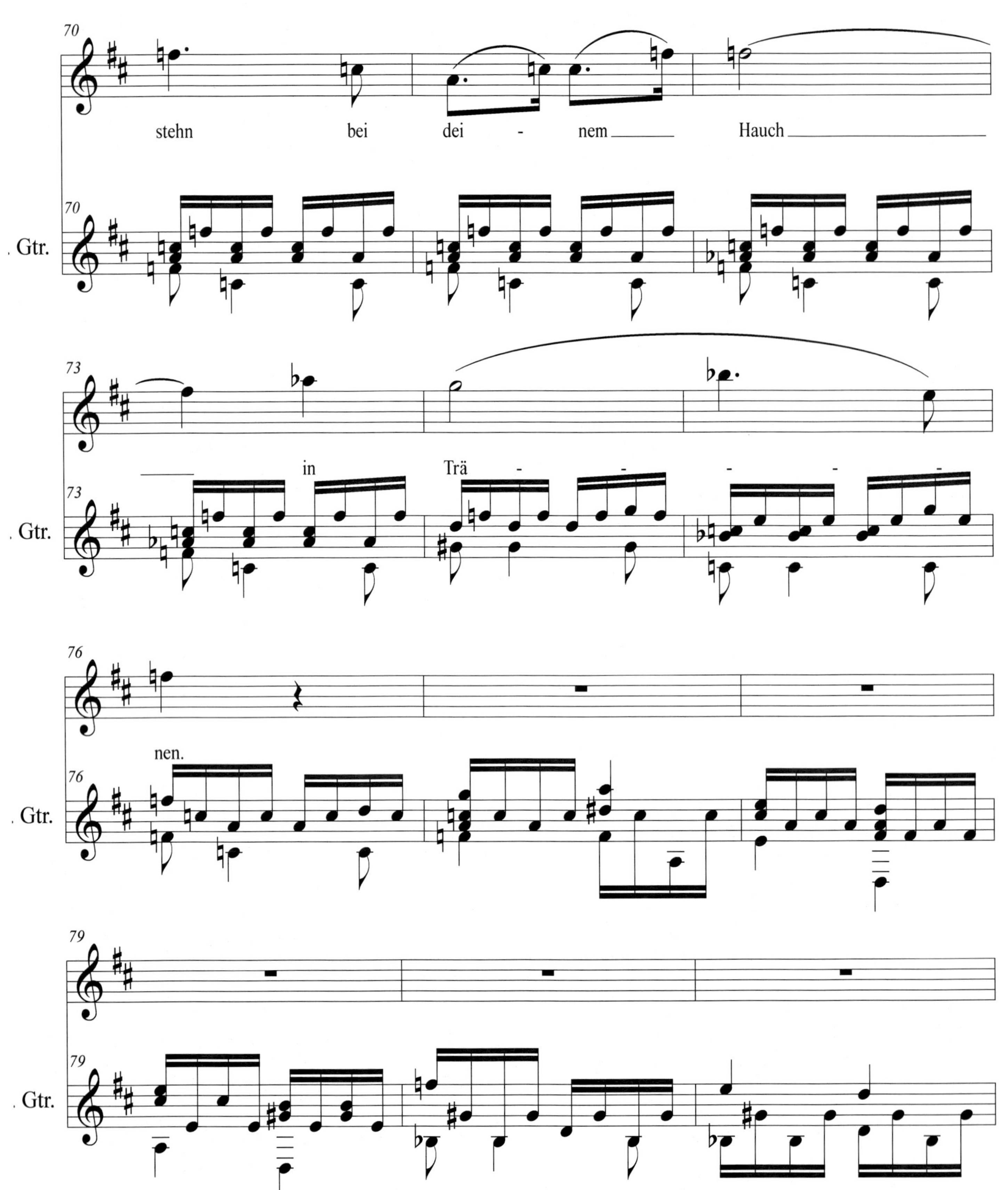
70
stehn
bei
dei
-
nem
Hauch
70
. Gtr.
73
in
Trä
-
-
-
-
-
73
. Gtr.
76
nen.
76
. Gtr.
79
79
. Gtr.

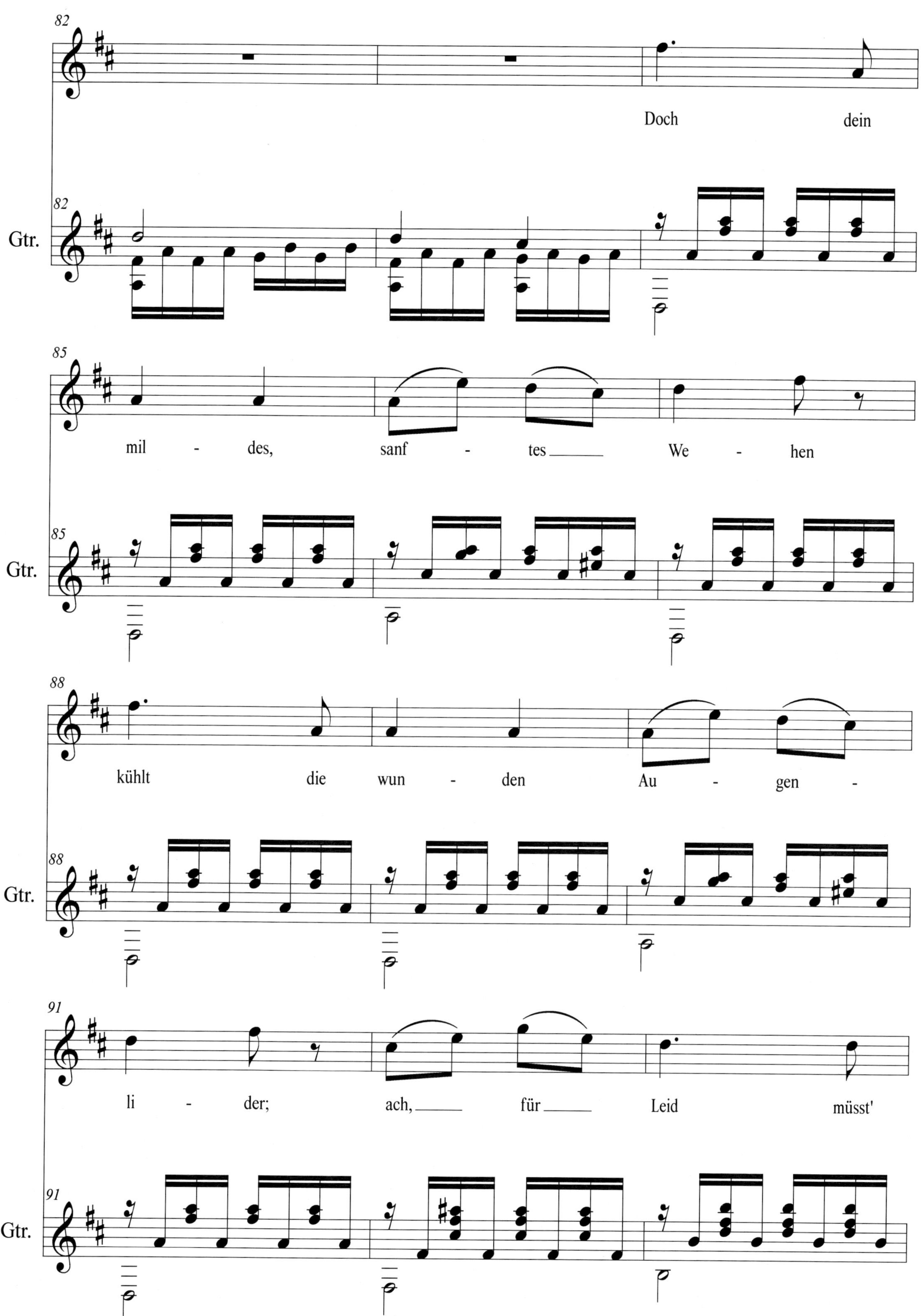
82
Doch dein
Gtr.
85
mil - des, sanf - tes We - hen
Gtr.
88
kühlt die wun - den Au - gen -
Gtr.
91
li - der; ach, für Leid müsst'
Gtr.

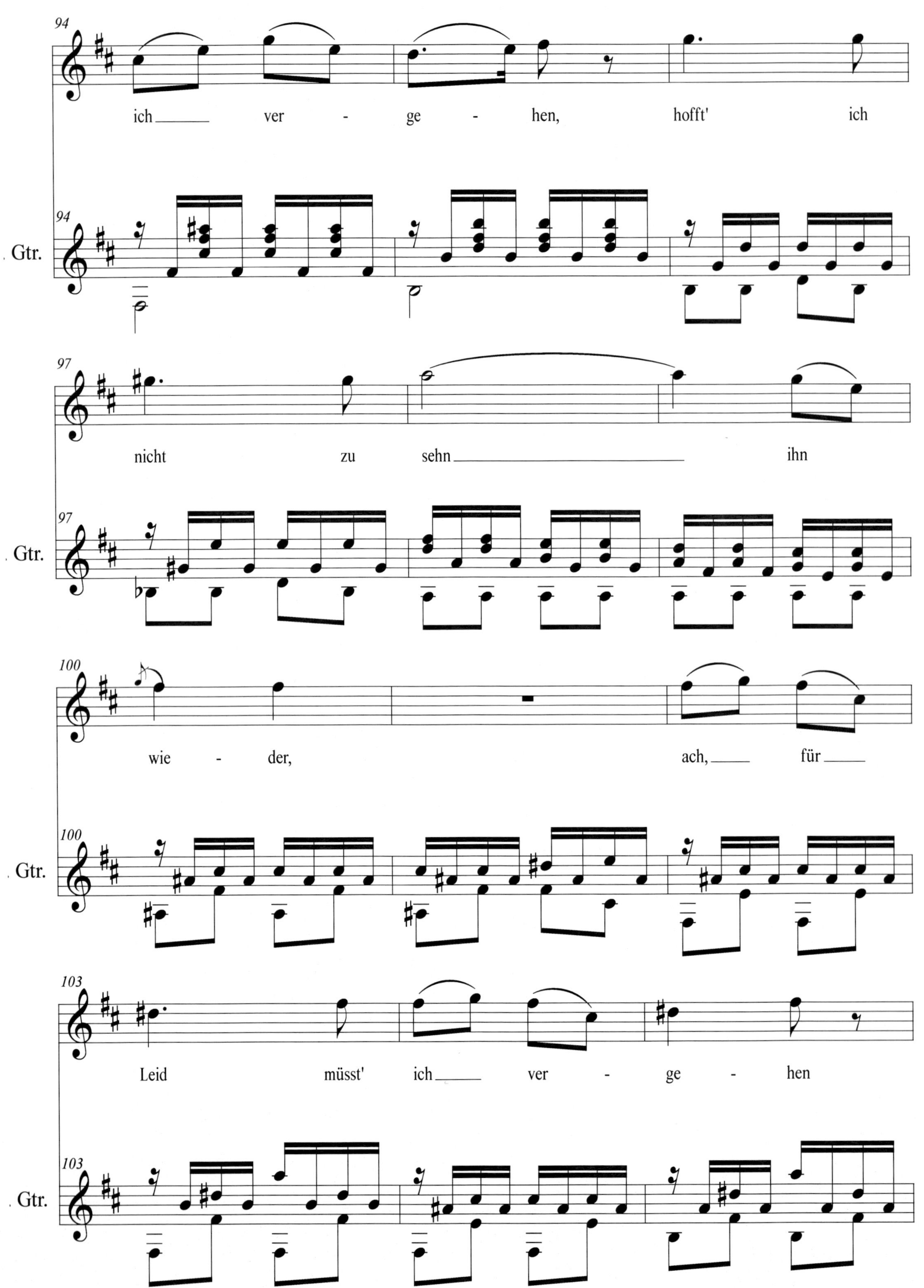
94
ich ver - ge - hen, hofft' ich
94
Gtr.
97
nicht zu sehn ihn
97
Gtr.
100
wie - der, ach, für
100
Gtr.
103
Leid müsst' ich ver - ge - hen
103
Gtr.

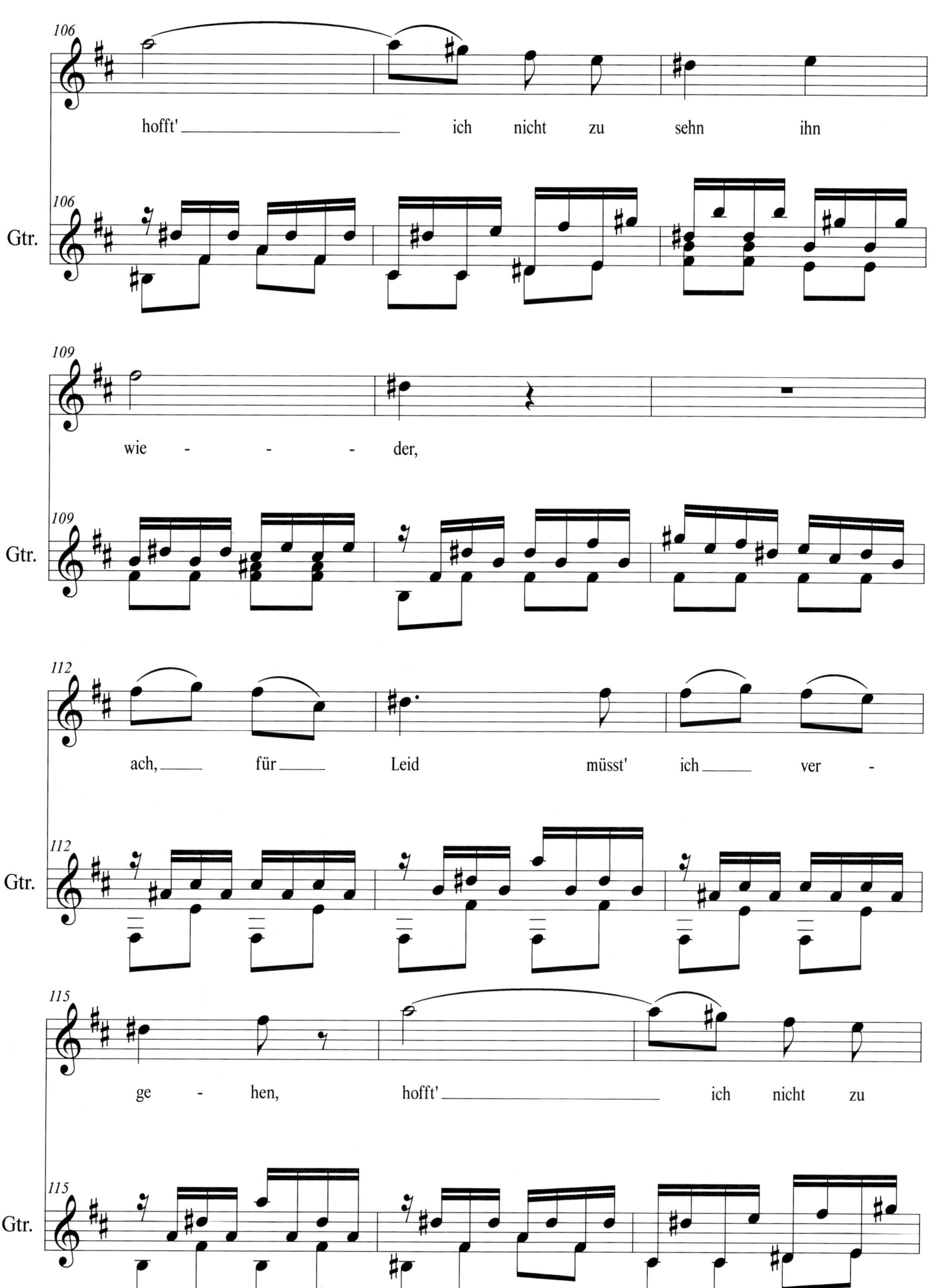
106
hofft' ich nicht zu sehn ihn
106
Gtr.
109
wie - - - der,
109
Gtr.
112
ach, für Leid müsst' ich ver -
112
Gtr.
115
ge - hen, hofft' ich nicht zu
115
Gtr.

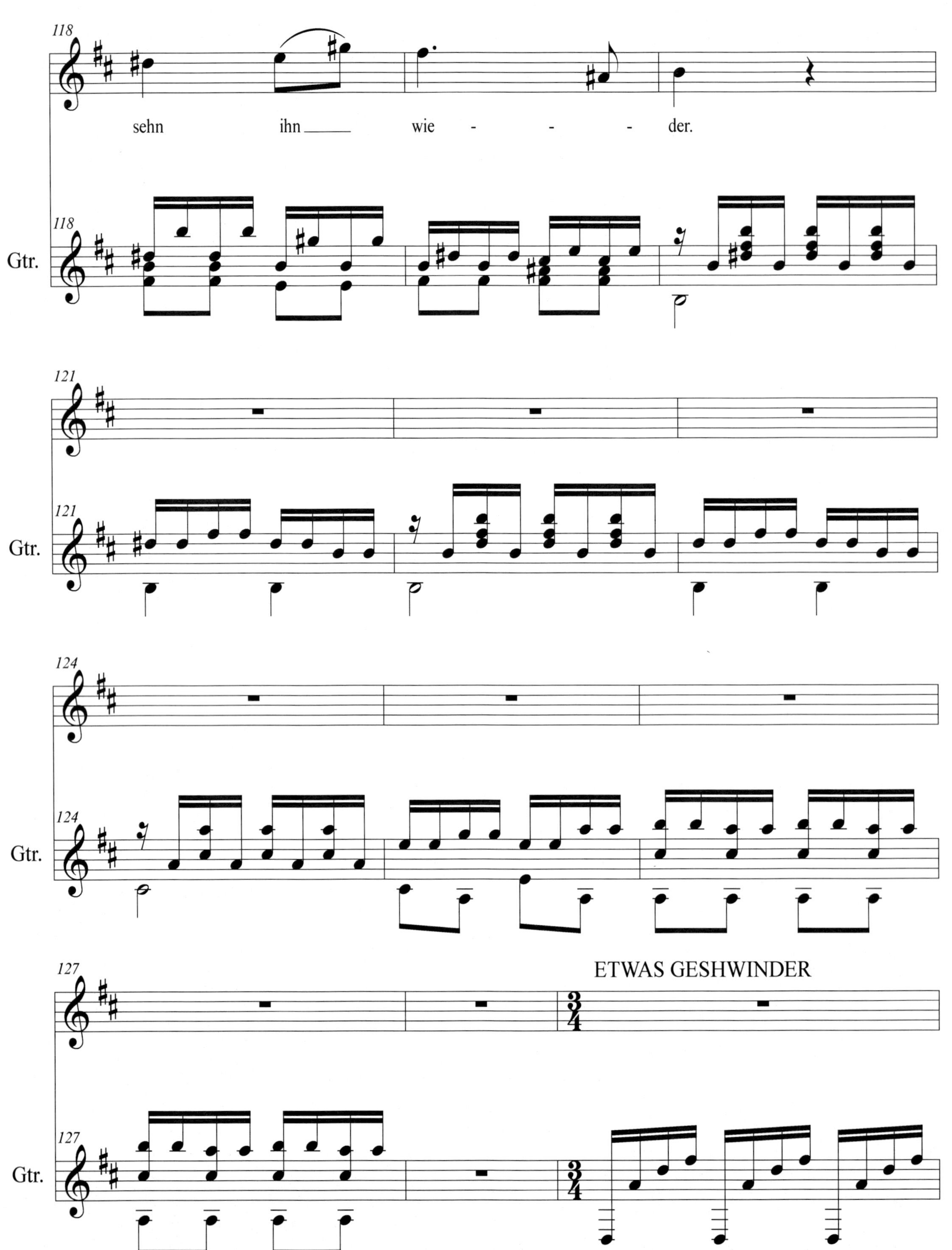
118
sehn ihn wie - - - der.
118
Gtr.
121
121
Gtr.
124
124
Gtr.
127
ETWAS GESHWINDER
127
Gtr.

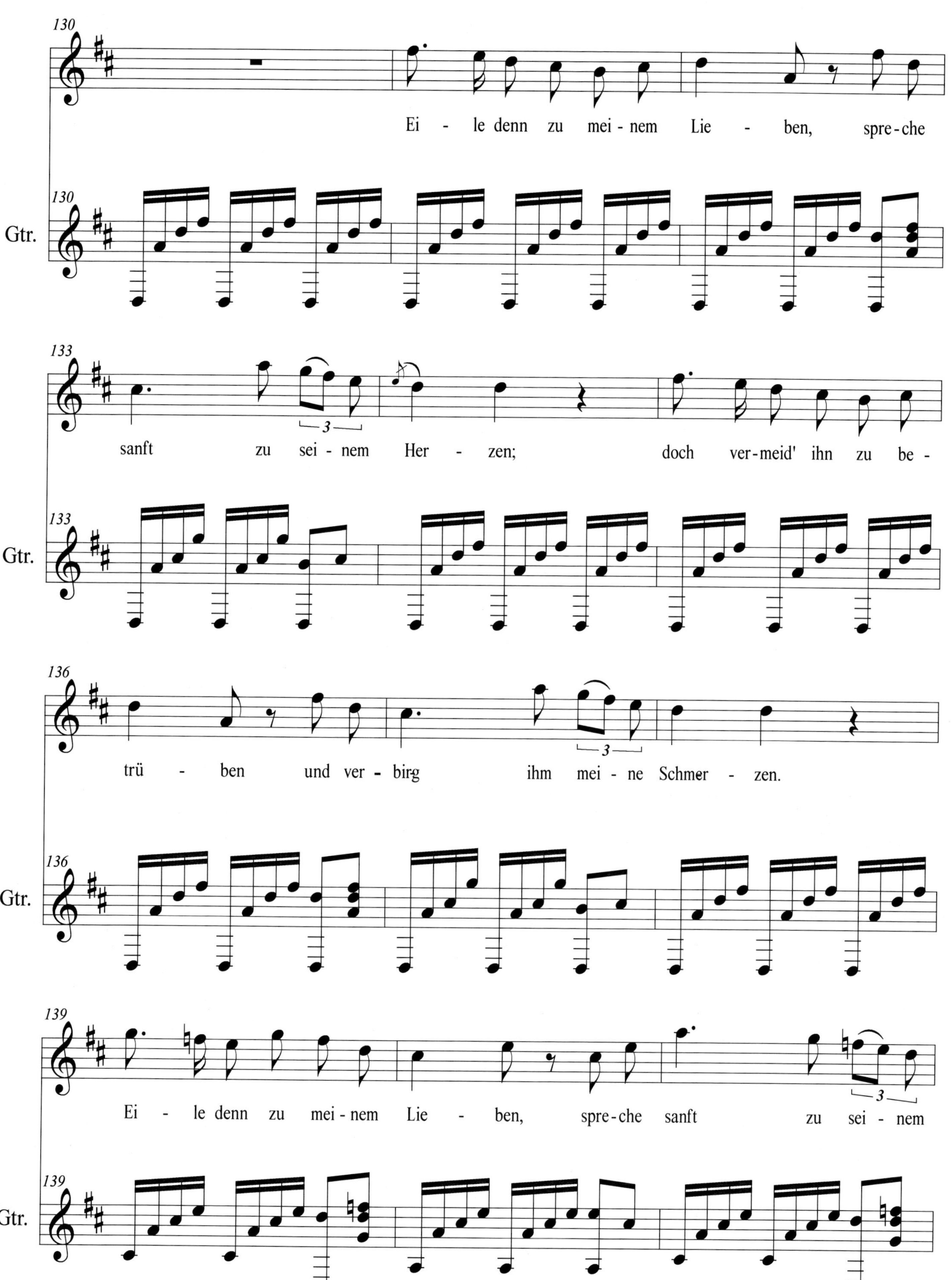
130
Ei - le denn zu mei - nem Lie - ben, spre - che
130
Gtr.
133
sanft zu sei - nem Her - zen; doch ver - meid' ihn zu be -
3
133
Gtr.
136
trü - ben und ver - birg ihm mei - ne Schmer - zen.
3
136
Gtr.
139
Ei - le denn zu mei - nem Lie - ben, spre - che sanft zu sei - nem
3
139
Gtr.

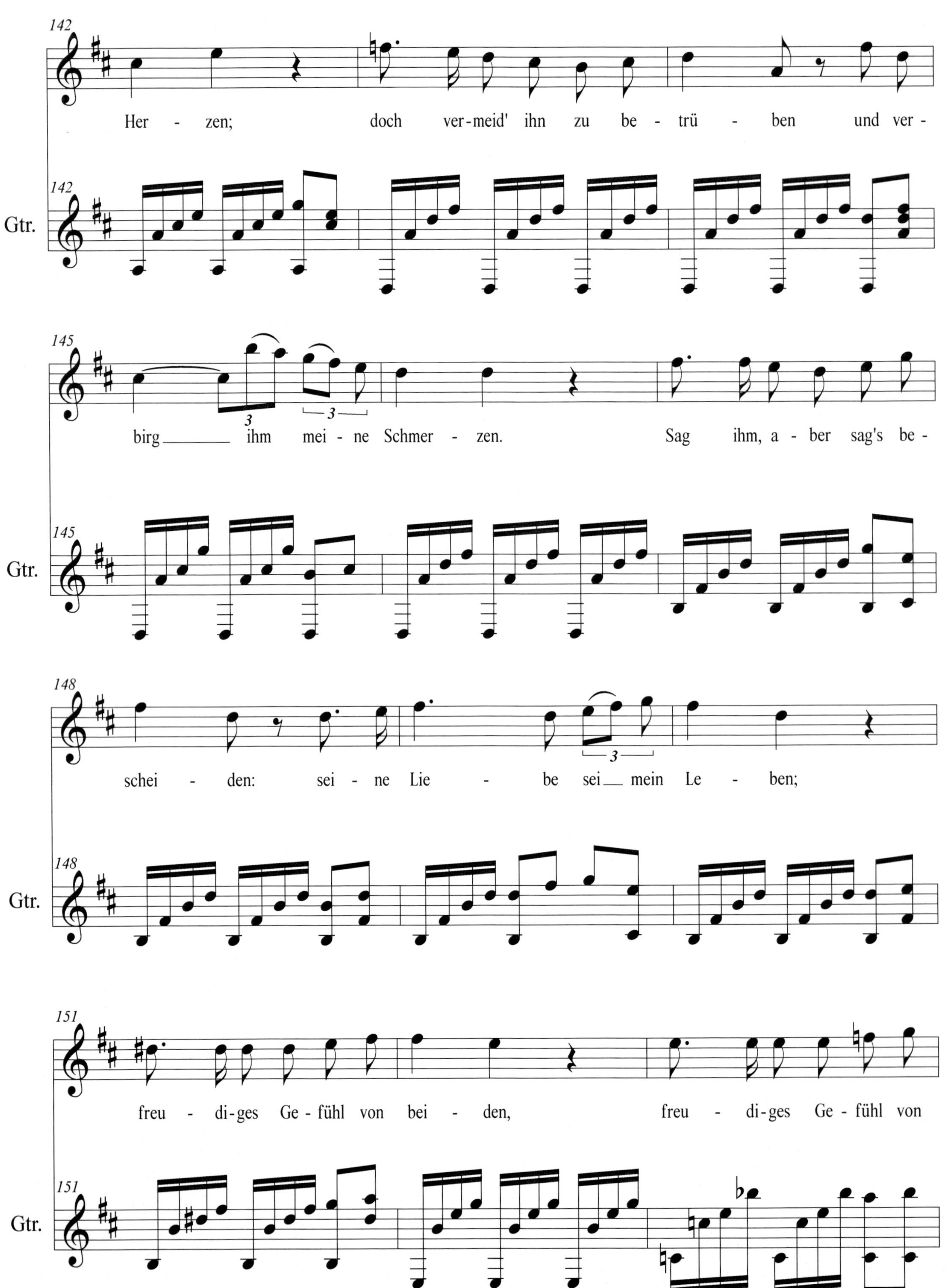
142
Her - zen; doch ver-meid' ihn zu be - trü - ben und ver -
142
Gtr.
145
birg ihm mei - ne Schmer - zen. Sag ihm, a - ber sag's be -
145
Gtr.
148
schei - den: sei - ne Lie - be sei mein Le - ben;
148
Gtr.
151
freu - di-ges Ge - fühl von bei - den, freu - di-ges Ge - fühl von
151
Gtr.

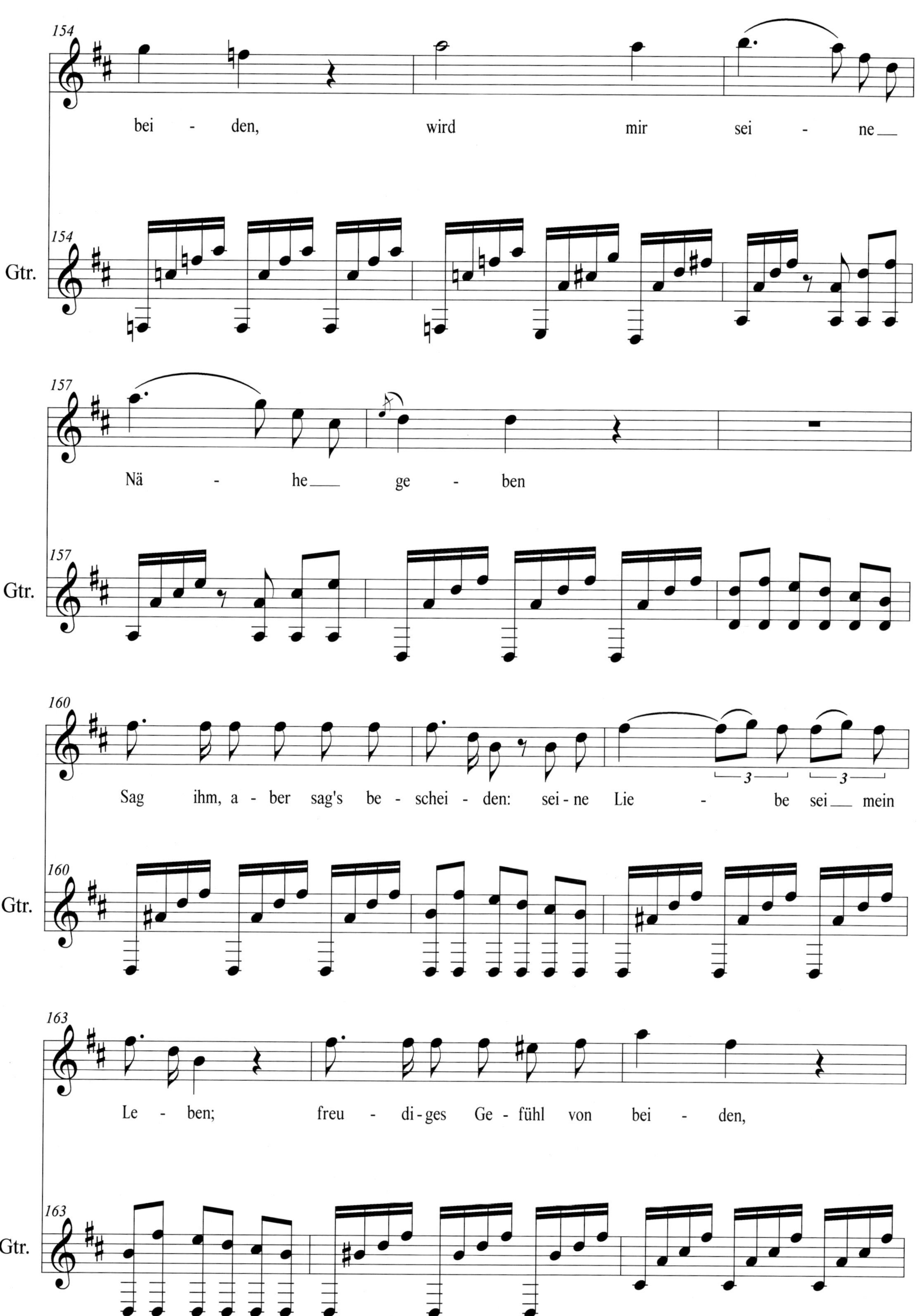
154
bei - den, wird mir sei - ne
Gtr.
157
Nä - he ge - ben
Gtr.
160
Sag ihm, a - ber sag's be - schei - den: sei - ne Lie - be sei mein
3
3
Gtr.
163
Le - ben; freu - di - ges Ge - fühl von bei - den,
Gtr.

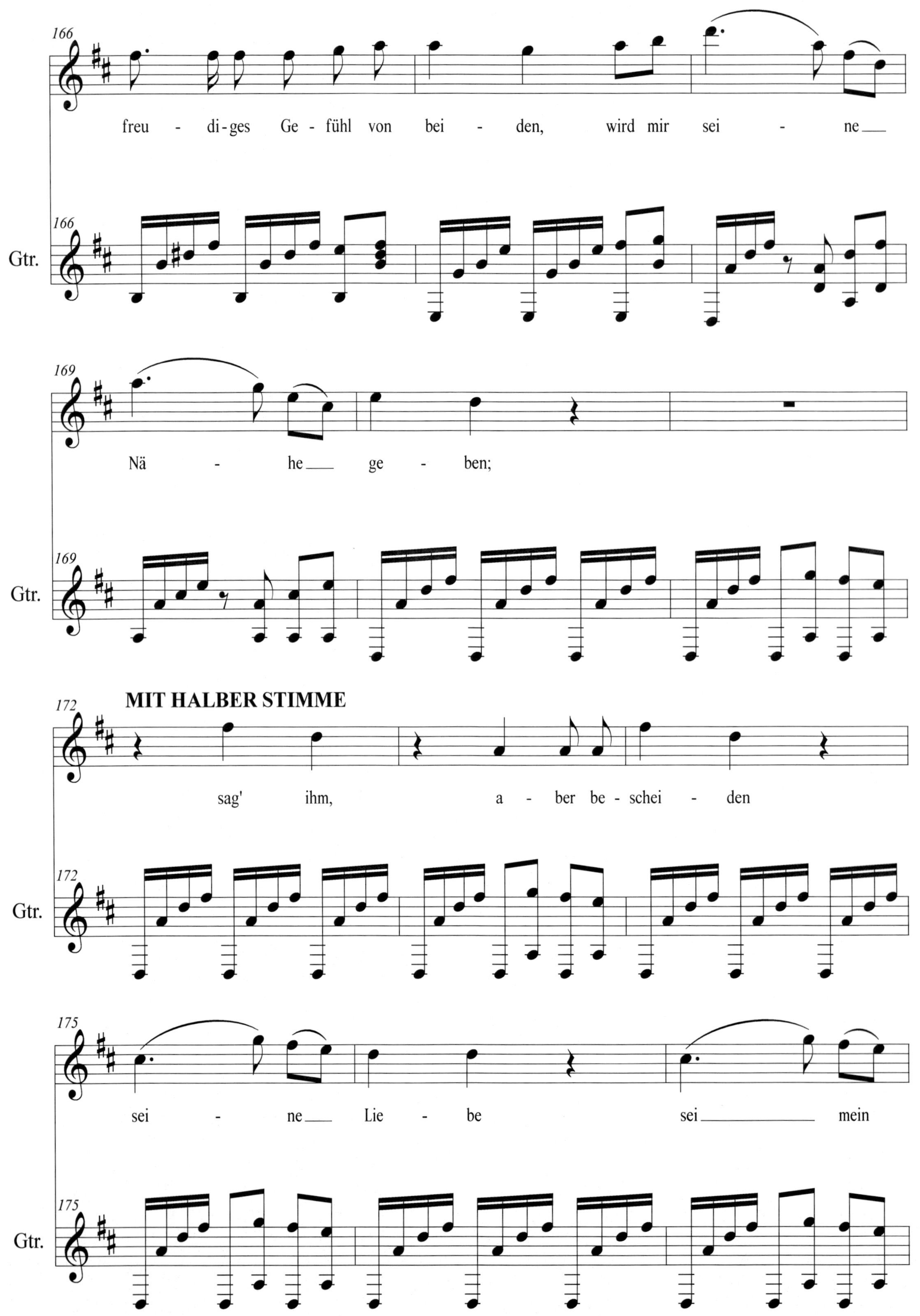
166
freu - di-ges Ge - fühl von bei - den, wird mir sei - ne
Gtr.
169
Nä - he ge - ben;
Gtr.
172
MIT HALBER STIMME
sag' ihm, a - ber be - schei - den
Gtr.
175
sei - ne Lie - be sei mein
Gtr.

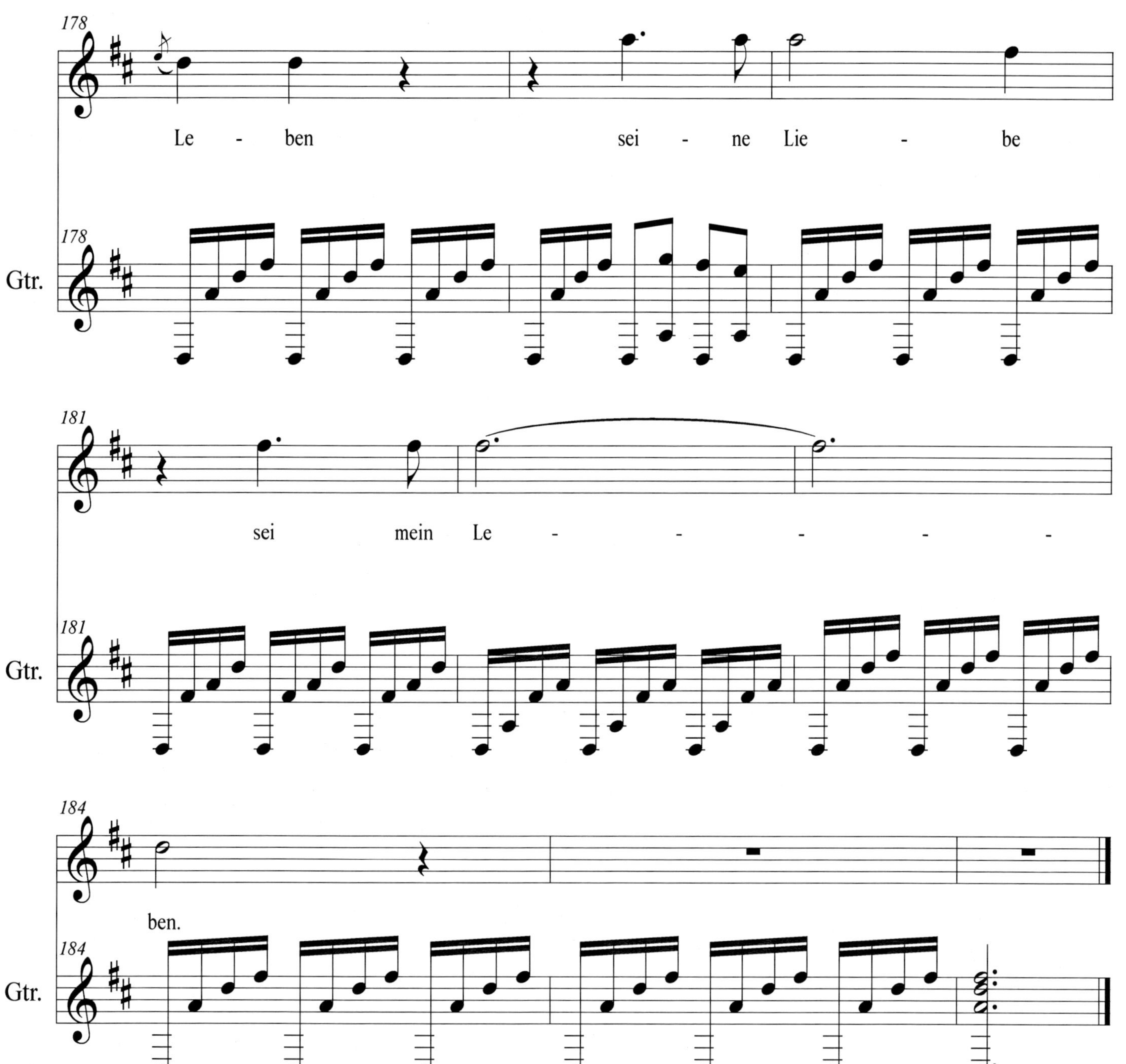
178
Le - ben sei - ne Lie - be
Gtr.
181
sei mein Le - - - - -
184
ben.

Score

17

Sei Ariette

Op. 95, No. 1

Andantino espressivo

♩ = 70

Mauro Giuliani

Voice

Guitar

Om- bre a-me - ne a - mi - che pian - te il mio

4

be - ne il ca - ro a - man - te chi mi di - ce o - ve n'an-

Gtr.

7

dò? chi mi di - ce o - ve n'an - dò? Zef - fi-

Gtr.

10

ret - to lu - sin - ghie - ro, a lui vo - la mes - sag -

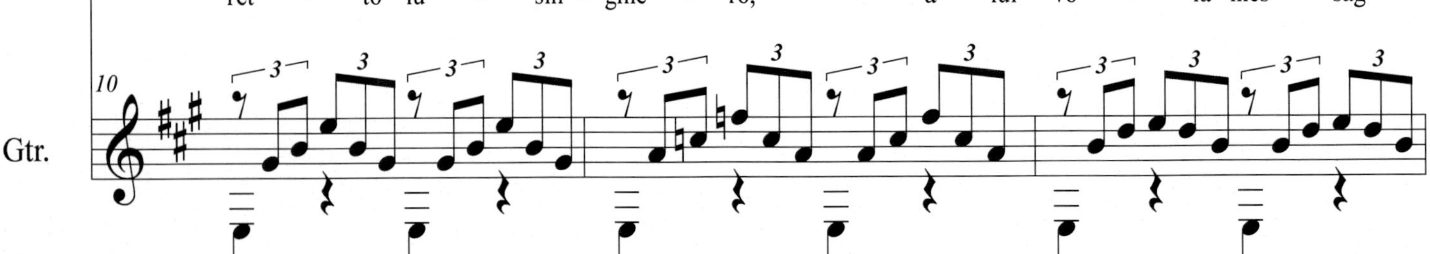

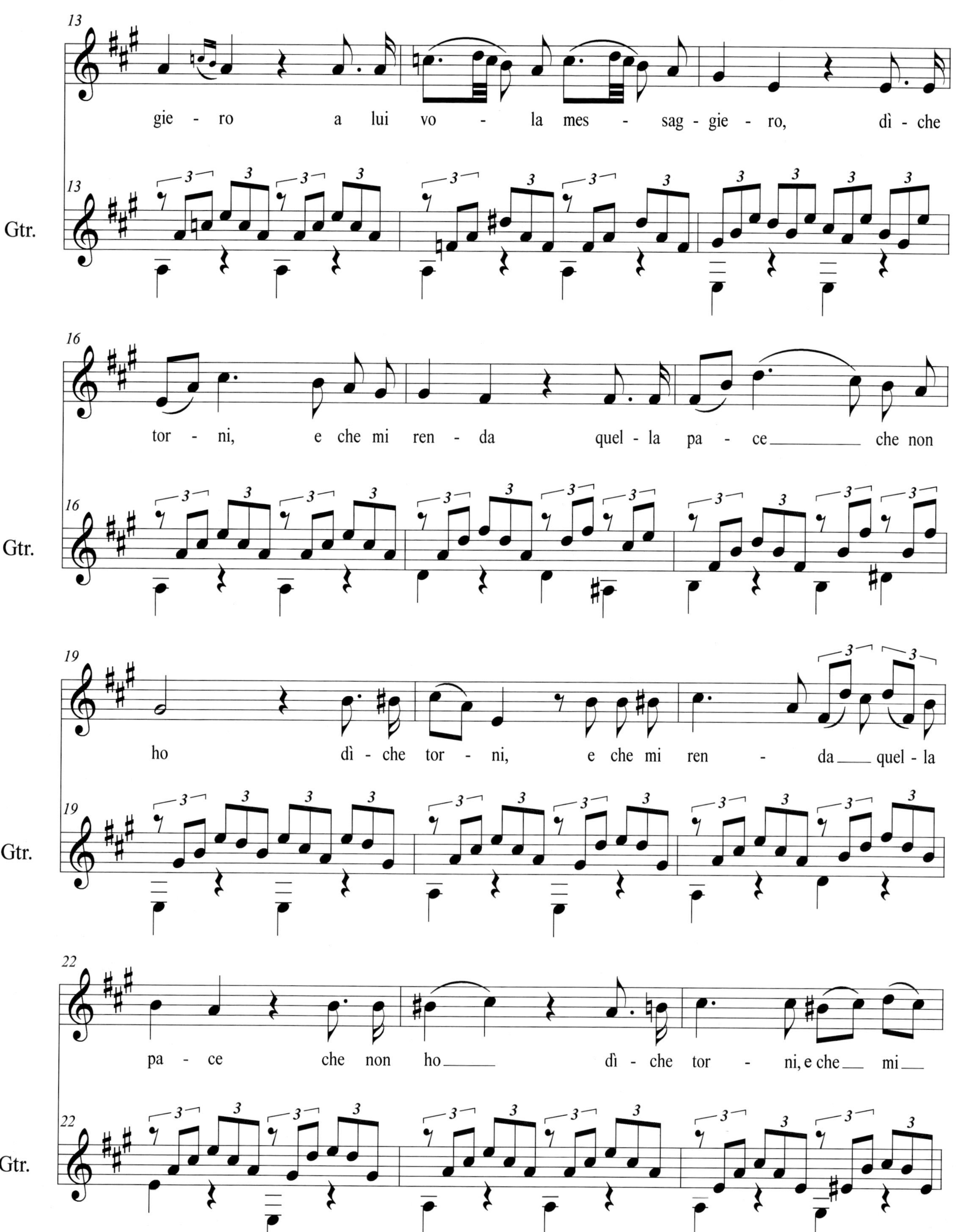
13
gie - ro a lui vo - la mes - sag - gie - ro, dì - che
Gtr.
16
tor - ni, e che mi ren - da quel - la pa - ce che non
Gtr.
19
ho dì - che tor - ni, e che mi ren - da quel - la
Gtr.
22
pa - ce che non ho dì - che tor - ni, e che mi
Gtr.

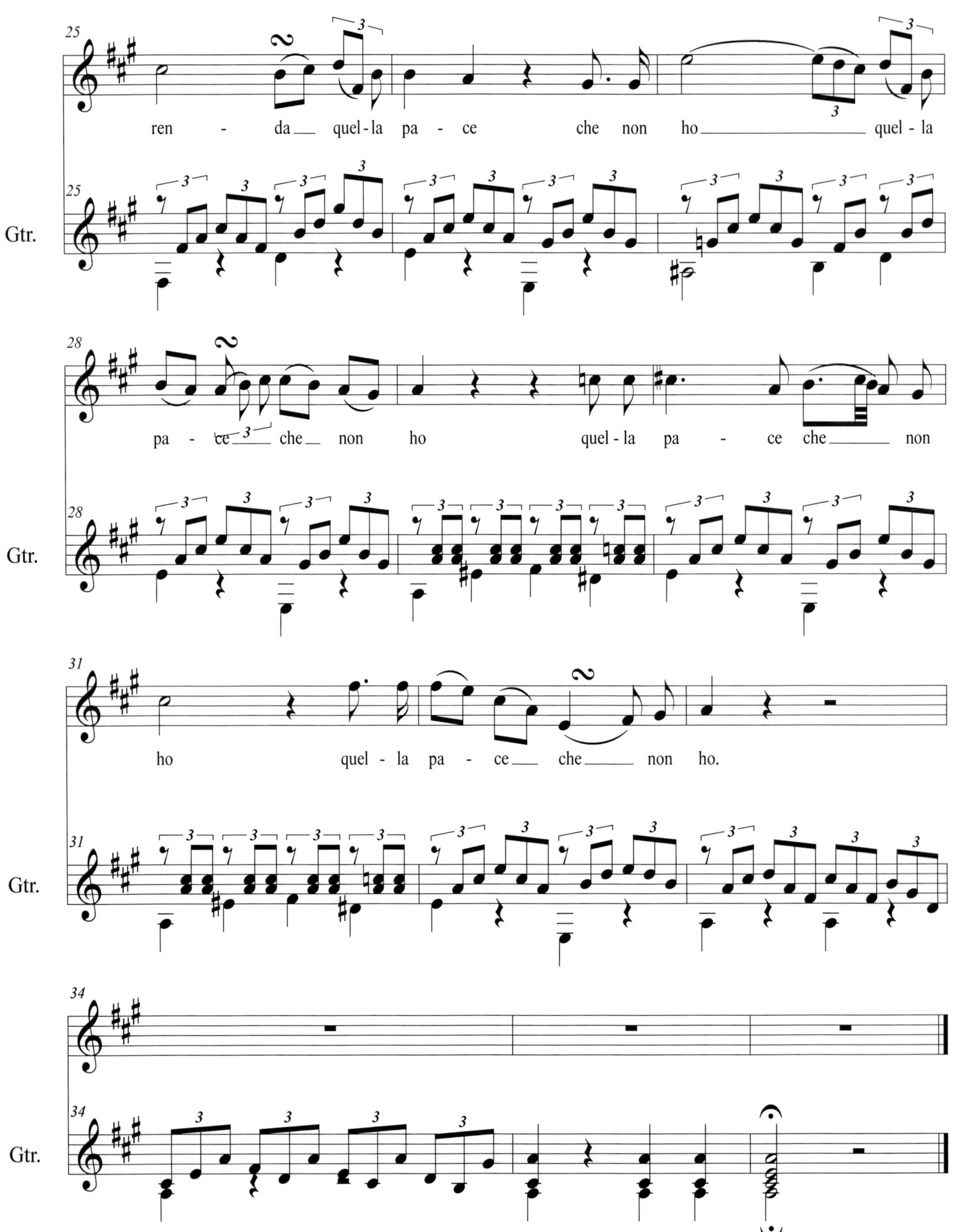
25
ren - da quel-la pa - ce che non ho quel-la
Gtr.
28
pa - ce che non ho quel-la pa - ce che non
Gtr.
31
ho quel - la pa - ce che non ho.
Gtr.
34
Gtr.

Score

18

Sei Ariette

Op. 95, No. 2

Allegretto Agitato

Mauro Giuliani

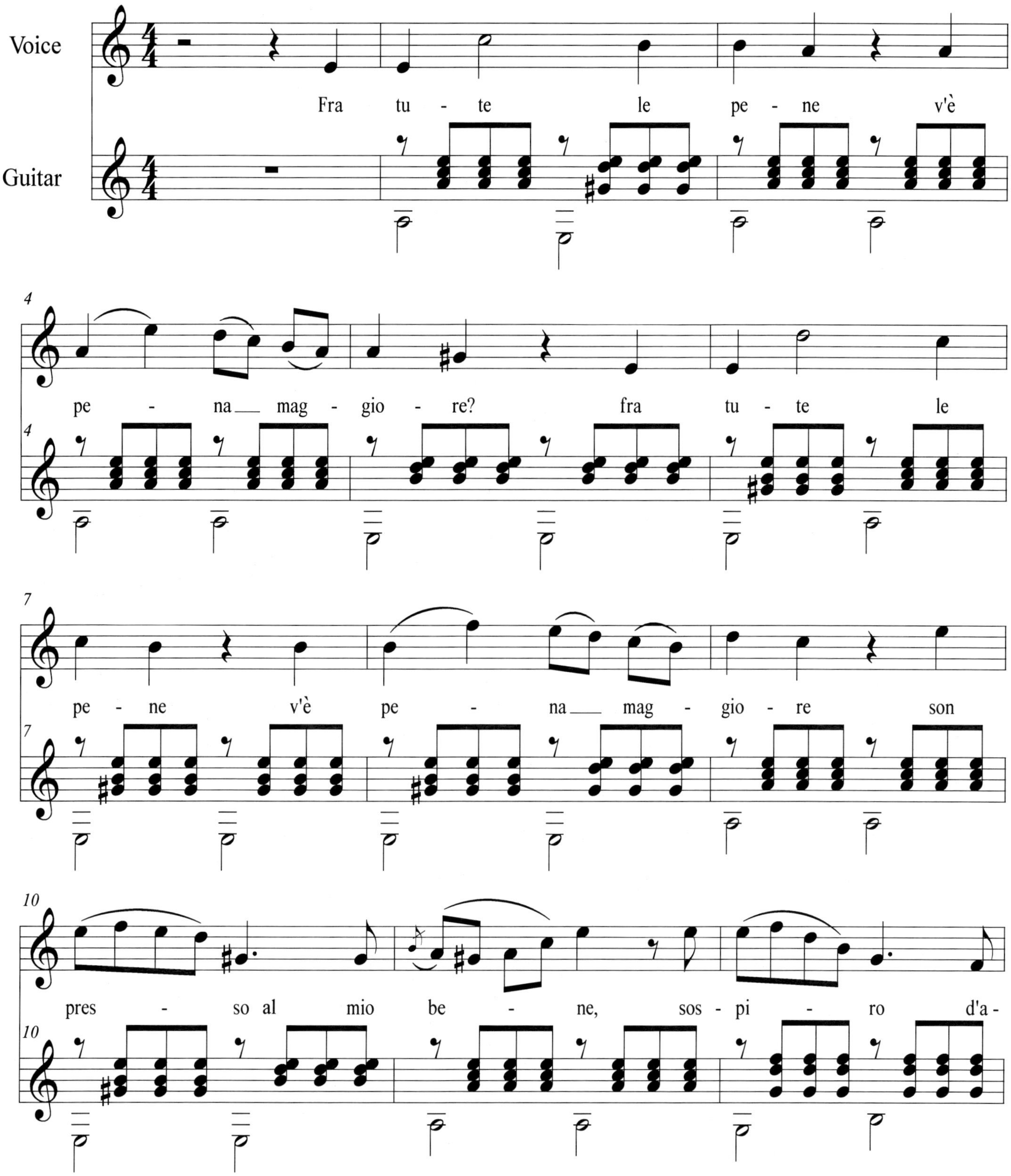

Voice

Guitar

Fra tu - te le pe - ne v'è

4

pe - na mag - gio - re? fra tu - te le

Gtr.

7

pe - ne v'è pe - na mag - gio - re son

Gtr.

10

pres - so al mio be - ne, sos - pi - ro d'a -

Gtr.

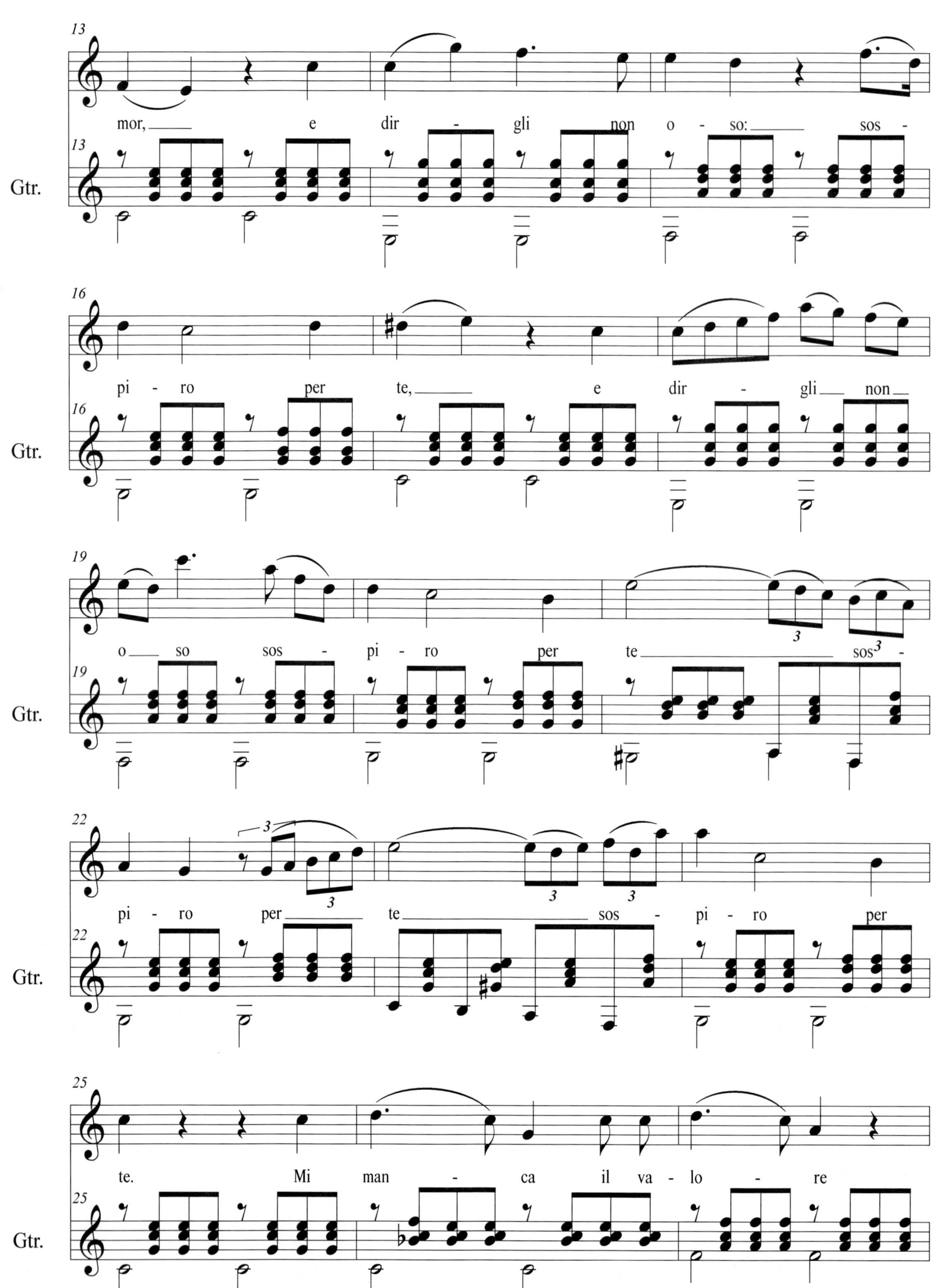
13
mor, e dir - gli non o - so: sos -
13
Gtr.
16
pi - ro per te, e dir - gli non
16
Gtr.
19
o so sos - pi - ro per te sos -
19
Gtr.
22
pi - ro per te sos - pi - ro per
22
Gtr.
25
te. Mi man - ca il va - lo - re
25
Gtr.

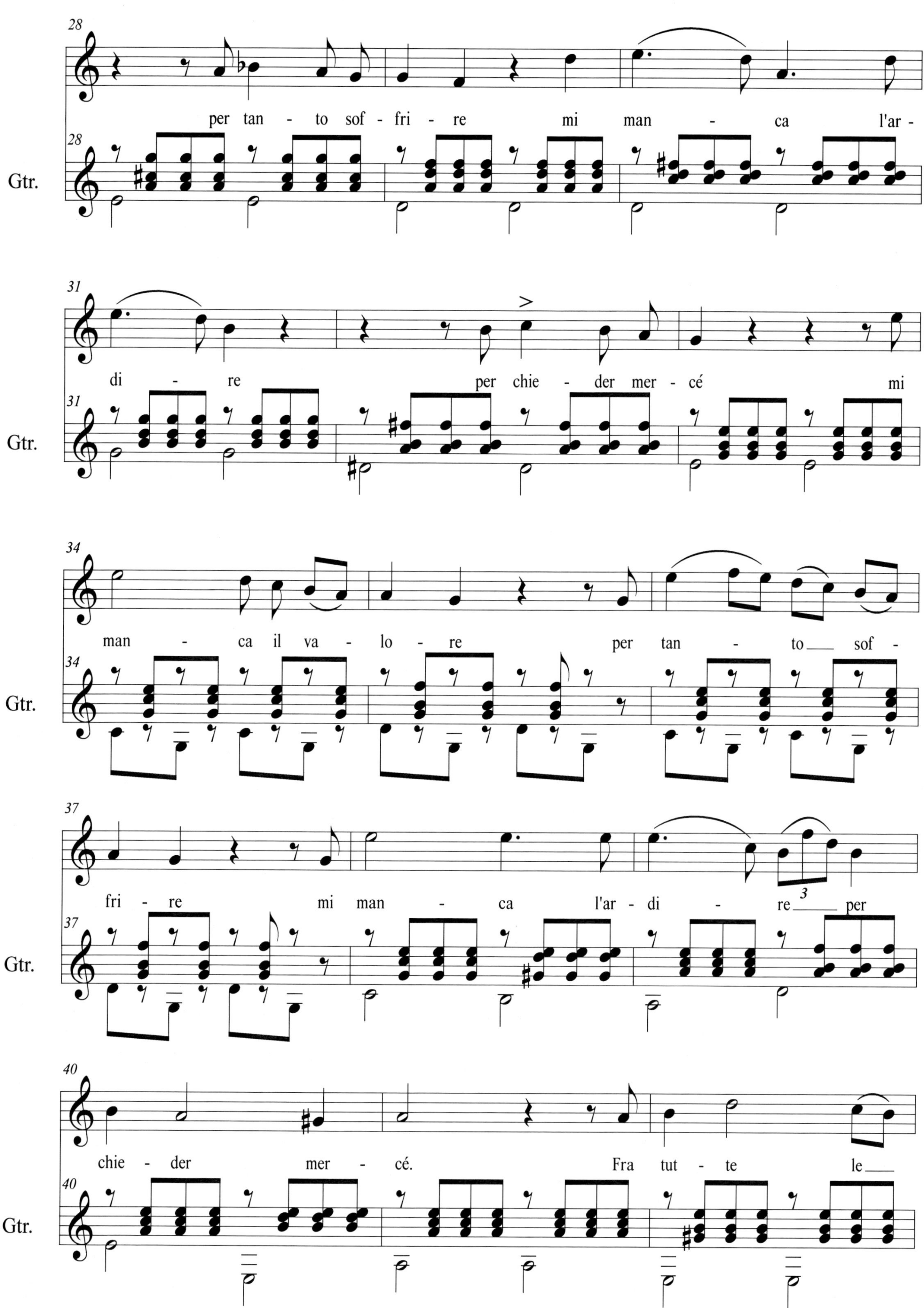
28
per tan - to sof - fri - re mi man - ca l'ar -
Gtr.
31
di - re per chie - der mer - cé mi
Gtr.
34
man - ca il va - lo - re per tan - to sof -
Gtr.
37
fri - re mi man - ca l'ar - di - re per
3
Gtr.
40
chie - der mer - cé. Fra tut - te le
Gtr.

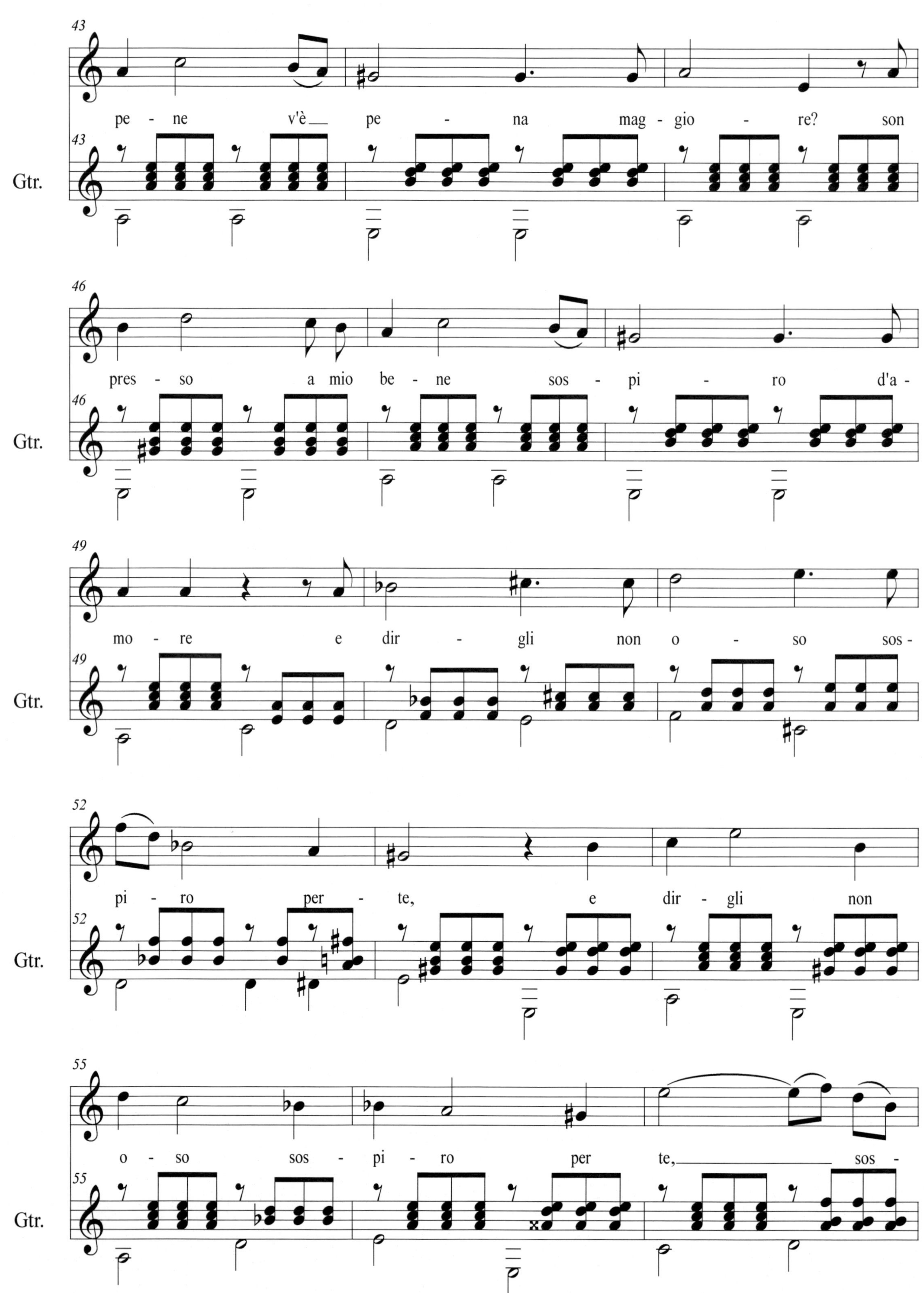
pe - ne v'è pe - na mag - gio - re? son
Gtr.
pres - so a mio be - ne sos - pi - ro d'a -
Gtr.
mo - re e dir - gli non o - so sos -
Gtr.
pi - ro per - te, e dir - gli non
Gtr.
o - so sos - pi - ro per te, sos -
Gtr.

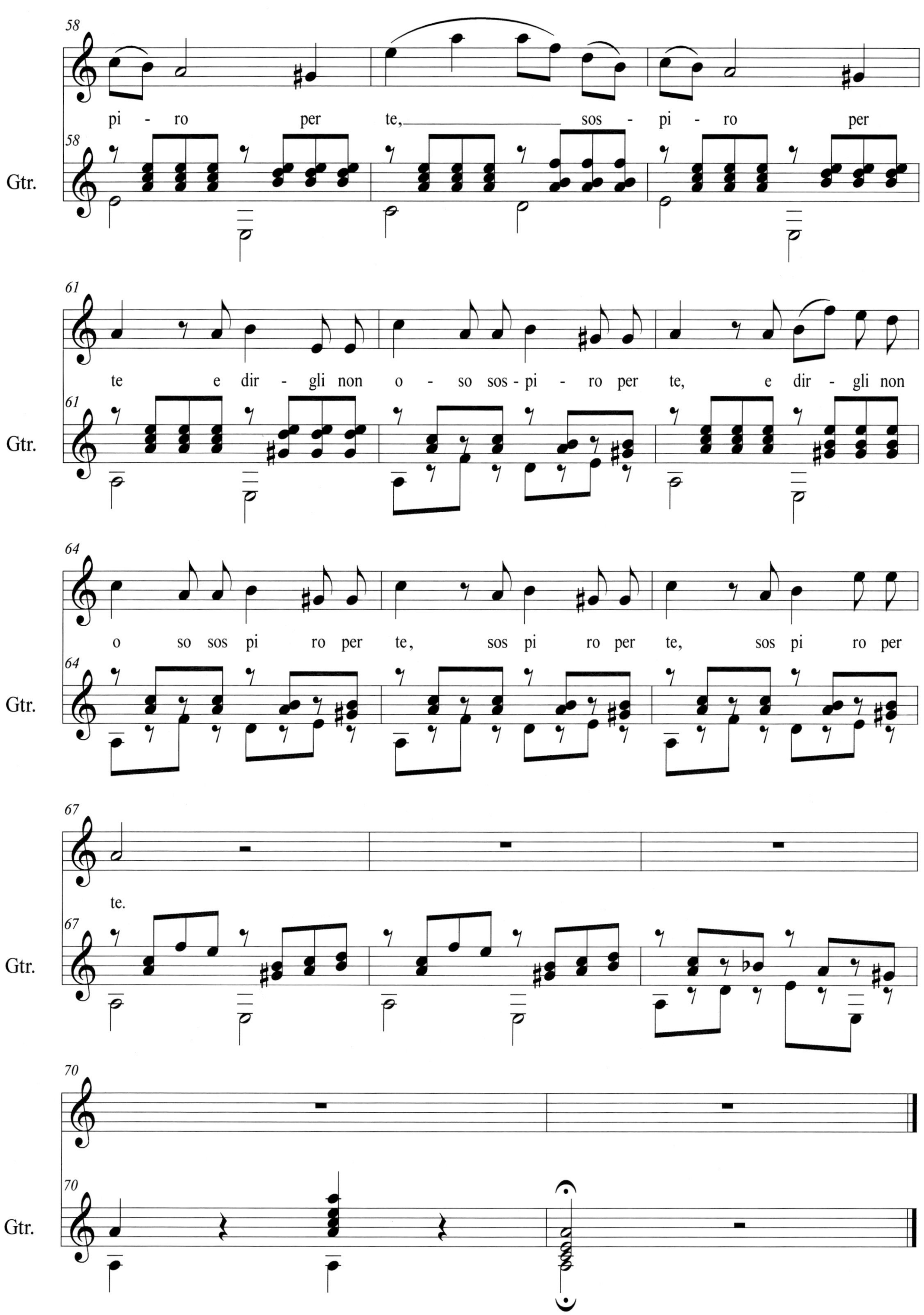
58
pi - ro per te, sos - pi - ro per
Gtr.
61
te e dir - gli non o - so sos - pi - ro per te, e dir - gli non
Gtr.
64
o so sos pi ro per te, sos pi ro per te, sos pi ro per
Gtr.
67
te.
Gtr.
70
Gtr.

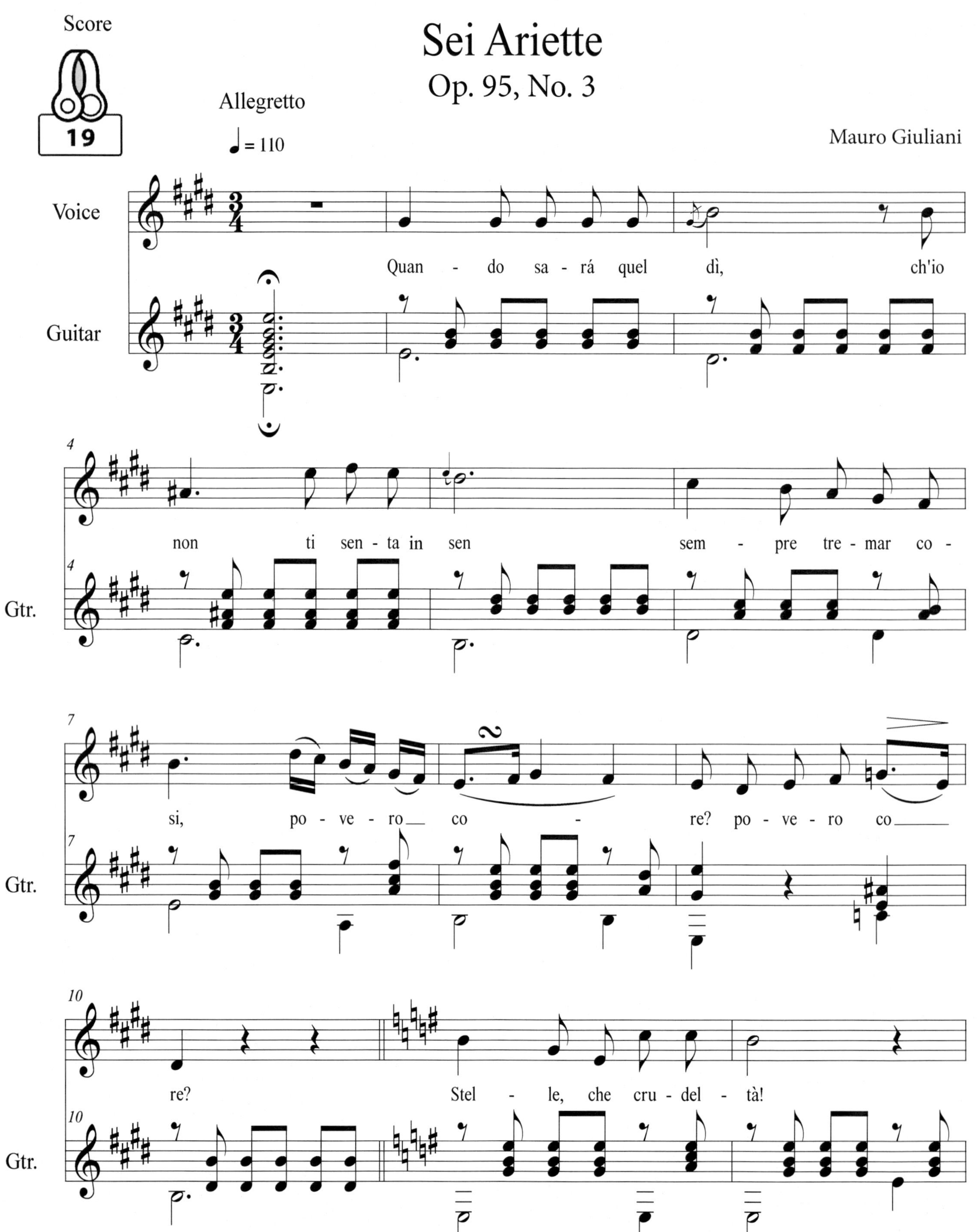
Score
19
Sei Ariette
Op. 95, No. 3
Allegretto
♩ = 110
Mauro Giuliani
Voice
Guitar
Quan - do sa - rá quel dì, ch'io
non ti sen - ta in sen sem - pre tre - mar co -
Gtr.
si, po - ve - ro co - re? po - ve - ro co
re? Stel - le, che cru - del - tà!

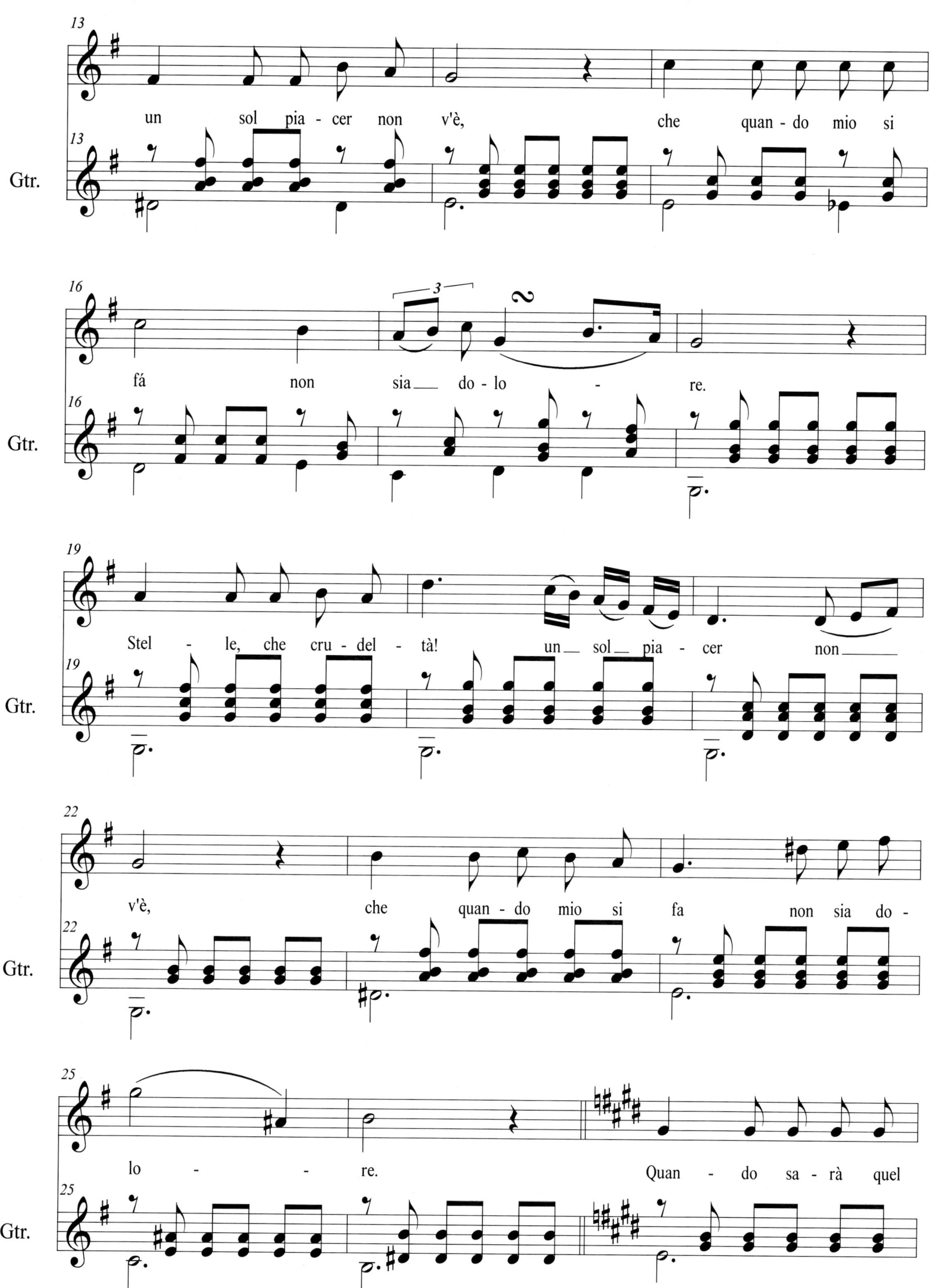
un sol pia - cer non v'è, che quan - do mio si
Gtr.
fá non sia do - lo - re.
Gtr.
Stel - le, che cru - del - tà! un sol pia - cer non
Gtr.
v'è, che quan - do mio si fa non sia do -
Gtr.
lo - re. Quan - do sa - rà quel
Gtr.

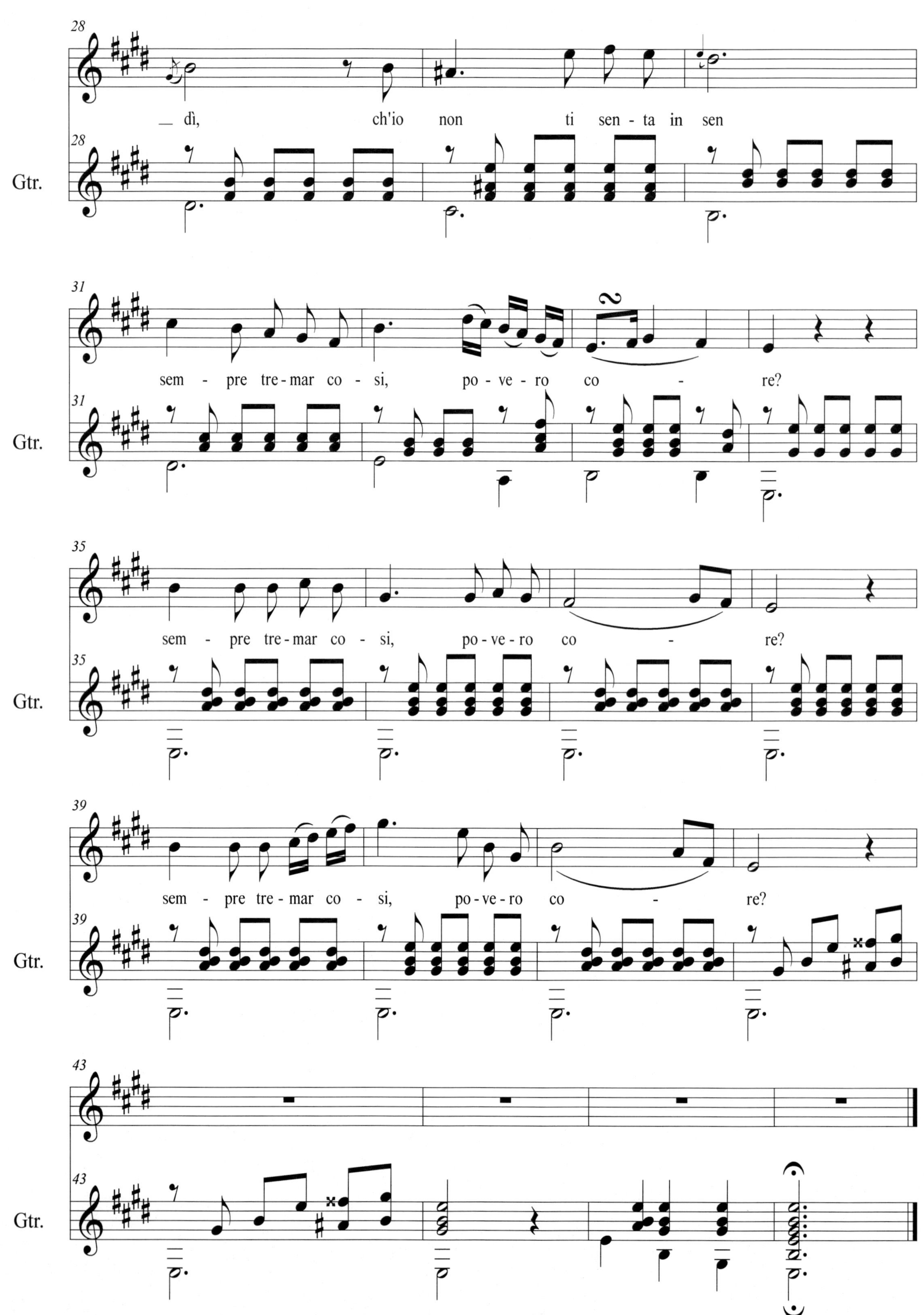
28
_ dì, ch'io non ti sen - ta in sen
Gtr.
31
sem - pre tre - mar co - si, po - ve - ro co - re?
Gtr.
35
sem - pre tre - mar co - si, po - ve - ro co - re?
Gtr.
39
sem - pre tre - mar co - si, po - ve - ro co - re?
Gtr.
43
Gtr.

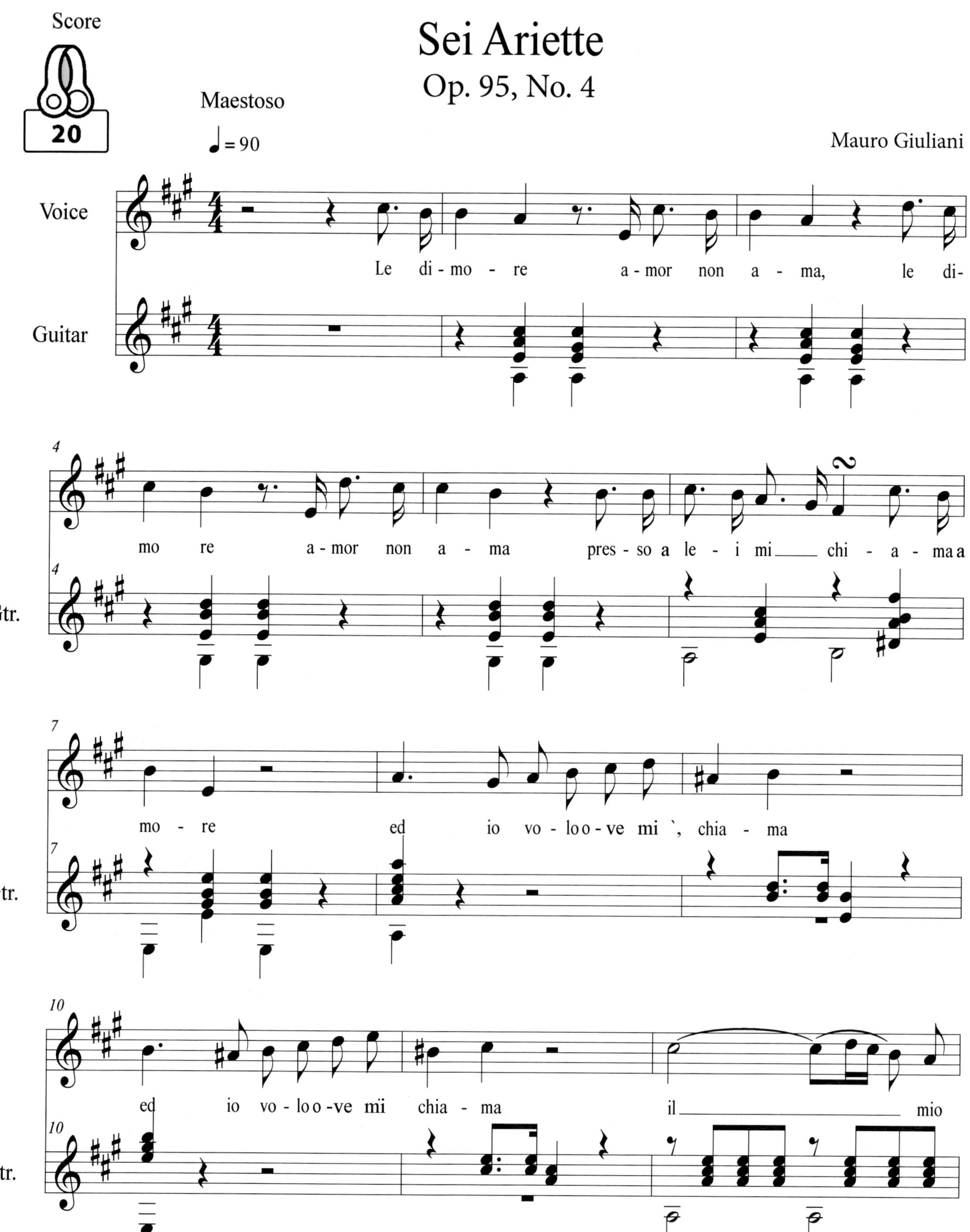
Score
20
Sei Ariette
Op. 95, No. 4
Maestoso
♩ = 90
Mauro Giuliani
Voice
Guitar
Le di - mo - re a - mor non a - ma, le di-
mo re a - mor non a - ma pres - so a le - i mi chi - a - ma a
mo - re ed io vo - lo o - ve mi `, chia - ma
ed io vo - lo o - ve mi chia - ma il mio
Gtr.

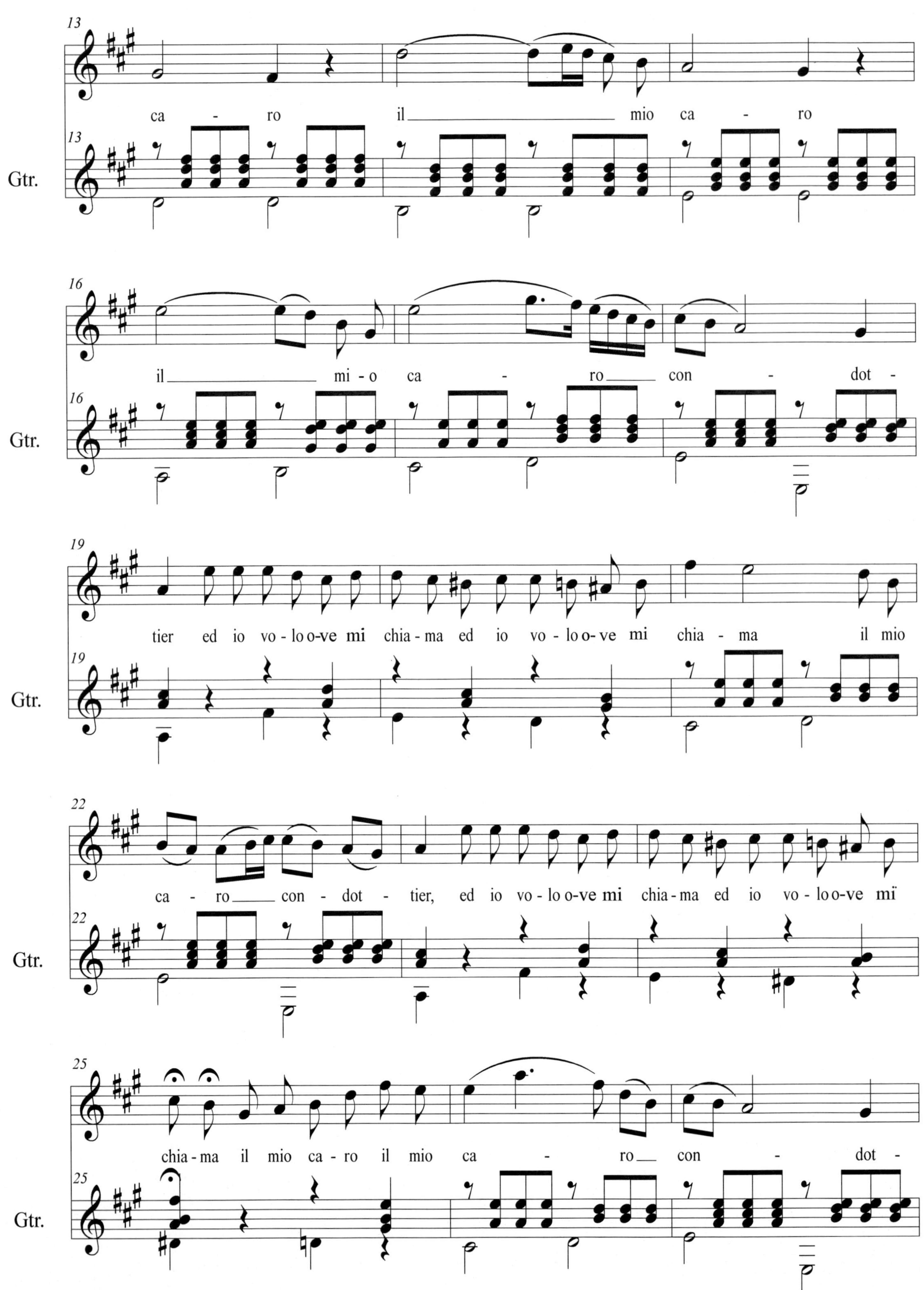
13
ca - ro il mio ca - ro
Gtr.
16
il mi - o ca - ro con - dot -
Gtr.
19
tier ed io vo - lo o-ve mi chia - ma ed io vo - lo o-ve mi chia - ma il mio
Gtr.
22
ca - ro con - dot - tier, ed io vo - lo o-ve mi chia - ma ed io vo - lo o-ve mï
Gtr.
25
chia - ma il mio ca - ro il mio ca - ro con - dot -
Gtr.

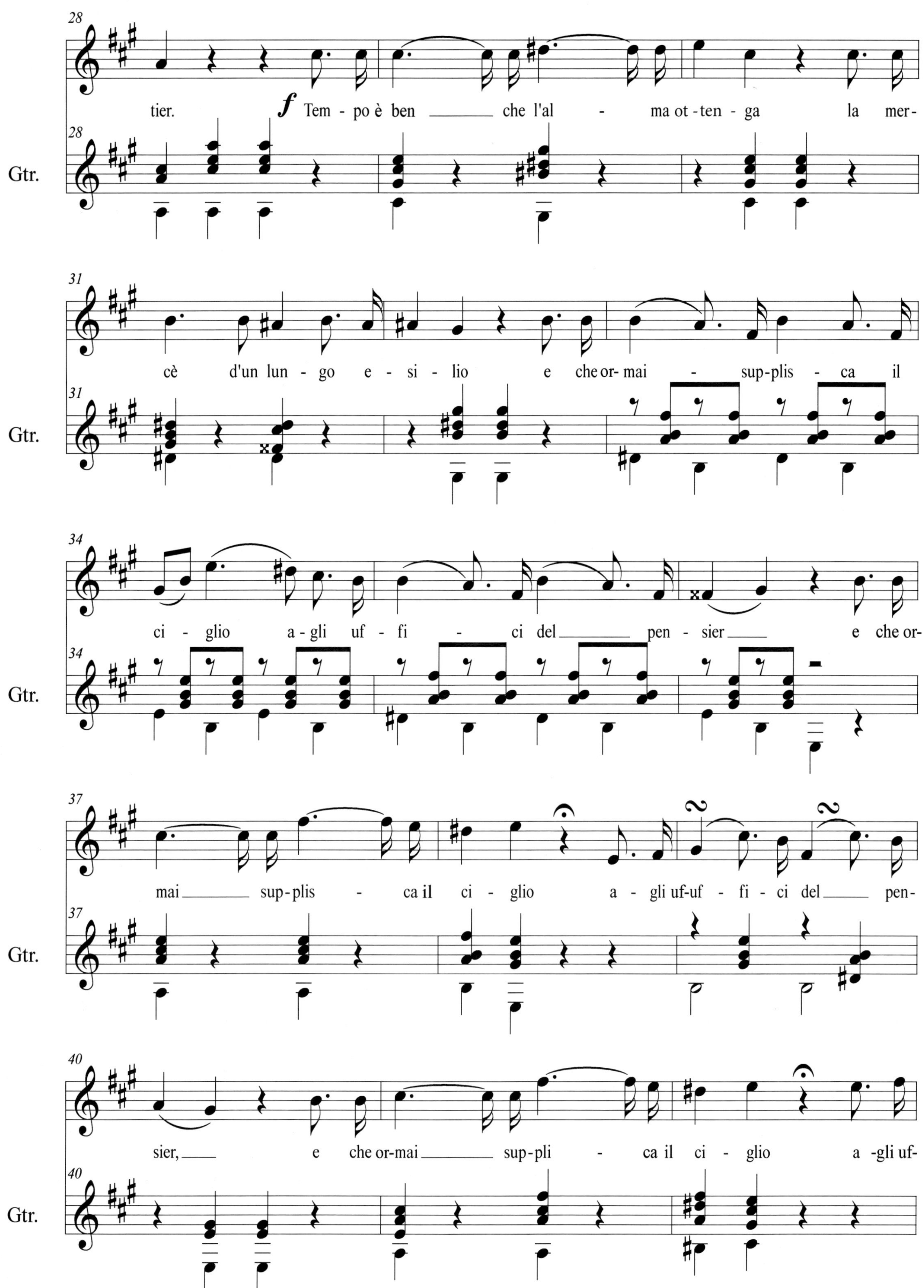
tier. f Tem - po è ben ___ che l'al - ma ot - ten - ga la mer-
Gtr.
cè d'un lun - go e - si - lio e che or- mai - sup- plis - ca il
Gtr.
ci - glio a - gli uf - fi - ci del ___ pen - sier ___ e che or-
Gtr.
mai ___ sup- plis - ca il ci - glio a - gli uf-uf - fi - ci del ___ pen-
Gtr.
sier, ___ e che or-mai ___ sup- pli - ca il ci - glio a -gli uf-
Gtr.

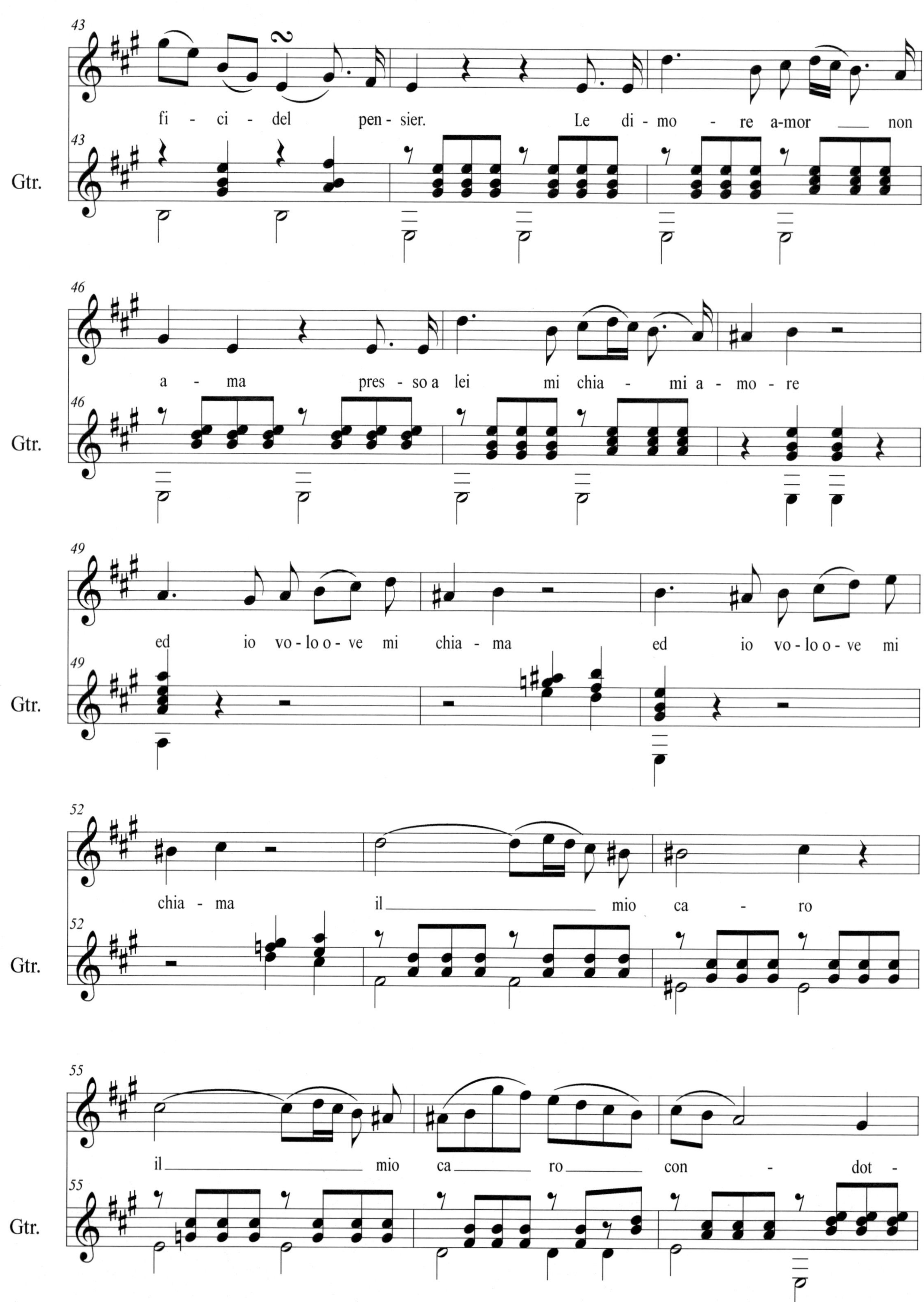
43
fi - ci - del pen - sier. Le di - mo - re a-mor non
Gtr.
46
a - ma pres - so a lei mi chia - mi a - mo - re
Gtr.
49
ed io vo - lo o - ve mi chia - ma ed io vo - lo o - ve mi
Gtr.
52
chia - ma il mio ca - ro
Gtr.
55
il mio ca ro con - dot -
Gtr.

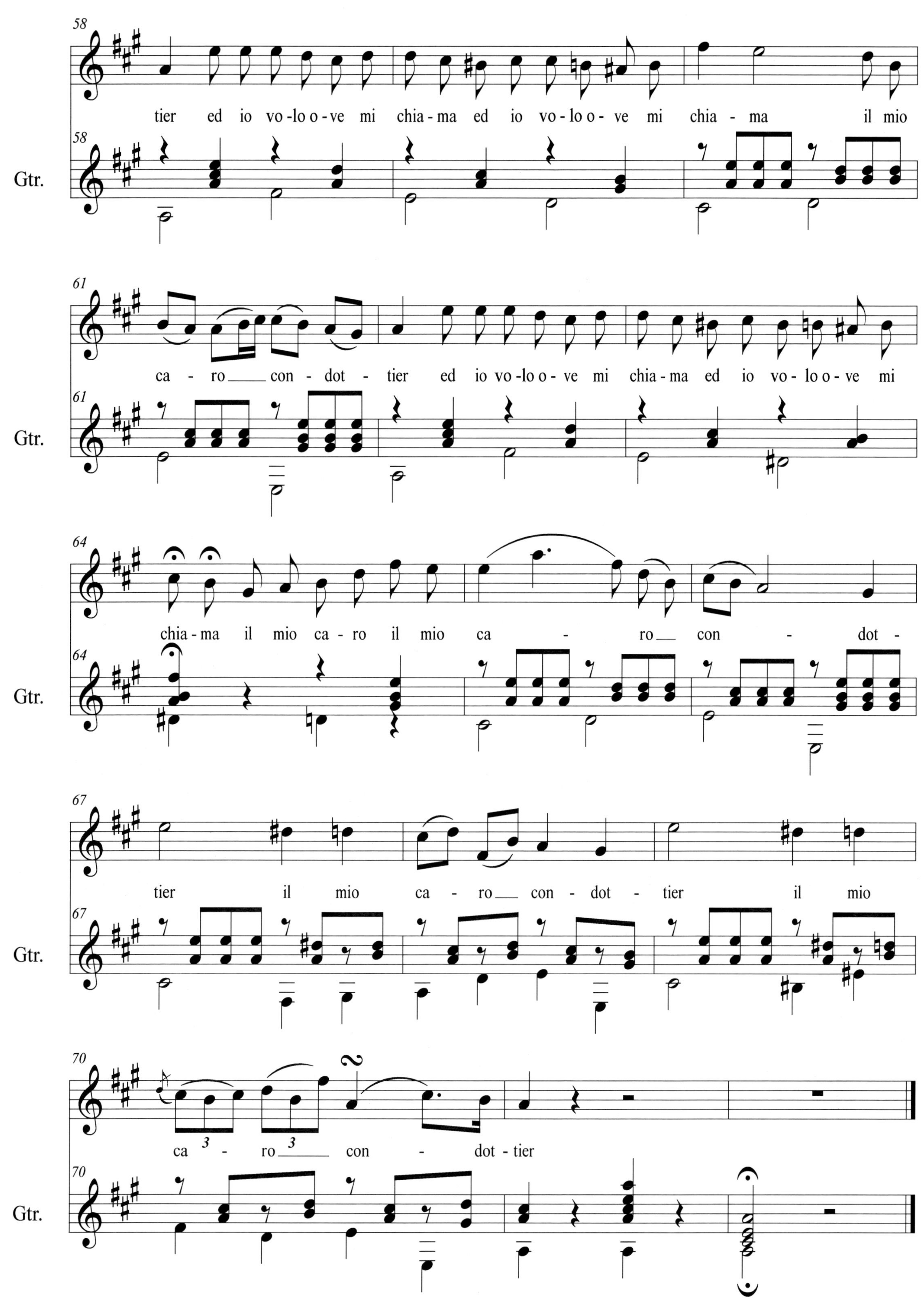
58
tier ed io vo-lo o-ve mi chia-ma ed io vo-lo o-ve mi chia - ma il mio
Gtr.
61
ca - ro con - dot - tier ed io vo-lo o-ve mi chia-ma ed io vo-lo o-ve mi
Gtr.
64
chia-ma il mio ca-ro il mio ca - ro con - dot -
Gtr.
67
tier il mio ca - ro con - dot - tier il mio
Gtr.
70
ca - ro con - dot - tier
Gtr.

Sei Ariette

Op. 95, No. 5

Mauro Giuliani

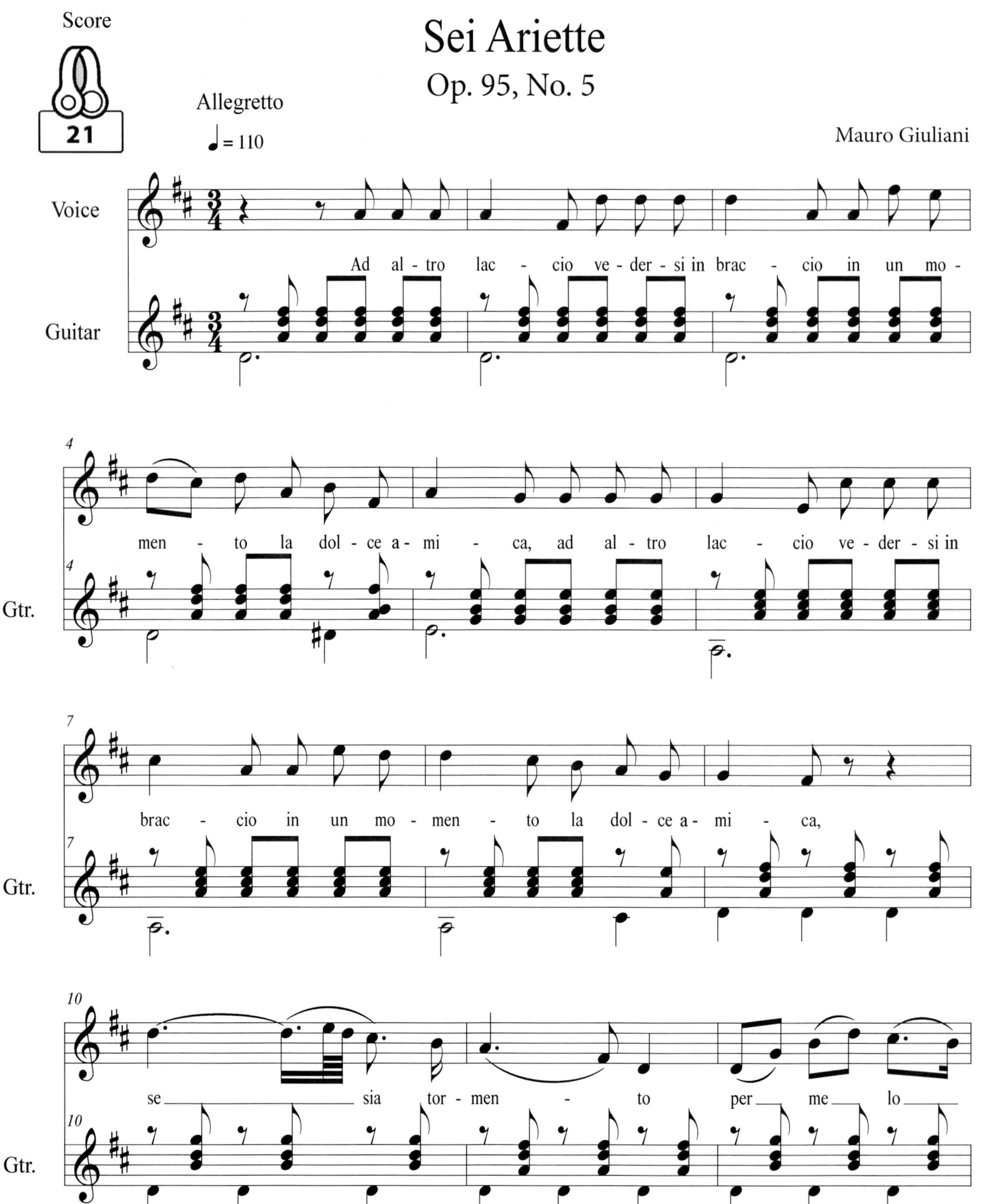

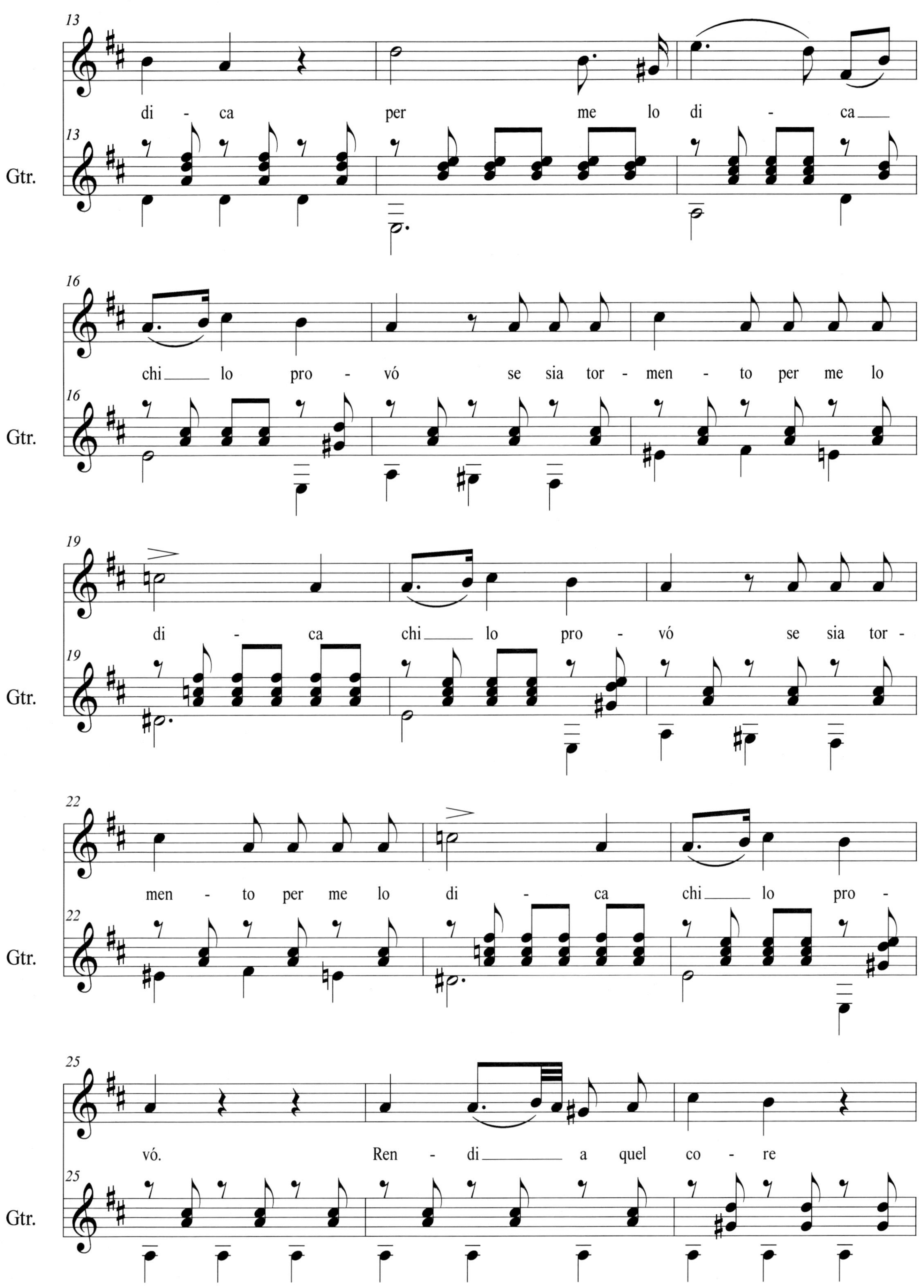
13
di - ca per me lo di - ca
Gtr.
16
chi lo pro - vó se sia tor - men - to per me lo
Gtr.
19
di - ca chi lo pro - vó se sia tor -
Gtr.
22
men - to per me lo di - ca chi lo pro -
Gtr.
25
vó. Ren - di a quel co - re
Gtr.

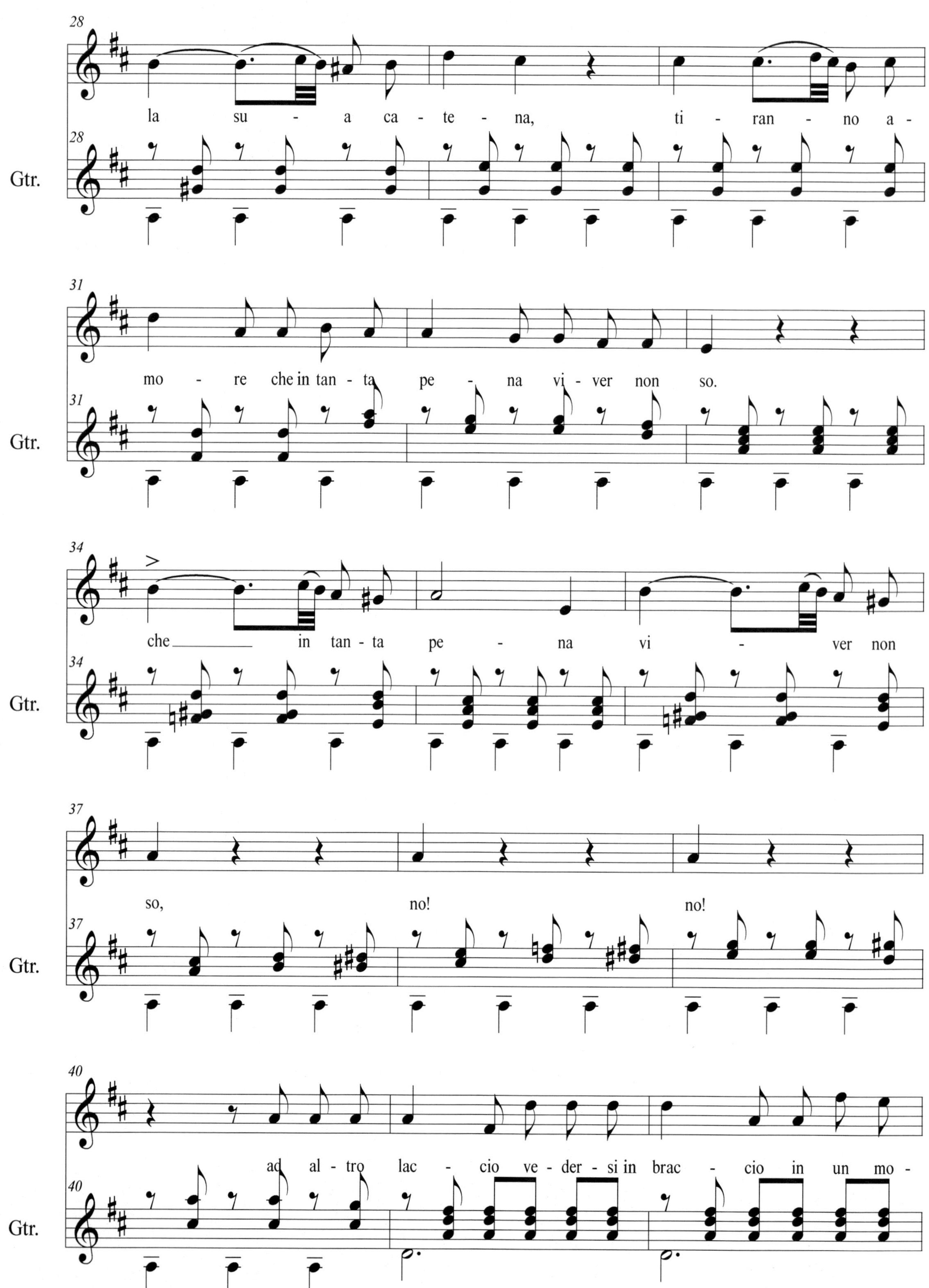
28
la su - a ca - te - na, ti - ran - no a -
Gtr.
31
mo - re che in tan - ta pe - na vi - ver non so.
Gtr.
34
che in tan - ta pe - na vi - ver non
Gtr.
37
so, no! no!
Gtr.
40
ad al - tro lac - cio ve - der - si in brac - cio in un mo -
Gtr.

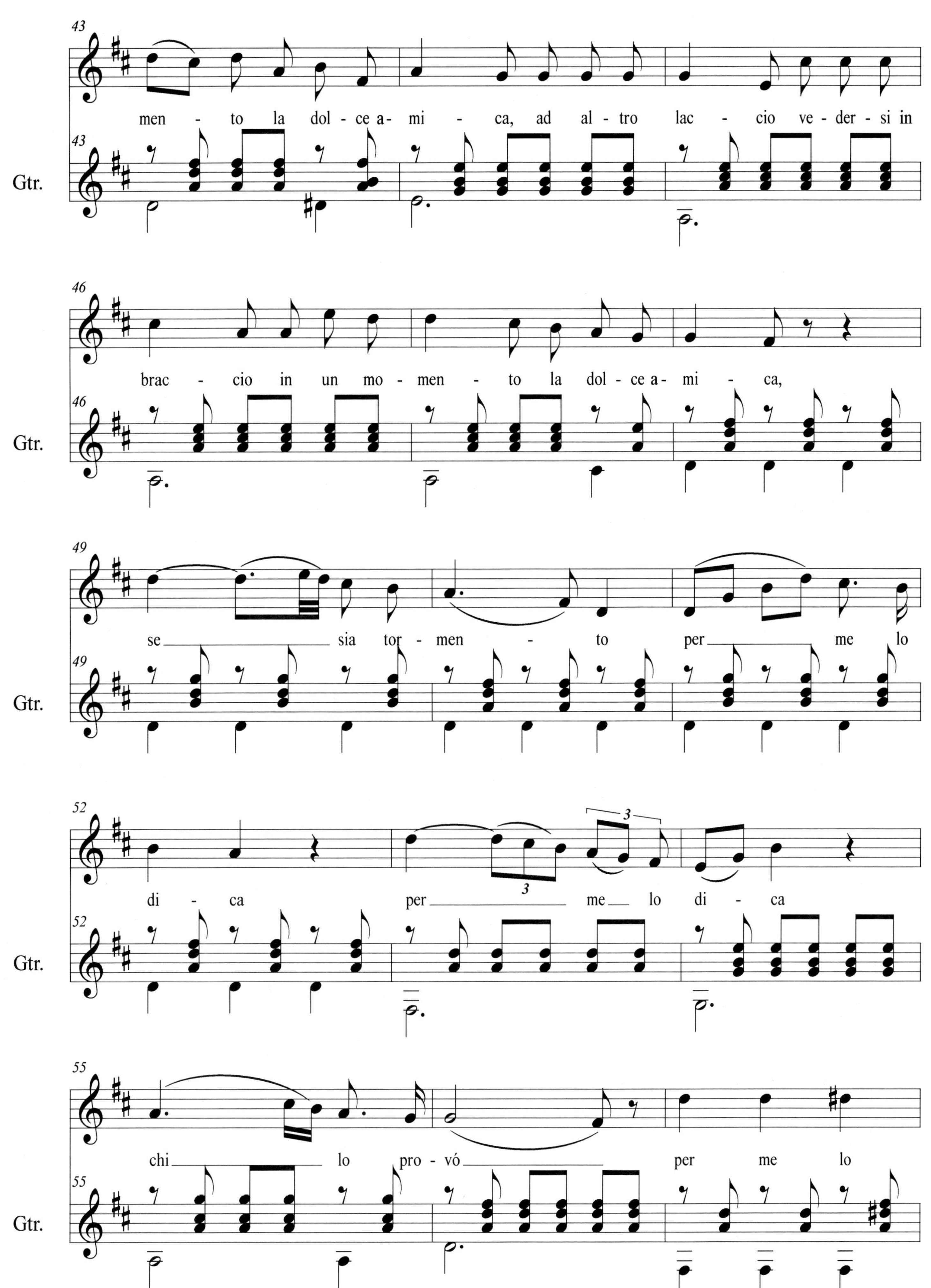
43
men - to la dol - ce a - mi - ca, ad al - tro lac - cio ve - der - si in
Gtr.
46
brac - cio in un mo - men - to la dol - ce a - mi - ca,
Gtr.
49
se sia tor - men - to per me lo
Gtr.
52
di - ca per me lo di - ca
Gtr.
55
chi lo pro - vó per me lo
Gtr.

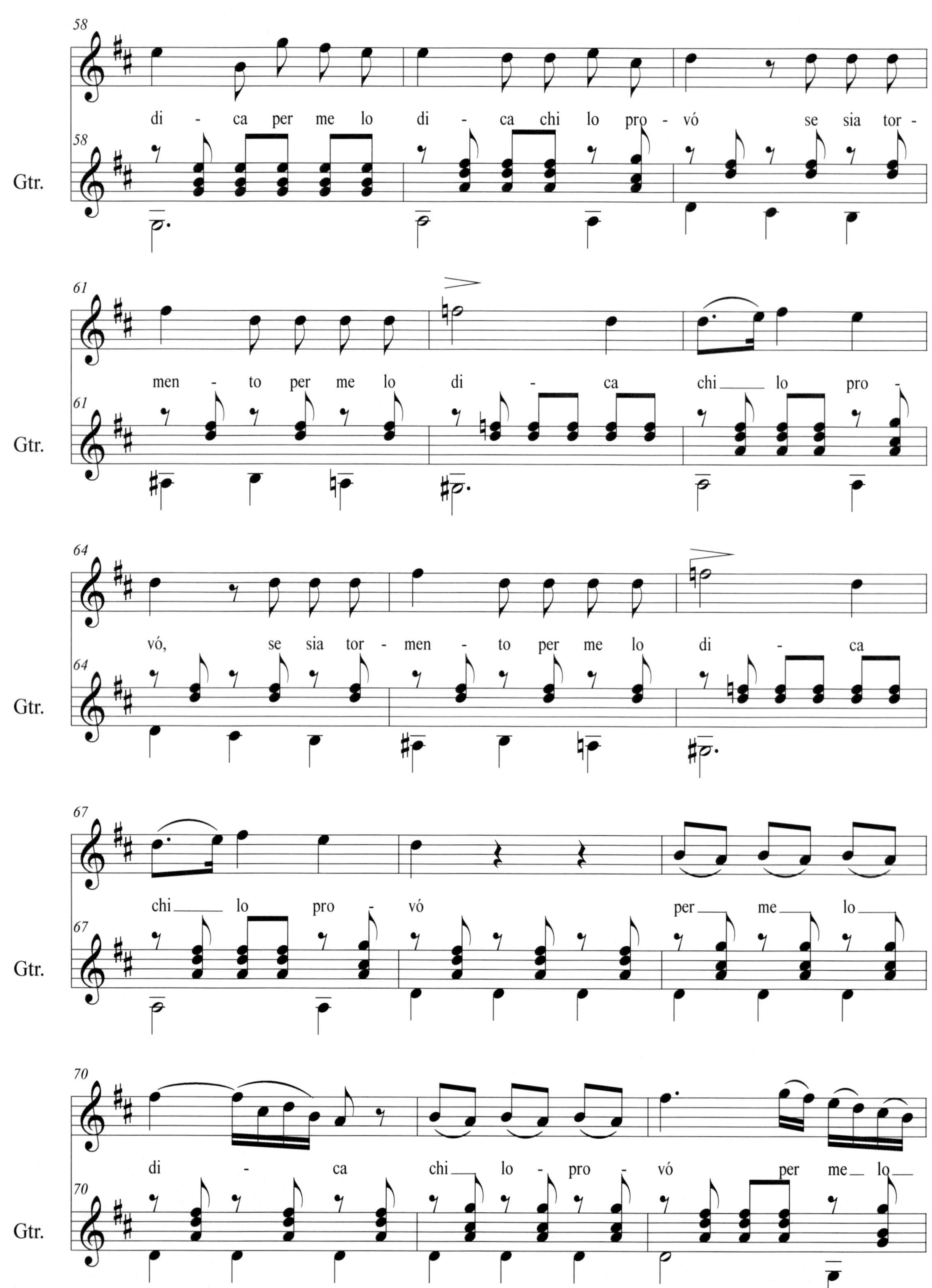
58
di - ca per me lo di - ca chi lo pro - vó se sia tor -
Gtr.
61
men - to per me lo di - ca chi lo pro -
Gtr.
64
vó, se sia tor - men - to per me lo di - ca
Gtr.
67
chi lo pro - vó per me lo
Gtr.
70
di - ca chi lo - pro - vó per me lo
Gtr.

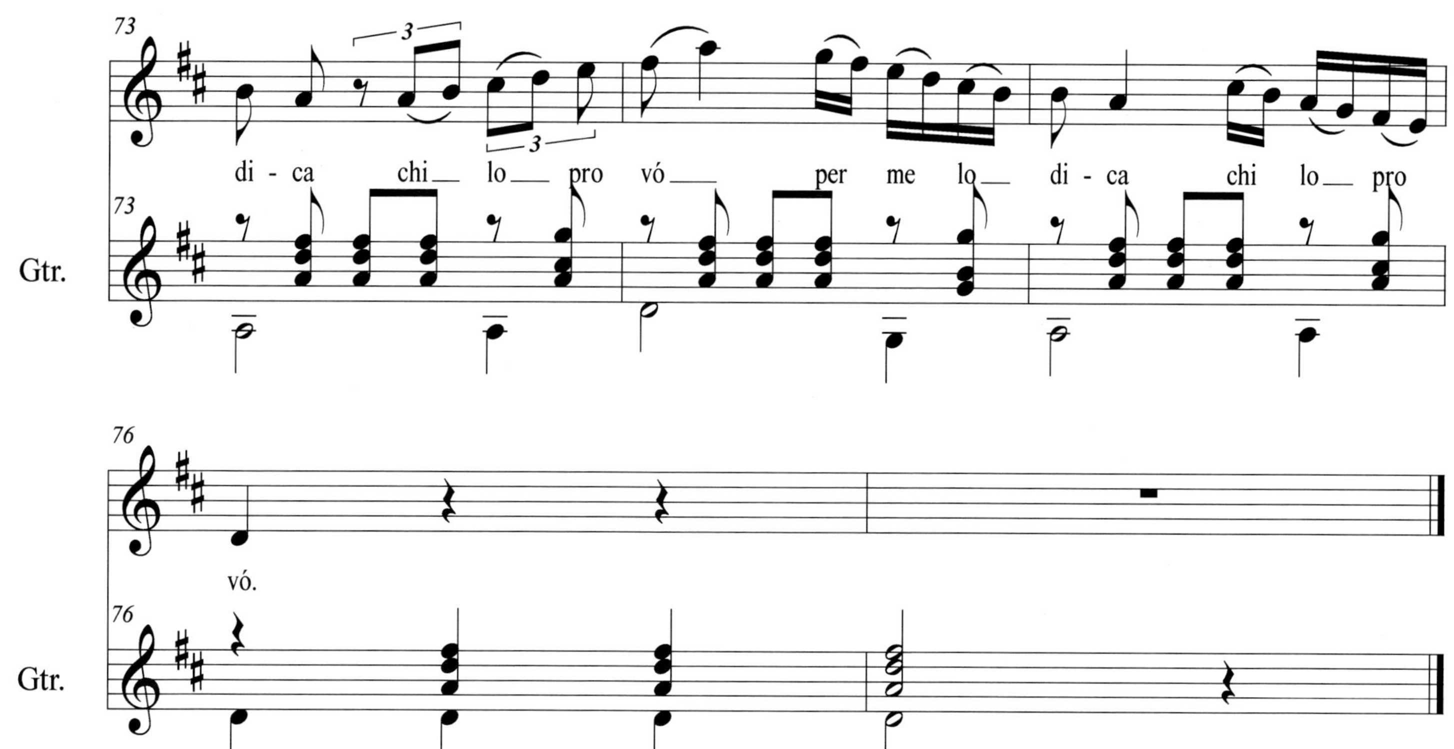
73
di - ca chi lo pro vó per me lo di - ca chi lo pro
Gtr.
76
vó.
Gtr.

Sei Ariette

Op. 95, No. 6

Mauro Giuliani

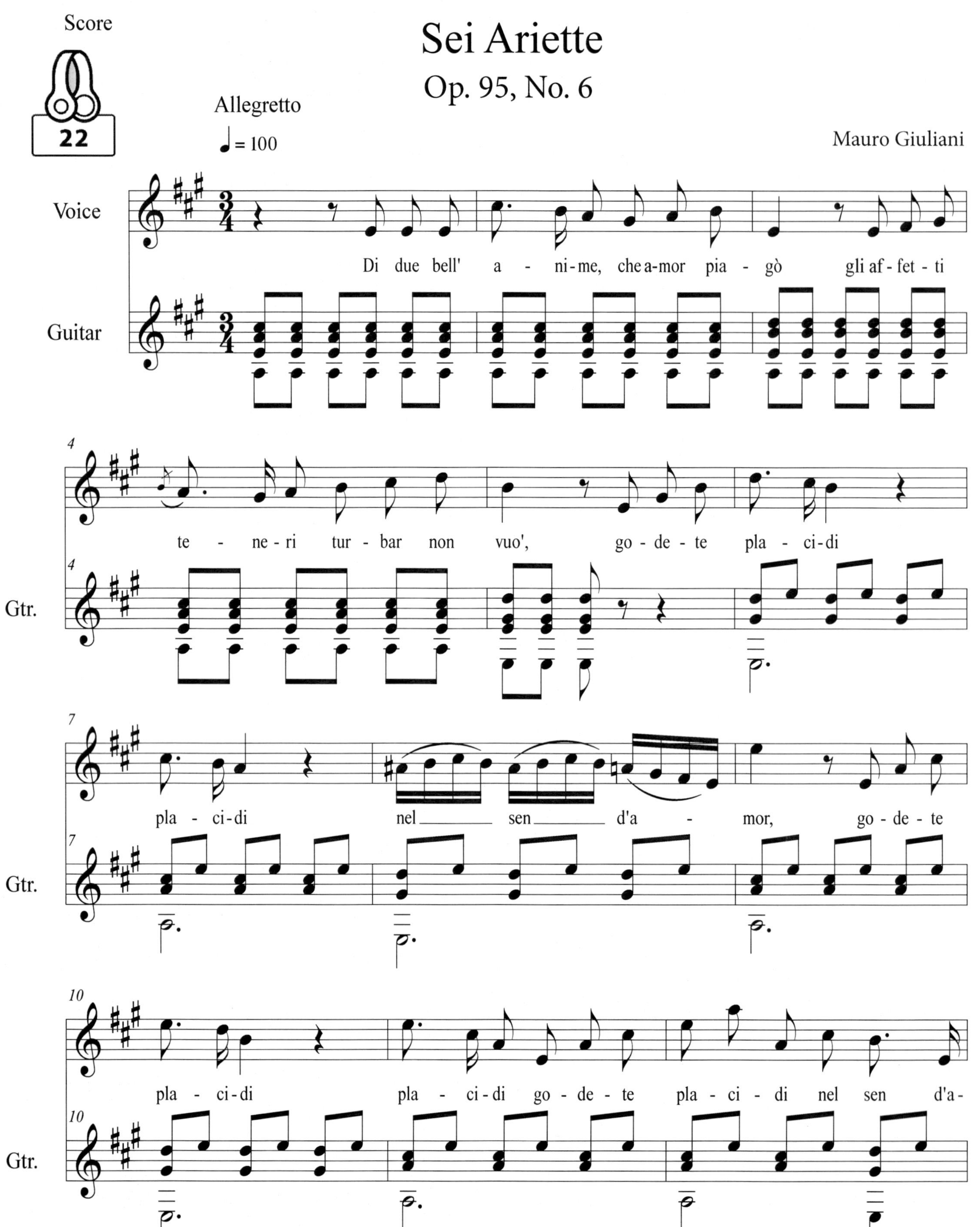

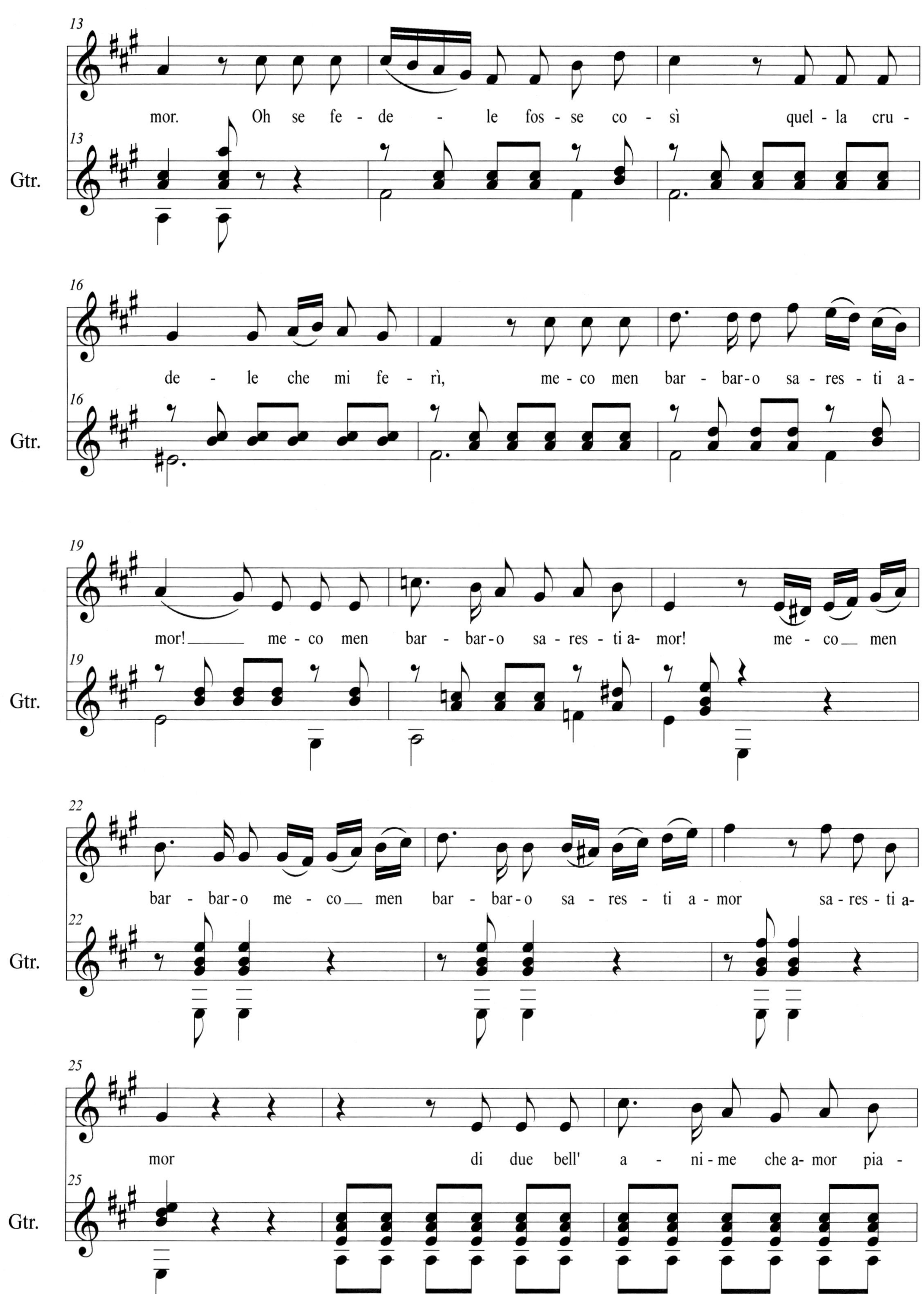
13
mor. Oh se fe - de - le fos - se co - sì quel - la cru -
Gtr.
16
de - le che mi fe - rì, me - co men bar - bar-o sa - res - ti a -
Gtr.
19
mor! me - co men bar - bar-o sa - res - ti a - mor! me - co men
Gtr.
22
bar - bar-o me - co men bar - bar-o sa - res - ti a - mor sa - res - ti a -
Gtr.
25
mor di due bell' a - ni - me che a - mor pia -
Gtr.

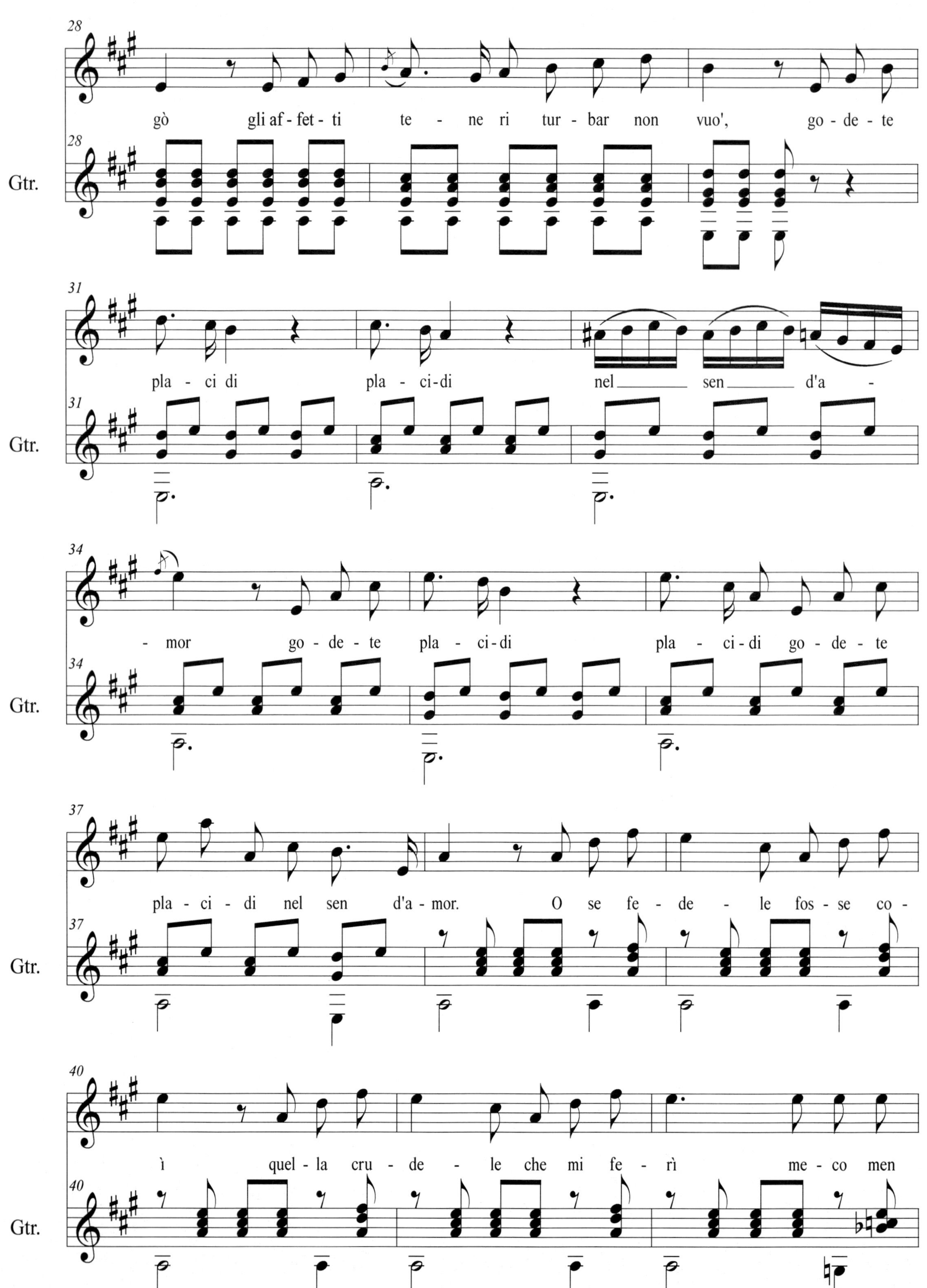
28
gò gli af - fet - ti te - ne ri tur - bar non vuo', go - de - te
Gtr.
31
pla - ci di pla - ci-di nel sen d'a -
34
- mor go - de - te pla - ci-di pla - ci-di go - de - te
37
pla - ci - di nel sen d'a - mor. O se fe - de - le fos - se co -
40
ì quel - la cru - de - le che mi fe - rì me - co men

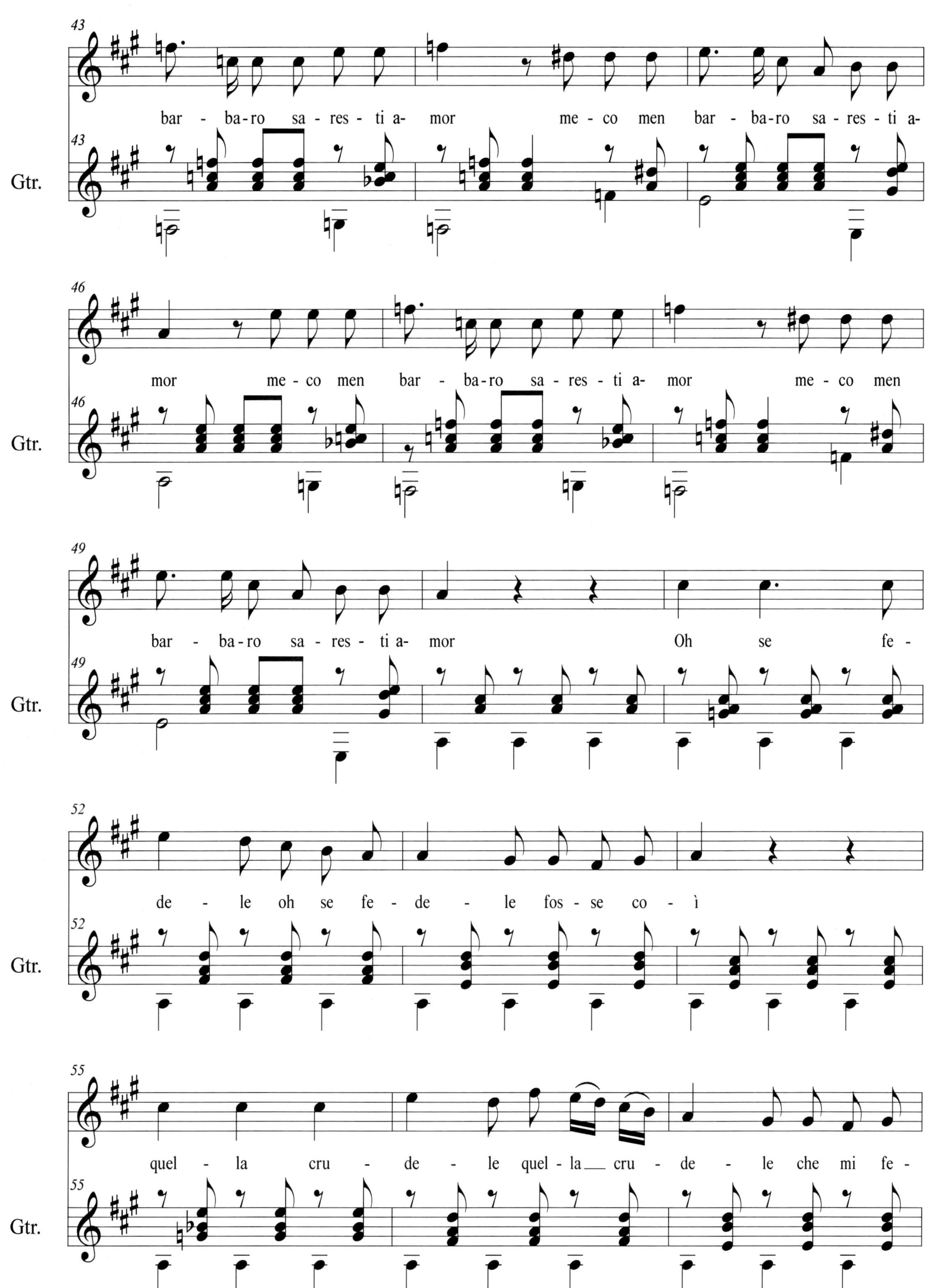
43
bar - ba-ro sa - res - ti a- mor me - co men bar - ba-ro sa - res - ti a-
Gtr.
46
mor me - co men bar - ba-ro sa - res - ti a- mor me - co men
Gtr.
49
bar - ba-ro sa - res - ti a- mor Oh se fe -
Gtr.
52
de - le oh se fe - de - le fos - se co - ì
Gtr.
55
quel - la cru - de - le quel - la cru - de - le che mi fe -
Gtr.

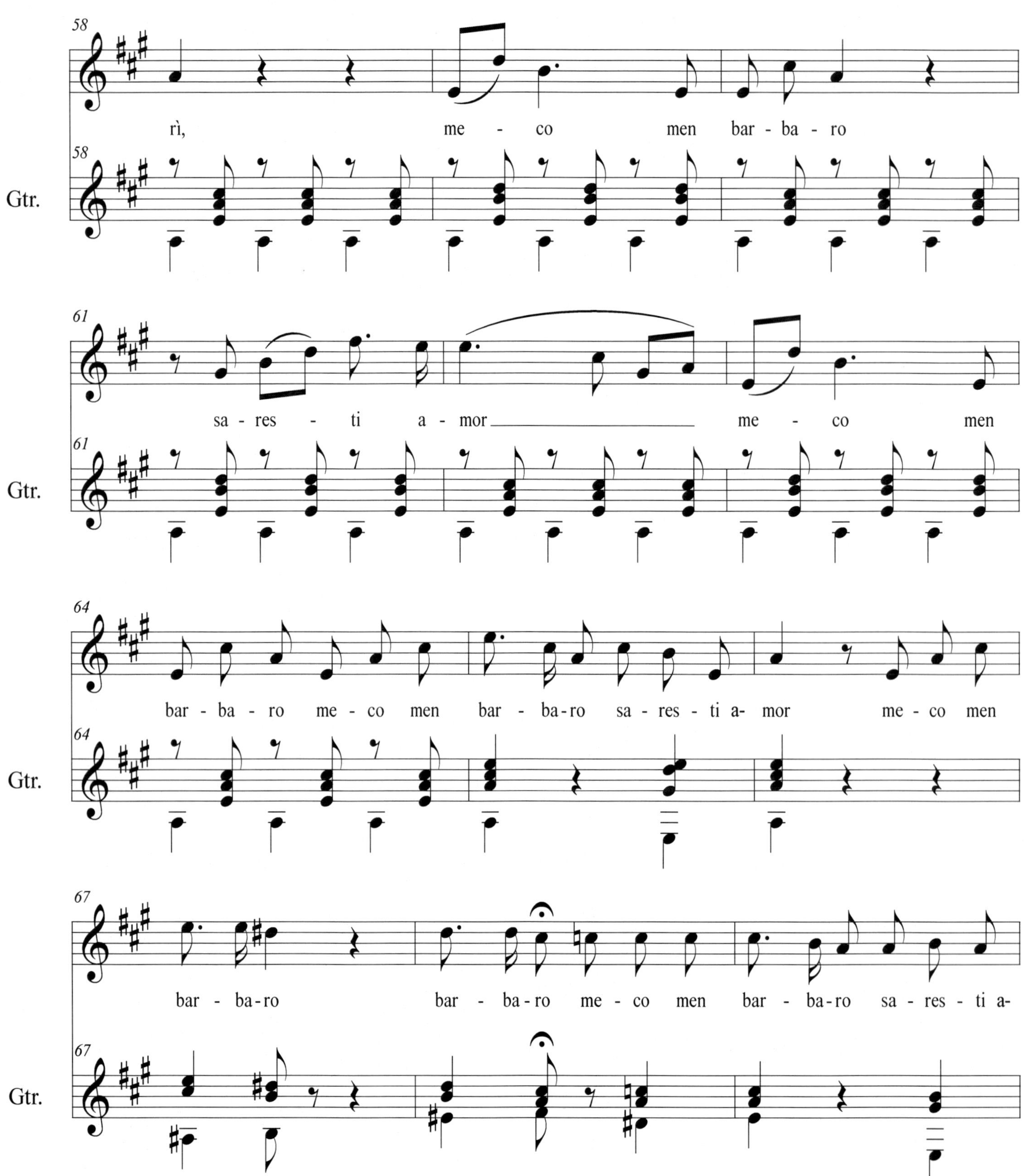
58
rì, me - co men bar - ba - ro
58
Gtr.
61
sa - res - ti a - mor me - co men
61
Gtr.
64
bar - ba - ro me - co men bar - ba-ro sa - res - ti a- mor me - co men
64
Gtr.
67
bar - ba-ro bar - ba-ro me - co men bar - ba-ro sa - res - ti a-
67
Gtr.

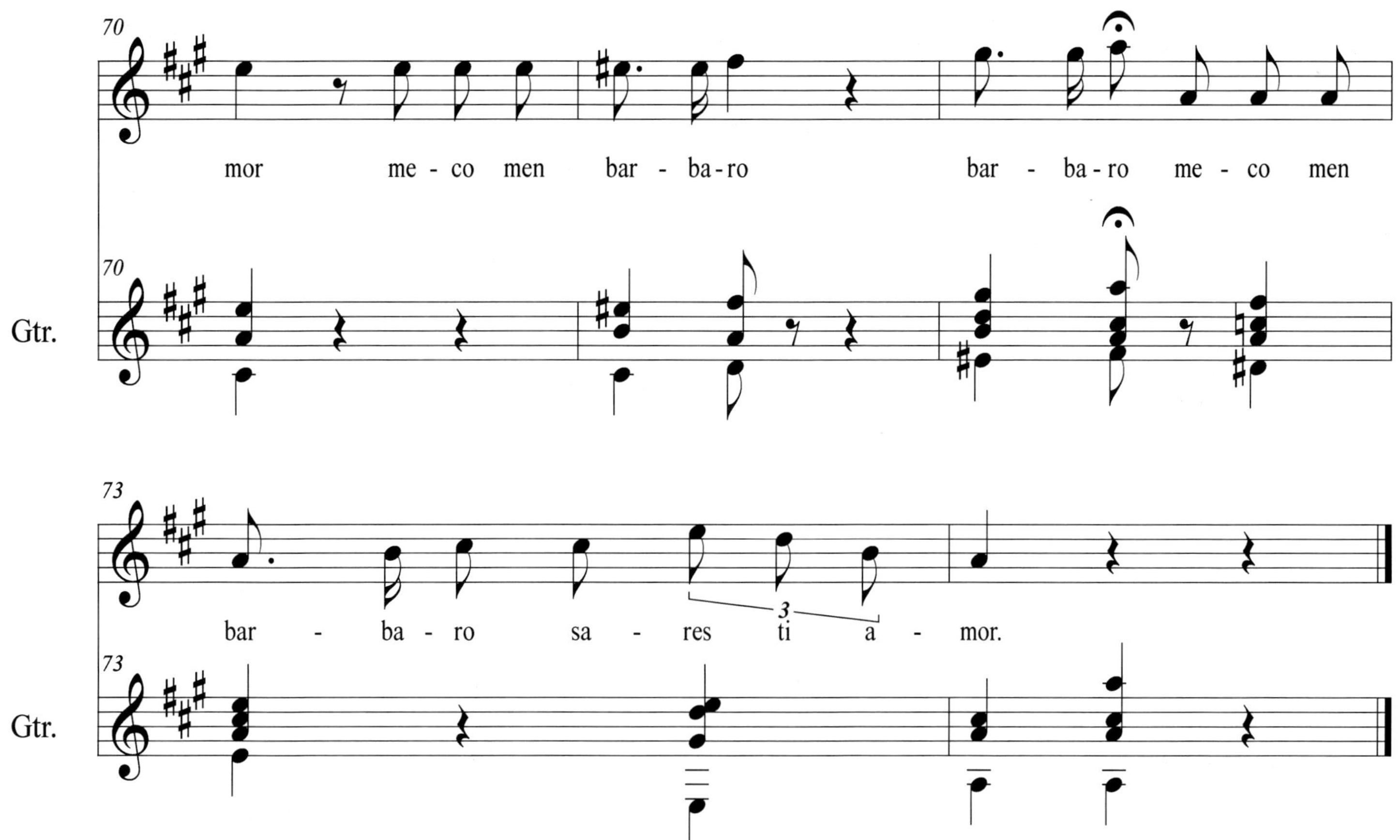
70
mor me - co men bar - ba-ro bar - ba-ro me - co men
Gtr.
73
bar - ba - ro sa - res ti a - mor.
3
Gtr.

Other Mel Bay Classic Guitar Books

Angel Romero in Concert
Classical Guitarist's Gig Book (Cruz)
Deluxe Album of Classic Guitar Music (Castle)
Folio of Great Classic Guitar Solos (Castle/M. Bay)
Néstor Ausqui Collection
The Classical Guitar Gig Book (Cruz)
The Complete Laurindo Almeida Anthology of Guitar Solos
Transcriptions for Classical Guitar (Witmyer)
6 Neapolitan Songs for Solo Classic Guitar (Scheldt)
A Dozen Italian Diversions for Guitar Solo (DeBenedetti)
Airs and Ballads for Classic Guitar (Lehmann-Haupt)
Arias for Acoustic Guitar: Operatic Melodies for Solo Guitar (Edwards)
Ashokan Farewell Guitar Arrangement (Ungar/Lehmann-Haupt)
Christmas Songs for Classical Guitar (Castle)
Ciclos: Music of the Sephardic Jews for Classic Guitar (Akiva)
Civil War Suite for Classical Guitar (Brew)
Classical and Flamenco Guitar Solos and Etudes (Elysa Hochman/Jason Hochman)
Classical Guitar Tunes - Fun Solos to Play (Calmes)
Classical Guitar Tunes - Gospel Favorites (Calmes)
Classic Tangos (Halen)
Complete Works of Scott Joplin: 52 PIano Rags, Waltzes & Marches Transcribed for Guitar Solo (De Chiaro)
Contemporary Irish Music for Classic Guitar Solo (Feeley)
Devotion: Sacred Solos for Guitar (W. Bay)
Favorite Hymns for Classical Guitar (Castle)
Five Popular Persian Ballads for Solo Guitar (Afshar)
Five Women Composers Arranged for Guitar (Newman)
Folk songs and Dances of the Jewish People for Acoustic Guitar (Back)
Early American Hymn Favorites for Classical Guitar (Miric)
Great American Marches, Polkas & Grand Concert Waltzes for Acoustic Guitar (Back)
Greek Traditional Music for Acoustic Guitar (Borjanic)
Irish Folk Songs for Classical Guitar (Marsh)
Melodies of the Far East for Guitar (Tuan Vu)
Nineteen Gilbert & Sullivan Favorites Arranged for Classical Guitar (Marrington)
O'Carolan Favorites for Classic Guitar (Böger)
Romantic Arias for Classical Guitar (Eckels)
Russian Folk Songs for Guitar Solo (Borjanic)
Solo Guitar Hymnal: Classic Guitar Solos for the Liturgical Calendar Year (Bass)
Stephen Foster for Classic Guitar (Böger)
The Christmas Book - Carols Arrangeds for Acoustic Guitar (Barreiro)
The Holiday Gig Book (Johnstone)
Traditional Christmas Favorites for Classical Guitar (Siktberg)
Turlough O'Carolan Irish Harp Pieces for Classic Guitar (Böger)

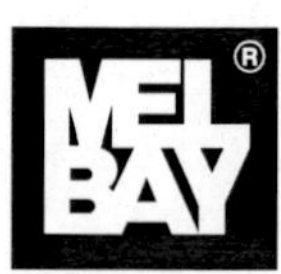

Other Mel Bay Classic Guitar Books

Wedding Favorites for Classical Guitar (De Chiaro)
Wedding Music for Classical Guitar (Boydston)
Baroque Transcriptions for Classic Guitar (Rodriques)
Bartolotti: A Performance Edition of Suites (George)
Best of Bach for Classic Guitar (Castle)
Chromatic Fantasia and Fugue in D Minor BWV 903 by J. S. Bach (Ausqui)
Domenico Scarlatti: 30 Sonatas (Zanon)
Essential Bach: Arranged for Guitar (Afshar)
Essential Baroque Guitar (Siktberg)
J. S. Bach Transcriptions for Classic Guitar (Calderon)
J. S. Bach Cello Suite #1 (Lorimer)
J. S. Bach French Suite Number 5 in C Major (Ausqui)
J. S. Bach: Six Unaccompanied Cello Suites Arranged for Guitar (S. Yates)
J. S. Bach: The Two Part Inventions (Wyman)
Music of Girolamo Frescobaldi for Classic Guitar (Shepard-Smith)
Scarlatti and Weiss for Guitar (Afshar)
The Baroque Guitar in Spain and the New World (Koonce)
Treasures of the Baroque Volume 1 (Grimes)
Treasures of the Baroque Volume 2 (Grimes)
Treasures of the Baroque Volume 3 (Grimes)
65 Gradually Progressive Pieces and 6 Studies from Opus 241 by Carulli (Roberts)
Anthology of 19th Century Studies (Beck/Postlewate)
Best of Carulli (Castle)
Best of Tarrega (Castle)
Chopin for Acoustic Guitar (R. Yates)
Complete Chopin Mazurkas (Aron)
Edvard Grieg: 16 Lyric Pieces (R. Yates)
Franz Schubert Arranged for Guitar (Calderon)
Guitar Transcriptions of Francisco Tárrega (Ballam-Cross)
J. K. Mertz: Original Compositions for the Classic Guitar (Reuther)
Johannes Brahms: Hungarian Dances for Solo Guitar (Estovos)
La Melanconia by Mauro Giuliani arranged by Pepe Romero
Masters of Russian Composition: Alexander Borodin & Antoly Lyadov arr. by Rovshan Mamedkuliev
Padovec Collection (Dojcinovic)
Parlor Gems (Mayes)
Peer Gynt Suite: Op 46 plus Solveig's Song (R. Yates)
Selected Operatic Fantasies of Mertz (Torosian)
Woodland Sketches by Edward MacDowell (R. Yates)
7 Studies for Guitar (Hull)
24 Pieces for Guitar by Gilbert Isbin
25 Etudes Esquisses (Garcia)
A Tribute to Guitar Masters (Ramos)

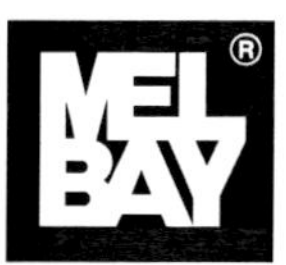

Other Mel Bay Classic Guitar Books

Andrew York: 3 Dimensions for Solo Guitar
Anthology of Dimitri Fampas Music for Guitar (E. Fampas)
Classic Koshkin (Koshkin/Koonce)
Contemporary Anthology of Solo Guitar Music (Postlewate)
Contemporary Guitar Composers of the Americas (Multiple Authors)
Contemporary Pieces for Classical Gutar (Jakola)
Conversation Pieces (Long)
Diego Barber Compositions for Classical Guitar
Gordon Mizzi: Saints and Fireworks
Gordon Mizzi: Song of the Sea
Guitar Compositions by Carlos Dorado
Guitarra Solista (Juan Martin)
Homage to Villa-Lobos and Other Compositions (Postlewate)
Introspect (Pellegrin)
Jazz Goes Classic (Multiple Arrangers)
Les reflets de l'obscurite for Classical Guitar (Schwizgebel)
Lyrical Solos (W. Bay)
Master Anthology of New Classical Guitar Solos (Multiple Composers)
Rock Goes Classic (Multiple Arrangers)
Solos for Guitar (F. Hand)
The Contemporary Guitar: An Anthology of New Music (S. Yates)
The Jovicic Collection (Dojcinovic)
Well Tempered Blues (Beauvais)
Barrios for Flute and Guitar (Stover)
Cantabile/Mandolin & Guitar (Baldassari/Mock)
Christmas Carols for Flute and Guitar (Gendron)
Classical Pieces for Flute and Guitar (Waters)
Contradanzas Habañeras for Guitar and Flute by Manuel Saumell (Barreiro)
Cuban Dances for Guitar and Flute by Ignacio Cervantes (Barreiro)
Early American Melodies for Flute and Guitar (Welch)
Gilbert and Sullivan Favorites for Voice and Guitar (Silverman)
Guitar/Flute Duets on Celtic Favorites (Luft)
Gypsy Songs of Russia & Hungary: Guitar/Vocal (Silverman)
Johann Sebastian Bach: 69 Sacred Songs for Voice and Guitar (Stegmann)
Laurindo Almeida-Brazilian Reflections (Guitar and Soprano Voice)
Laurindo Almeida: Duets for Clarinet and Guitar
New Classics for Guitar & Cello or Viola
Songs of the British Isles for Guitar (and Voice) (Silverman)
Spanish Dances, Opus 12 by Moszkowski for Guitar and Flute (Baxter)
The Complete Laurindo Almeida Anthology of Guitar and Flute Duets
The Joy of Flute and Guitar (Marlow)
Wedding Music for Flute and Guitar (Gendron)

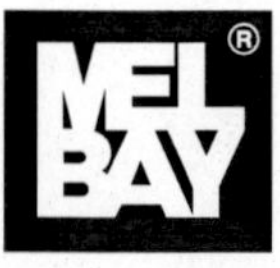